Reglobalisation

Since the end of the Cold War, globalisation has been the dominant political and economic trend. But what is China's role in globalisation? What is China's vision of the world? This title offers a fresh and stimulating account of how China's involvement in globalisation has changed over time, and how its role in leading the reglobalisation process is profoundly reshaping the world.

Introducing an innovative theoretical framework in the shape of reglobalisation, this book discusses China's strategies and challenges while interacting with the international community. The book provides several illuminating case studies, such as the Belt and Road Initiative (BRI), the Asian Infrastructure Investment Bank (AIIB), and the strategies of the Chinese technology firm Alibaba. Rich in data and bold in argument, the book provides an extraordinarily dynamic depiction of how China's encounter with the outside world has not only transformed itself, but also reshaped the global order.

As the first systemic and book-length study of reglobalisation, this volume will appeal to researchers and students of politics and Chinese studies and contemporary Chinese politics in particular.

Dong Wang is an Associate Professor at the School of International Studies and Executive Director of the Institute for Global Cooperation and Understanding (iGCU) at Peking University.

Dejun Cao is a Lecturer at the School of International Studies at Remin University of China.

China Perspectives

The *China Perspectives* series focuses on translating and publishing works by leading Chinese scholars, writing about both global topics and China-related themes. It covers Humanities & Social Sciences, Education, Media and Psychology, as well as many interdisciplinary themes.

This is the first time any of these books have been published in English for international readers. The series aims to put forward a Chinese perspective, give insights into cutting-edge academic thinking in China, and inspire researchers globally.

To submit proposals, please contact the Taylor & Francis Publisher for China Publishing Programme, Lian Sun (Lian.Sun@informa.com)

Recent titles in politics partly include:

Shortening the Distance between Government and Public in China II
Methods and Practices
Liu Xiaoyan

Fiscal Policy and Institutional Renovation in Support of Innovative Country Building
Jia Kang

Avoiding the "Thucydides Trap"
U.S.-China Relations in Strategic Domains
Dong Wang and Travis N. Tanner

Syrian Civil War and Europe
Zhao Chen, Zhao Jizhou and Huang Mengmeng

Reglobalisation
When China Meets the World Again
Dong Wang and Dejun Cao

China in the Eyes of the Japanese
Wang Xiuli, Wang Wei and Liang Yunxiang

For more information, please visit https://www.routledge.com/China-Perspectives/book-series/CPH

Reglobalisation
When China Meets the World Again

Dong Wang and Dejun Cao

LONDON AND NEW YORK

This book is published with financial support from the Chinese Fund for the Humanities and Social Sciences.

First edition published 2021
by Routledge
2 Park Square, Milton Park, Abingdon, Oxon, OX14 4RN

and by Routledge
52 Vanderbilt Avenue, New York, NY 10017

Routledge is an imprint of the Taylor & Francis Group, an informa business

© 2021 Dong Wang and Dejun Cao

The right of Dong Wang and Dejun Cao to be identified as authors of this work has been asserted by them in accordance with sections 77 and 78 of the Copyright, Designs and Patents Act 1988.

All rights reserved. No part of this book may be reprinted or reproduced or utilised in any form or by any electronic, mechanical, or other means, now known or hereafter invented, including photocopying and recording, or in any information storage or retrieval system, without permission in writing from the publishers.

Trademark notice: Product or corporate names may be trademarks or registered trademarks, and are used only for identification and explanation without intent to infringe.

English Version by permission of Social Sciences Academic Press (China).

British Library Cataloguing-in-Publication Data
A catalogue record for this book is available from the British Library

Library of Congress Cataloging-in-Publication Data
A catalog record has been requested for this book

ISBN: 978-0-367-64916-6 (hbk)
ISBN: 978-1-003-12693-5 (ebk)

Typeset in Times New Roman
by Deanta Global Publishing Services, Chennai, India

Contents

	List of Figures	vi
	List of Tables	vii
	Introduction	1
1	Embracing globalisation and China's narrative	8
2	From Globalisation to Reglobalisation	26
3	Inclusive development and interconnected thinking	47
4	The Belt and Road Initiative and global governance	63
5	The Asian Infrastructure and Investment Bank pushes forward reglobalisation	92
6	Digital Economy 2.0 and Alibaba's reglobalisation story	106
7	The mechanism of reversal pressure and the experience of special economic zones in China	120
8	Embracing the era of reglobalisation	139
	Conclusion: Reglobalisation: When China meets the world again	153
	Index	157

Figures

1.1	The percentages of trade in goods of the world's major economies	13
1.2	Illustration of the embedded style of national rise in the era of globalisation	15
1.3	The network expansion model of the Belt and Road	20
2.1	The transformation of reglobalisation: from verticalisation to flattening	35
2.2	BRICS countries' share of world population in 2016	37
2.3	Four types of globalisation	39
3.1	The inclusive spirit conveyed by the Belt and Road Forum for International Cooperation	49
4.1	Bilateral trade between China and the countries along the Belt and Road economic corridor	64
4.2	The macro economic benefits of Asian interconnectivity (transportation, communications, and energy)	69
4.3	Illustration of the trade flow along the Belt and Road: From 2001 to 2007 to 2014	74
6.1	The transaction volume of China's mobile payments	108
6.2	The rapid development trend of cross-border e-commerce in china	112
6.3	Development pattern of world artificial intelligence technology in 2016	117

Tables

1.1	The history of China's three-time participation in globalisation	11
3.1	China's partnership network	55
4.1	The national conditions of the 65 countries along the Belt and Road in 2016	66
4.2	China's investments and construction contracts in countries along the Belt and Road	70
4.3	The national competitiveness and stages of development of countries along the Belt and Road economic corridor	75
4.4	Analysis of the factors influencing China's surrounding economic corridors	80
4.5	Potential projects of cooperation and competition of the Belt and Road Initiative	85
5.1	Capital gap for infrastructure buildup in Asia from 2010 to 2020	96
5.2	The expansion of the Asian Infrastructure Investment Bank	98
5.3	Comparison of the rules of the Asian Infrastructure Investment Bank and the World Bank	99
6.1	ECI indexes of countries along the Belt and Road	110
6.2	The sharing connotation of eWTP	111
7.1	China's new zones, special economic zones, development zones, and free-trade zones	122
7.2	The '1+3+7' pattern of China's pilot free-trade zone	124
7.3	Selected overseas industrial parks established by China	128
8.1	Projects by the Center for International Knowledge on Development	143
8.2	A roadmap for China to take Part in leading reglobalisation	145

Introduction

The end of the Cold War marked the arrival of the era of globalisation. In a sense, the Cold War turned out to be the first global contest of different ideas and powers in the history of humankind. The formation of the global order has been undergoing a process of continuous revolution and evolution. In the context of the macro trends of globalisation, the Cold War was like a huge wave on a calm sea, and only after the wave had passed did people realise that it was only a brief episode and that globalisation would still remain the macro trend of human history. In the context of systemic transformation, the political and military partial rise of China in the Cold War bipolar structure made China an important driving force in dismantling and reconstructing the old order. China took part in the reconstruction of the global order of the Cold War era. From the standpoint of the classic 'Kissingerians', the interaction of China and the global order during the Cold War merely underwent a process of 'renormalisation' wherein China went from a so-called 'revisionist' state, challenging the post-WWII world order dominated by the West, back to a state following a realist approach involving the balance of power.[1] However, such a Kissingerian narrative depicts China more as a state that was passively shaped by the world order. Interestingly, this binary perspective that puts China as the 'Other', adopted by the Kissingerians, has been inherited by Western observers after the Cold War. In their eyes, the central question of a rising China and the global order is how to reintegrate China into the global order dominated by the West. The simple binary viewing of China as an Other in opposition to the existing order is not only deeply Western-centric, but also out of touch with the reality of the evolving world order because China has increasingly become a major force in shaping and reconstructing the world order since the end of the Cold War. This binary view will inevitably become an absurd paradox: China is in reality part of the existing order, yet it is not its 'legitimate' member.

The year 2008 marked a historical fault line clear as day: the huge success of the Beijing Olympic Games and the enormous destruction of the global financial crisis both took place in the same year, in marked contrast to each other, demonstrating a 'scissors effect'. China, which had maintained a low profile for a long time, entered the global centre stage years earlier than expected. When the United States, as a superpower, was busy scratching its head while dealing with its domestic and foreign problems, China proposed systematic new thinking on

2 *Reglobalisation*

the reform of the international order and global governance system in a spirited and confident manner. The global stage was familiar yet strange to China at the same time. It was familiar because China, though once marginalised, had always been within the global system and never left it. It was strange because the global order stood at a crossroads. The global financial crisis, beginning in the United States, exposed the weaknesses and ailments of the existing order, yet sparked new forces to cure itself. After Donald Trump was elected the 45th president of the United States, the global hegemon quickened its pace of forsaking its own global responsibilities. Trump's 'America First' slogan implied an antiglobalisation consciousness and strategy. Faced with international disorder and a hegemon with an inward-looking tendency, China actively played a constructive role worthy of a rising state, but it does not seek to destroy or escape the arrangement of the existing international institutions. Instead, it has merged itself into the existing international system, exerting its own unique influence. This influence speaks to a kind of reform that balances continuity and change. The complementarity and creativity of such a reform will comprehensively enhance the vitality, efficacy, and inclusiveness of the existing international institutions.

There is an ancient Chinese poem that goes: 'A thousand sails pass by the wrecked ship, and ten thousand saplings shoot up beyond the withered tree'. New contradictions are always born out of old ones, and new life always springs up from old life. Building on the existing body of international order, China has strived to propose new ideas instead of old ones and provide new regimes and rules of global governance in a creative way in order to smoothen the operations of the international system. In contrast to traditional 'creative destruction', reglobalisation seeks to upgrade globalisation in a mild and flexible manner, advocating an all-win situation that includes most people rather than a hegemonic one-sided win. Since the 2008 global financial crisis, China has played an impressive role in global governance. Anchored on the peaceful development strategy, Chinese diplomacy has increasingly turned toward so-called '*fenfa youwei*' (striving to accomplish something). However, China has always emphasised the importance of partnerships and communal action when it proposes any new thinking on the international order. China is beginning to propose constructively global reform plans ranging from multilateral economic and financial organisation structures and platforms (e.g. the Asian Infrastructure and Investment Bank, the BRICS Bank or the New Development Bank, the Belt and Road Initiative, and Boao Forum for Asia) to regional security governance structures (e.g. the Shanghai Cooperation Organisation, the Conference on Interaction and Confidence Building Measures in Asia, and the Xiangshan Forum) and to cultural-psychological ideas of sharing (e.g. the new Asian security concept, a community of shared future for humankind). The new round of globalisation facilitated by China's rise has created a development mode involving mutual consultation built on the foundation of reflection upon the existing world order. This diverse and open governance mode of networked consultation had no fixed centre or hegemon. Instead, it approaches different issues with one side as the advocate and many sides participating, giving weight to the comparative advantages of all participants. The reason China

Introduction 3

advocates communal participation in globalisation is that the binary, compartmentalised, and fragmented nature of the existing global order has ensured that the so-called 'liberal international order' is dominated by only a few countries. As an emerging power born out of the old process of globalisation, China has a responsibility to repair and upgrade the current global structure. We can imagine that once China, a great power, gets to work, old globalisation must be expanded. Once the expansion is complete, the efficiency of globalisation will be enhanced qualitatively. This process can be called 'reglobalisation'.

Viewing the global order from China's perspective, we focus on this central question: when China, as a heterogenous great power with the largest population in the world, returns to the centre stage of world power, how will the changes in the rules of globalisation caused by its rise affect the interactions between the domestic and international orders? To understand China is to understand globalisation, for China is already an important and integral part of globalisation; and to have a discussion on reglobalisation is to think about how China will reshape globalisation and the global order. The concept of reglobalisation tries to understand the new features of the global order and mainly illustrates three points. First, expansion is an advanced form of global governance reform. When a piece of cloth does not fit a person anymore, do we continue to apply patchworks to it, or do we face reality and re-tailor another one for this grownup? A new round of expansion does not mean throwing away the old clothes, but instead expanding and enlarging them. The relationship between the old and the new clothes cannot be understood properly with a simple dichotomy. They merge into a special piece of clothing that is both old and new. Such is expansion and upgrading, not destruction. Second, emerging economies, such as China, have long been on the bandwagon of globalisation and have benefited from the global public goods provided by the hegemon; however, the hegemon has now begun to undermine the very global order that it once built. Faced with such dramatic historical transformations, what should emerging economies strive to do? How should the new round of globalisation avoid the drawbacks of traditional globalisation? These questions are litmus tests for emerging countries. Different countries may propose different answers, but China, as a big rising power with the most potential, must have its own answers. Third, the wave of globalisation has led to China's rise in the twenty-first century, bringing China, which was once hidden in the periphery, all of a sudden to the centre of the world stage. China and the United States are on the same latitude, but on opposite longitudes and in different hemispheres. When the West sees a familiar yet strange China on the rise, how can it adjust itself to try to shoulder shared responsibilities together with China? How will China avoid the strategic dilemmas of a rising state? Will the imbalance of world order, coupled with the imbalance of great powers' mentalities, cause another tragedy of great power politics?

This book has at least two points of departure. First, at a theoretical level, we hope to bring forth a brand new perspective with which to understand the relationship between China's rise and the global order. It is safe to say that China's rise is the central focus of current research on international relations, not only in China

4 *Reglobalisation*

but also in global academic circles. In the past 40-odd years since China joined the most recent round of globalisation, it has achieved a great deal that the rest of the world has admired. It has changed courses in a gradual manner that the West does not fully appreciate. Never before in human history has another country or region achieved such spectacular economic development in such a short period of time. When it comes to understanding China, Western scholars have always missed the mark like 'scratching an itch through one's boot', as the Chinese saying goes. Discussions on the interaction between China's rise and the global order among international academic and policy circles have long analysed such interactions from a static perspective, simply attributing it to the inevitable conflict between an established power and a rising one. This book, however, proposes that we should, from a dynamic perspective, treat China as an inherent variable of globalisation and focus on the interactions between China and other actors. This book defines the process of reglobalisation as the expansion of globalisation and focusses on the analysis of institutional changes and systemic equilibrium to make theoretical contributions.

Second, this book seeks to use China's responsibilities in the era of globalisation as a point of departure and, in discussing how Chinese scholars view the world, to incorporate China's thinking and plans into the discussions on the global order in transformation. In a more inclusive frame of mind, we need to see China as an experimental field for globalisation, so as to transcend the idea of zero-sum games and to reduce the risk of the globalisation process being torn apart between rival camps.

Based on these analyses, this book tries to put forward four major propositions for discussion.

The first proposition is that globalisation was embedded in and born out of the coming apart of the Cold War. The end of the Cold War marked the true arrival of the era of globalisation. Globalisation indicates not only competition, but also an expansion of the international order, which has gone from International Order 1.0, which was limited to Europe, to International Order 2.0 in which the world was governed jointly by Europe and the US, and then to International Order 3.0, comprising a cross-Pacific partnership that includes the transatlantic West and China along with other partners. More and more countries are being integrated into the process of reglobalisation. The Cold War marked the first time in human history when different ideas and powers competed with each other at a global scale. It was an instance of dramatic representation in the reconstruction of the global order. From the perspective of systemic change, China's political and military partial rise in a bipolar system has made China the most important force in the dissolution and reconstruction of the existing order. During the Cold War, China contributed to the world revolution as a leader of the Third World, facilitating the rebuilding of the global order in those times. From the classic standpoint of the Kissingerians, the relationship between China and the global order was a process of 'renormalisation', that is, China went from a so-called 'revisionist' state challenging the post-WWII global order led by the West back to a realist state following the principle of the balance of power. Yet from this point of view, China was

Introduction 5

shaped more by the global order than it shaped the global order. This is a binary perspective that sees China as an Other, which is deeply tinged with Western-centrism and colossally out of touch with the progression of the global order.

Second, the major challenges facing China's reentry into the world are the heterogeneity of its identity and the homogeneity of the rules of international order. When Western leaders talk about such an order, they often express a preexisting Western-centric point of view, as though they had claimed ownership over the current international order. In such Western discourse, talk of China usually comes with a clear tone of exclusivity: Is China going to challenge and even overthrow the existing rule-based order? In their eyes, the existing so-called liberal international order is a set of norms and rules constructed by states led by the US and its allies. There is clearly a sense of condescending arrogance in such a discourse: 'You must behave well in order to become a member of the existing, rule-based international order'. Such a mindset is in itself ludicrous. China is inside and outside the international order at the same time, as if in quantum physics. Then, is China a member of the existing order at all? It has obviously been part of the postwar order; its economic success, no less, is a result of its acceptance of market rules. However, in the Western liberal narrative, China does not seem to be a legitimate part of the global mainstream because its identity is considered heterogeneous when compared with that of most Western countries. Therefore, when Western decision-makers and scholars look upon the existing international order using the concept of the liberal international order, they see China as a 'black hole', as an Other that needs to be educated and changed. This thinking is clearly limited and may cause further distrust between China and the West.

Third, the expectations of the international community for China are ever rising, but China's ascent, like that of a plane flying from the troposphere to the stratosphere, is not complete and is at a point where it encounters the high risk of uncertainty. More countries are openly acknowledging China's de facto position as a global power, lauding its great achievements in economic and financial governance while also seeing much room for it to improve in its handling of security affairs. Objectively speaking, in terms of providing ideas and capabilities, China is still some distance away from being a truly global leading power.[2] It already plays an important role in the transformation and reshaping of the international order, but it still has a long way to go before it can acquire a legitimate leadership role. For any great power to rise, just like a plane, it must endure the tumult of taking off before entering the stages of ascending and cruising. For an emerging power, the stages of taking off, ascending, and cruising are those when it faces the most pressure. In the current East Asian order, China's international behaviour is not only pressured by the hegemon, but also diverted by neighbouring countries. This dual pressure raised the costs of China's rise and reduced the space for its military rise as a rational strategic option. On the one hand, as there are both strategic distrust and contradictions between China and the hegemonic system with the US as the centre, the American alliance system will force China to maintain the current order. On the other hand, China's soft and hard powers are not yet completely in line with the expectations of smaller neighbouring countries, so it

6 Reglobalisation

cannot truly win all-around support from the international community on major strategic issues. The US, as the hegemon in East Asia, enjoys the luxury of wasting away strategic resources that are easily obtained from other countries and in a sense beyond ideology, the luxury of relying on resources both within the system and outside the system, thus increasing the forces hedging against China. In contrast, a rising power must meet the needs of both the hegemon and the international community, so it often applies a hedging strategy of wooing small countries for their support and seeking to conciliate with the hegemon.

The fourth and final proposition to be made is that China needs to strike a balance between self-restraint and outward involvement. Since the reform and opening up era, China's strategic objectives in international order have been humble and inward-looking. However, the ideological contradictions between China and the US are not gone forever but are only mitigated and hidden. When their capabilities are getting closer, it is possible that such ideological frictions may return, as the tensions in US-China relations in the past 2 years have shown. Consequently, both sides need to maintain strategic self-restraint of their own forces, which is by no means easy. Strategic self-restraint is a rare virtue in international politics, the importance of which both sides must come to realise. Whereas the arguments in recent years in China about '*taoguang yanghui*' (keeping a low profile and biding time) indicate that a foreign policy of '*fenfa youwei*' (striving to accomplish something) is increasingly a preference of the Chinese government. There is a growing domestic consensus in China that it should increase its capabilities of obtaining resources, expand international participation, and be a leader in global affairs as a great power. In the era of globalisation, to embed China's rise in the existing international system is an optimal choice to reduce the pressure on its rise.[3] The rising power needs to have enough strategic composure and patience, adopt prudent and wise strategies, and develop its capabilities of obtaining resources.

This book is divided into eight chapters. Chapter 1 provides an overview of China's history since the mid-nineteenth century of participating in the various processes of globalisation. The chapter highlights China's leading role in the reglobalization process since 2008, by emphasizing the unique embedded rise of China. Chapter 2 begins with a critical review of the dilemma facing the old globalisation. It then provides a definition of reglobalisation, followed by a typology of four types of globalisation: closed globalisation, involuted globalisation, disembedded globalisation, and inclusive globalisation. Chapter 3 evaluates the philosophical foundations of reglobalisation, including China's inclusive philosophy and the Confucian relational thinking. Chapters 4–6 provide three case studies of China's role in leading the process of reglobalisation. Chapter 4 seeks to demonstrate how China's flagship Belt and Road Initiative (BRI) is in fact in accord with the core characteristics of reglobalisation. Chapter 5 surveys China's leadership role in developing the Asian Infrastructure Investment Bank (AIIB) and how that has contributed to the process of reglobalisation. Showcasing Alibaba's cutting-edge innovations in promoting the digital economy 2.0, Chapter 6 tells the story of reglobalisation of one of the world's most successful high-tech companies. Chapter 7 suggests that reglobalisation is a two-way street: China embraces

Introduction   7

globalisation by carrying out innovative economic reforms, which in turn helps to reshape the process of reglobalisation. Chapter 8 envisions a three-stage roadmap of China leading the process of reglobalisation. The book concludes by emphasizing that China has already become an important driving force for reshaping the globalisation process. When China meets the world again, the reglobalisation process that such an encounter unleashes is bound to shape and reshape the world in the years and decades to come.

Notes

1 Henry A. Kissinger, *World Order*, London, UK: Penguin Books, 2015.
2 Wang Dong, 'Cong Munihei kan Zhongguo yu guoji zhixu' ['Viewing China and the International Order from Munich'], *Xuexi shibao* [*Study Times*], 29 February 2016, p. 2.
3 Sun Xuefeng, *Zhongguo jueqi kunjing: lilun sikao yu zhanlue xuanze* [*Dilemma of China's Rise: Theoretical Reflections and Strategic Options*], Beijing: Social Sciences Academic Press, 2011; Kai He and Huiyun Feng, 'China's Bargaining Strategies for a Peaceful Rise: Success and Challenges', *Asian Security*, Vol. 10, No. 2, 2014, pp. 168–187.

1 Embracing globalisation and China's narrative

Be it a black cat or a white cat, a cat that can catch mice is a good cat.

Deng Xiaoping, the chief architect of
China's Reform and Opening Up, talking
about development, *Selected Works of Deng
Xiaoping, Vol. I*

We have negotiated for 15 years ... Black-haired men have turned into grey-haired men.

Comments of the former Chinese premier
Zhu Rongji about China's long and winding
road into the World Trade Organization
(WTO), 1999

In February 2016, the China COSCO Shipping Corporation was founded out of the merger of the two major shipping companies in China, the China Ocean Shipping (Group) Company and China Shipping Container Lines, and was officially listed on the Shanghai Stock Exchange. The new megacorporation boasted of 1,114 ships of various kinds as well as 85.32 million deadweight tonnes shipping capacity in total, more than any other shipping company in the world. Its enormous size and capabilities have become the epitome and a symbol of China's rise.[1] In keeping with its fast expanding material strength, China's ability in institutional innovation has also been rising rapidly. In 2010, a shipping capability trading platform dedicated to world-leading innovation was officially launched in Shanghai, the shipping and financial centre of China. The Shanghai Shipping Freight Exchange Company (SSFEC) introduced the model of shipping derivatives trading, giving rise to the unique 'Shanghai standard' in international shipping.[2] In the meantime, the Shanghai Pilot Free Trade Area initiated a new round of synchronisation of Chinese and international reforms, in accordance with the Belt and Road Initiative (BRI). Compared with the previous rounds of reforms, this one had a distinct feature, which was to link China's development completely with globalisation. Forty years ago, China's reform and opening up focussed on solving domestic problems of economic development. The language concerning globalisation in

Embracing globalisation and China's narrative 9

the reform plan merely served as a backdrop for domestic reforms; there were few reform measures linking domestic and international development, but China has now progressed from domestic reforms to global ones, striving to lead in new trends in globalisation. Based on the matrix of the existing world order, new, innovative global governance regimes and rules are being devised by China in a creative manner. One can imagine that once China's huge engine begins working, the old globalisation process must be expanded to be more tolerant and inclusive to pursue new, all-win trends in international coexistence. We may define the current globalisation process as 'reglobalisation' instead of as 'new globalisation' because, rather than starting afresh, China is pushing for the enlargement of this process to upgrade the existing global framework through internal and international reforms.

1.1 The globalisation process and the Chinese reorientation

The concept of globalisation originated in Western society and eventually came to be accepted and used throughout the world, which itself embodies the process of globalisation. For a long time, China has been considered a passive recipient of the concept and theories of globalisation, with its biggest influence on it being the choice to embrace the tide in the late 1970s after numerous struggles. However, in retrospect, China had already begun its true embrace of globalisation because it was doubtless a major participant in the globalisation process in the first three decades of the 20th century. Shanghai was a first-rate global metropolis, swarming with international tourists, the number of which equalled that of London, Tokyo, and Paris. Chinese students, revolutionary activists, and businessmen were a pretty common sight all over the world. A far larger percentage of the faculty of then Yenching, Peking, and Tsinghua Universities studied abroad than that of the faculty of famous Chinese universities today, and most students at that time wrote their theses in English.[3] These signs of internationalisation show that China did not try to close its doors to the outside world even when it was a weaker country and faced the dual crises of international turmoil and domestic revolutions. The tides of globalisation slipped silently through China's half-open doors.

The process of globalisation is generally considered to contain several wavelengths, the latest of which stems from the international economic and trade relations of the 1970s as well as from the rapid growth of non-state actors. Yet, seen in a larger historical narrative beginning from the mid- and late nineteenth century, after its first close encounter with the rest of the world, China was forced to participate in the Western-dominated globalisation process, which has left behind countless bitter memories. It is more appropriate to say that China then was embroiled rather than participated in globalisation, for China, still stuck in its delusions of being 'the only celestial kingdom', was coerced into the tides of globalisation by Western gunboats and became a peripheral actor that was exploited and squeezed in the system. However, it was precisely that process that gave China a chance to open its eyes and take a look at the strange world outside. Later came the realisation that to save itself and to ensure its survival, China had to overcome its own challenges

10 *Reglobalisation*

and keep up with the rest of the world both culturally and ideationally. With that, China's socialisation into the global community began, its national consciousness was born through continuous trials and errors. In 1902, Liang Qichao, one of China's foremost intellectual leaders in the early twentieth century, first proposed the idea of the 'Chinese people'. The Chinese government has since increasingly seen the world system in terms of national interest, power politics, and international law. As a result, China's first encounter with globalisation in modern times and its embroilment into the international system initiated its own reforms and modernisation. This ancient civilisation was 'resocialised' by Western rules.

The westernisation and constitution movements during the late Qing dynasty expedited China's involvement in the international society. China also played an important role as a participating nation in WWI and WWII, but with the establishment of the People's Republic in 1949, China completely leaned into the Soviet Camp to rid itself of Western influence. The US and China quickly became ideological rivals and fought each other in the Korean War. The US imposed comprehensive sanctions on China, while China considered American imperialism its Number 1 enemy. In the 1960s, China began 'hitting with both fists', largely staying out of the Socialist and Capitalist Camps. The Cultural Revolution swept China into an era of 'ultra-left' ideologies and closed its doors to globalisation. It was the Third Plenary Session of the Eleventh Central Committee of the Chinese Communist Party in 1978 that brought China back and began its reform and opening up. Only this time, China actively made the historical transformation of rejoining the international society and globalisation process. The historic reform and opening up was China's second embrace of globalisation. Different from its first socialisation after the Opium Wars, China made a conscientious choice to 'change itself and impact the world'.[4] This second embrace was aimed at modernisation based on the modern nation-state rather than on accepting sovereignty, nationalism, and other already internalised notions of modern times. Compared with its first attempt at globalisation, the reform and opening up was China's own choice, a decision to benefit itself through cost-benefit analysis. In China's official narrative, the reform and opening up did not begin in a treacherous environment, but rather during an era of strategic opportunity and in a conducive environment. Before it began its reforms, the United Kingdom and the United States both came up with 'neoliberal' policies in the 1970s and 1980s that advocated less government interference and the expansion of overseas markets. US-Soviet détente and the rise of the East Asian 'tigers' created conducive trade conditions for China's participation in the international industrial reconfiguration. Deng Xiaoping, the chief architect of the reform and opening up, made the judgement that the theme of the times had turned from 'Wars and Revolutions' into 'Peace and Development'. However, until the 2008 global financial crisis, China's diplomacy had been following the strategy of keeping a low profile and biding time' and trying to fit in and learn from others instead of actively shaping international rules. Table 1.1 summarises China's three times of participation in globalisation."

From a larger historical perspective, globalisation represents repeated expansions of the world order. It started with Magellan's voyage around the world in the fifteenth century. Globalisation 1.0 was limited to Europe alone. With

Embracing globalisation and China's narrative 11

Table 1.1 The history of China's three-time participation in globalisation

Stages	Periods	China's Role	Motivation for Globalisation	Features of Interaction
The First Time	From the mid-nineteenth to the mid-twentieth centuries	Peripheral/passive actor	The gunboat policy of European imperial powers	One-directional, passive manner: China was forced into globalisation to learn under oppression
The Second Time	1979 to 2008	Central/active participant	US-dominated Western liberalist economy	One-directional, active manner: China was embedded in globalisation process for mutual growth
The Third Time	Since 2009	Core/active shaper	The Beijing Consensus and the Washington Consensus complementing and competing with each other	Two-directional, active manner: China actively shaping globalisation to expand and upgrade it

Note: Table compiled by the authors.

the development of the Industrial Revolution and the integration of the entire Western world into globalisation, Globalisation 2.0 (British hegemony) and 3.0 (American hegemony) began to take shape with a transatlantic joint governance model. Later, when the Cold War divided and then united the world, the era of China's reform and opening up and transpacific cooperation began, launching Globalisation 4.0.[5] Theoretically, the relationship between great powers and the rest of the world has four development paradigms: revolution, evolution, devolution, and involution. A revolutionary relationship denotes a radical change or interruption, such as China's 'rebel' status from 1949 to 1979. An evolutionary development means that China forms a community of shared future with the world and is able to decisively facilitate the progress and growth of the world order when the international system is facing a major crisis, similar to the highly recognised role played by the US during the two World Wars. The devolution, degeneration, or deterioration of a great power's relations with the outside world usually happens when a fallen hegemon, in order to safeguard its former status, makes a last attempt by initiating preventive wars or expansive strategies. On either side of devolution and evolution lies the stage of involution, a transition period. After the revelry of 'the end of history' and the 'unipolar moment' following the end of the Cold War,[6] the West now faces more 'invisible' enemies, not only from the competition of non-Western countries,

12 *Reglobalisation*

but also in nontraditional security fields such as terrorism, financial turmoil, refugee crises, cyber security, and, above all, climate change. The first half of the twenty-first century is a crucial period for China's rise, in which profound changes will stem from the interaction of China's society and the international community and take place in Western societies, as can been seen from the most talked-about word 'change' in elections in almost every Western country. China is changing, the West is changing, and the whole world is changing.

1.2 China leading a new round of globalisation

The political influence of the 2008 global financial crisis is felt even today. After the collective involution of the West, the world increasingly turns to China. China understands that the setbacks of the West-led globalisation do not mean the end or demise of globalisation. Emerging economies, especially China, have taken up the baton for globalisation. On 17 January 2017, during his keynote speech at the World Economic Forum Annual Meeting in Davos, Switzerland, Chinese President Xi Jinping emphasised that 'just blaming economic globalisation for the world's problems is inconsistent with reality, and it will not help solve the problems'. He called upon nations to 'commit themselves to growing an open global economy … to remain committed to developing global free trade and investment, promote trade and investment liberalisation and facilitation through opening up and say no to protectionism'. He also pointed out that 'no one will emerge as a winner in a trade war. Pursuing protectionism is like locking oneself in a dark room. While wind and rain may be kept outside, that dark room will also block light and air'.[7] President Xi Jinping's landmark speech was widely hailed by the international community as bearing 'tremendous historic significance' and shouldering the leadership for supporting economic globalisation amidst the shadows of antiglobalisation, deglobalisation, and trade protectionism.[8] The interactive patterns between China and globalisation have changed directions in a profound way: China has grown from a student on the periphery of globalisation trying to fit in, into an important engine of the new round of reglobalisation. The transformation shall be explained in the following three ways.

First, the world's leading economic size and trade volume of China will have deep and far-reaching influence on global politics. In 2013, China surpassed the US and became the world's biggest trader of goods. China is now the largest trade partner to more than 120 countries and regions and is the largest export market for more than 70 countries and regions (see Figure 1.1). As the largest emerging economy, China will create enormous economic momentum for the world in the foreseeable future and will also give rise to a super middle-class consumer market. The synchronisation of China's domestic demand and its globalising efforts will produce a phenomenon of Chinese consumers supporting foreign economies all over the world. In 2009, the world's middle class comprised over 1.8 billion people, including 664 million from Europe, 525 million from Asia, and 338 million from North America. In 2020, the global middle-class population will rise to 3.2 billion, and according to the US National Intelligence Council (2012), this

Embracing globalisation and China's narrative 13

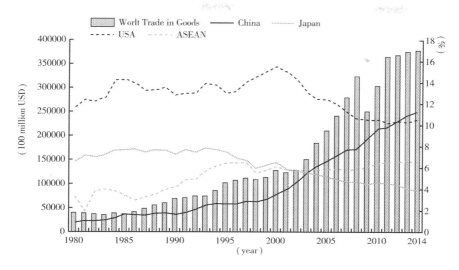

Figure 1.1 The percentages of trade in goods of the world's major economies*

number will be 4.9 billion in 2030. In this trend of rapid growth, China, India, and other Asian emerging markets will contribute the largest major middle-class consuming power: the middle-class population of China and India will account for 66% of that of the entire world; the consumption driven by that 66% will also take up 59% of the world's consumption, which, for this same group in 2009, was a mere 23%.[9] Before 2030, China will continue the trend of its lightning-fast growth of middle-class population, which alone will take up 75% of China's total population, exceeding the entire populations of Europe, the US, and Japan combined. It will truly be a world-shaking number.[10]

Second, China has shown great strength in exports and has become a net exporter of its economic, financial, and tourism development modes. In 2016, China surpassed the US to become the world's largest market for business travel. In 2015, Chinese citizens made 120 million trips overseas, generating $104.5 billion in travel expenses. These numbers increased from those of the previous year by 12% and 16.7%, respectively. Against the backdrop of economic downturns across the world, Chinese tourists have become more and more influential globally.[11] Additionally, in recent years, China's active foreign direct investment and acquisitions have been expanded in more areas. In the 15 years since China's entry into the WTO, its exports increased by 7.6 times, from $266.098 billion in 2001 to $2.276 trillion in 2015, while its imports increased by almost 6 times from $243.553 billion to $1.682 trillion during the same period. China has now become the world's biggest trading nation, the owner of the biggest stock of foreign exchange reserves, the second largest economy, and the biggest buyer of primary products of various kinds. These outstanding economic achievements have broad global appeal.[12] The

14 *Reglobalisation*

BRI, the Asian Infrastructure Investment Bank (AIIB), and other public goods have begun to be seen as the new business cards of China and signs of its 'soft power'. China has also pushed for the perfection of global financial governance regimes. In 2015, the volume of cross-border trade settled in renminbi (RMB) amounted to $1.1 trillion, which accounted for 30% of China's foreign trade and 3% of global trade. In 2000, RMB was nowhere to be seen in cross-border trade settlements. The internationalisation of RMB gained significant ground through bilateral agreements with Australia, Japan, Korea, Russia, and other major trade partners of China. The rise of RMB can become a constructive force in promoting change in Chinese and international currency systems. The reserve currency status of RMB in the International Monetary Fund (IMF) and the establishment of the New Development Bank and the AIIB demonstrate China's rising position in the world economy.[13] China's central bank has set up almost 20 RMB settlement centres in global financial strongholds such as Hong Kong, Singapore, New York, London, Frankfurt, and Doha.

Third, China has led the wave of globalisation and resisted the voices against deglobalisation with real action. Statistics show that in 2016, China's economic growth accounted for 33% of the world's total. The Chinese economy was the world's biggest economic engine. In March 2017, the manufacturing industry achieved steady growth again in most parts of Asia. China was the trendsetter yet again.[14] In recent years, China has actively increased imports and has safeguarded open and free trade globally. It has participated actively in structural reforms of the international economy and has contributed its wisdom and plans in global economic governance. The BRI and the AIIB are concrete actions in China's support of economic globalisation. The spirit of the BRI is to stress open cooperation, infrastructure connectivity, uninterrupted trade, the smooth flow of funds as well as facilitating understanding between different people. Globalisation promoted by the BRI benefits not only China, but also the participating economies along the Belt and Road. In 2016, among sunken international market demand, the economic and trade cooperation between China and the participating economies along the Belt and Road achieved a great deal: the total import and export volume amounted to $6.3 trillion, indicating an increase of 0.6% over the previous year; aggregated investment was $18.5 billion, which, in turn, created $1.1 billion in tax revenues and 180,000 jobs for those economies. China has made other concrete efforts to facilitate economic globalisation. It has pushed the construction of free-trade areas forward, playing a constructive and positive role in the negotiation of Regional Comprehensive Economic Partnership (RCEP) agreements. It is a staunch supporter of multilateral trade regimes, having facilitated the Doha Round trade negotiations and having taken real action to promote plurilateral trade agreement negotiations under a multilateral framework. China has also actively participated in the perfection of the global economic governance structure, making its voice heard in multilateral and regional platforms, such as G20, the BRICS (Brazil, Russia, India, China and South Africa) summit, and Asia-Pacific Economic Cooperation (APEC).[15]

1.3 The embedded style of national rise with Chinese characteristics

In the past 40 years of China's rapid rise, Chinese leaders have repeatedly declared that 'China's development is not to start anew on its own or get rid of existing institutions, but to find common ground in each other's strategies and complement each other's strengths'.[16] From China's perspective, its rise benefits from the international political and economic system formed after WWII. This means that, in its rise, China needs to accept the existing rules in order to join the current international system. Western international relations theory often refers to a rising state as a 'revisionist state', which is thought of as a nation actively seeking to change the world order,[17] while a 'status quo power' is one that builds, benefits from, and safeguards the existing world order, whose strategic objective is to keep and sustain the existing international system. Obviously, such a dichotomy is limited in perspective. If China's rise is the result of the existing international system, it stands to reason that China should have an enormous incentive to maintain the current system. It is also why China actively supports such institutions and concepts as the UN, the WTO, and free trade. As China's rise is embedded in the globalisation process, once it decides to join the tide of globalisation, it must change some domestic institutions that are incongruent with common international norms and practices. By the time of its entry into the WTO in December 2001, China's attitude toward multilateral institutions and WTO membership had already undergone changes. Its former sole motive to maximise its own trade benefits as a member of the General Agreement on Trade and Tariffs (GATT) had turned into comprehensive efforts to integrate with the global economic system and to internalise the rules in the domestic economic system. China's learning curve upon entering the WTO stems from the awareness that it ought not to be an exception.[18] Here, we will summarise the manner of China's deep integration into and its influence on the world's landscape and development as the *Embedded Style of National Rise* (see Figure 1.2).

The idea of 'embeddedness' comes from the prominent Hungarian-British philosopher Karl Polanyi, whose thinking was that material production and exchange activities are embedded in such social motivations as the sense of responsibility and honour and are thus realised spontaneously. Material fulfilment is the concomitant effect of social action; economic institutions are embedded in social ones and cannot operate alone.[19] This inspired the famous American sociologist Mark Granovetter to propose that behaviour and institutions are deeply confined by social relations and that one sort of social relations is embedded in others.[20]

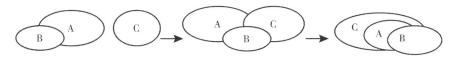

Figure 1.2 Illustration of the embedded style of national rise in the era of globalisation.

16 *Reglobalisation*

The biggest difference between China's rise and that of Germany or Japan is that the former is taking place against the backdrop of globalisation. In its rise, China has formed a symbiotic relationship with the global hegemon, to which American historian Niall Ferguson has referred as 'Chinamerica' or 'Chimerica'.[21] The historical background of China's rise is the opening up to the outside world; and this is a result of the embrace of and integration with the globalisation process. Without the trends of the globalisation era, China's rise would have been impossible – much like a body of water without a source or a tree without roots. Without the stable international order provided by the hegemon, China's rise would have been rife with setbacks. Hence, the mutually embedded, symbiotic relationship between China and the international community and between the rising power and the hegemon in this era of profound globalisation: without a prosperous China, the world would be in chaos; without the structure of the existing international order, China would not have been the world's largest trader. From the end of the Cold War to the outbreak of the 2008 financial crisis, the world was in a period of highly open globalisation and prosperity. China's rise benefited directly from it. In 2006, the US was the biggest trade partner of 127 countries, while China was that of 70. In 2011, the situation was entirely the opposite: China became the biggest trade partner of 124 countries, and the US was that of 76. In a span of just 5 years, China had surpassed the US to become the biggest trade partner of many countries, including US allies such as South Korea and Australia.[22] Granovetter used embeddedness metaphorically to imply two inseparable and symbiotic variables A and B, with A rooted in B in a codependent relationship.[23] Here, we can also use the same metaphor in China's relationship with globalisation: China, as an international actor, is always embedded in the international community, sometimes in a peripheral position, sometimes in a central position. After 2008, when faced with global trends against globalisation, a strong China, as an embedded, rising power, needed to stand up and assume more responsibilities to restore and improve the global system that had nourished and facilitated China's own development. Although the main constructs of the system are still left with Western marks, it did not stop China from giving the system some new momentum and meaning in a peaceful way of gradual progress. This is in line with the emphasis in traditional Chinese culture on 'the Way' or 'Dao', which is to go with the trend, making changes to some things while leaving others intact. Laozi, one of China's greatest philosophers and founder of Daoism, once famously put it, 'The Dao (Way) follows its own nature' (*dao fa zi ran*). China's development model of being embedded into the international system is the Dao to follow the trends of globalisation. Given its current obstacles, after measuring its capabilities, China is willing to take on the heavy task of furthering globalisation, and to meet others' expectations by carrying on with the Dao. China's rise is embedded in the existing order – it is not a replacement for it. Since 1978, the characteristics of Chinese diplomacy can be summed up into the following three strategies.

The first is the strategy to seek legitimacy in a gradual way, that is, to actively participate in existing international organisations and structures of international cooperation. The constructive responsibilities assumed by China are proportionate to the international influence it exerts. These international institutions and structures, such as the UN, World Bank, and WTO, mostly came into being in a process dominated by Western countries led by the US, forming the framework on which the post-WWII international system has relied. The crucial sign of the absence of China's challenge of the international order is that China has, since the 1980s, been more deeply receptive of and integrated into those organisations and platforms. Its increasing influence and level of involvement in the existing international system are demonstrated by the fact that it is deepening its participation, assuming greater responsibilities, and exerting more influence in those very organisations and platforms. For instance, part of the voting rights of the IMF have been transferred from the US and European countries to emerging countries, such as China. Chinese experts have also been named vice president of the World Bank and chief economist at the IMF. In November 2013, Hao Ping, China's Vice Minister of Education, was elected chair of the UNESCO General Conference for a 2-year term. China's power of influence and agenda-setting is also rising in G20 and APEC. Historically, the rise of a nation has not occurred within a short period of time, instead it is a process that requires legitimacy and patience. China has several thousand years of history and has patience dealing with issues pertaining to a power shift. Chinese leaders understand that international leadership is strongly associated with legitimacy and that China needs to embed itself into the existing system of international regimes to gradually be accepted by most countries.

The second is the strategy to invest in both reform and innovation. The flipside of China's increasing level of involvement and influence in the international system is the fact that, while following the existing multilateral international structures, China is also building new structures of international cooperation more proactively. These include certain bilateral structures. For example, under the WTO framework, China has established free-trade areas with Peru, Chile, Pakistan, New Zealand, Iceland, and Switzerland and is actively pushing for free-trade agreements with Australia, Mexico, Canada, Norway, and many other countries. If China signs free-trade agreements with Canada, Mexico, Brazil, and others, then those nations with free-trade relations with China will cover most of the membership of the Trans-Pacific Partnership grouping. Meanwhile, China is actively promoting the development of the international multilateral cooperation system. In the 1990s, China founded the Shanghai Cooperation Organization (SCO), a first of its kind for China. In the face of the Asian financial crisis, China initiated the China-Association of Southeast Asian Nations (ASEAN) Free Trade Area. Such forms of multilateral cooperation initiated by China have gained prominence in recent years. Just recently, either alone or with many other nations, China initiated and founded the BRICS Bank (proposed on 27 March 2013, in Durban, South Africa), as well as the AIIB (proposed on 2 October 2013, in Jakarta, Indonesia). China is actively pushing forward such multilateral cooperation mechanisms as the East Asia Free Trade Area, the SCO Energy Club, the SCO Free Trade Area, and the BRI. These measures are about nurturing and

18 *Reglobalisation*

creating new space and platforms for international cooperation without challenging existing international multilateral institutions; they are an incremental way of shifting the power structure of the international system.[24] By trying to set up new international rules, China can appropriately introduce and nurture more advanced global governance mechanisms that will not entirely replace the existing conventional international mechanisms.

The third is the strategy to produce consent. In the era of globalisation, countries depend on each other for their survival and interests. A rising power continues to strive for more international influence. What is different from before is that it must strive for coordinative and attractive influence rather than hierarchical and dominating power. Theoretically, influence can be attractive or coercive. Thus, international leadership can also be attractive or coercive. In the globalised modern international community, small- and medium-size countries have a stronger understanding of their rights and positions of equality. When a great power mainly exerts attractive influence, its leadership will be more popular globally. For instance, shortly after WWII, the US opened up its market to trade partners, which served as a key source of its international leadership. The US-led Bretton Woods System and Marshall Plan turned out to be very popular among its allies. On the other hand, when the US tried to force its leadership on others through the use of brute force and economic coercion, its legitimacy as a global leader was greatly compromised. For example, the US was heavily criticised when it launched the wars in Afghanistan and Iraq and led the intervention in Syria.[25] At present, the interaction and mutual influence between China and the rest of the world have reached new heights. China's influence on the rest of the world is increasing, while there are more factors affecting Chinese diplomacy. A confident China should learn to understand the thinking and concerns of other countries and pursue its interests in a diplomatic, peaceful, and more acceptable way. China should lead by attractive leadership and treat other countries as equals.[26]

The old rules created by the West after WWII and the new international rules created by China after 2008 are like the old branches and new buds of the same towering tree. Although, for a period of time, the public goods proposed by the rising state (new buds) will naturally replace those age-old international institutions that are unable to meet the demand of the times (old branches), it is not logically inevitable that the two will enter into a relationship of competition and zero-sum games. A big tree has enough vertical and horizontal space for old branches and new buds to weather storms together; the development of new international institutions is not at the expense of old institutions. In contrast, new buds will bring new life to the tree and provide new nutrients to the old branches, which is beneficial to its transformation and metabolism. An even more efficient and functional new platform needs to grow on top of the existing system. Such coexistence of old and new systems is another meaning of embeddedness. New global governance regimes that are truly tested need to continuously attract stakeholders to join in an accumulative and incremental manner, in order to achieve a 'coral reef effect' of healthy growth and eventually give birth to a new international system.

1.4 Understanding globalisation through network thinking

The best way for China to shape the world is not through power competition. Rather, China should do so by channelling its influence to the rest of the world via numerous pipelines in the diplomatic network. This soft governance of relationships can actively cultivate international social capital so that China's rise will be organically rooted in the international community. In other words, China's diplomatic transformation should go beyond linear thinking and link up the exogenous and endogenous variables of its national interests with an approach to the multidimensional connection.[27] In this view, interconnectivity itself is a strategic diplomatic resource that is more important than power. It should be noted that China's rise under globalisation is taking place in a networked world of global interdependence.[28] Since the beginning of the twenty-first century, the process of China's rise has involved a continuous integration into the outside world and the construction of networks with it. In recent years, China has taken the initiative to develop networks with neighbouring countries, while planting the element of '*guanxi*' (Chinese expression of the system of social networks and relationships) in these networks. The new pattern of Chinese diplomacy, has put forward its basic judgement of its surrounding environment by focussing on its relationship with other countries. In this respect, it has created a new structure of networks realised by the building of the Silk Road Economic Belt and the Twenty-First-Century Maritime Silk Road, or the BRI in short.[29] Today, China is working to construct its own hub linkages and to connect them widely with other networks in order to produce a radiating effect.

Globalisation needs new impetus in a period of transformation. China's relational thinking is consistent with the interconnectedness of reglobalisation. Since the 2008 financial crisis, there has been a growing worldwide consensus that China has become the world's new economic engine and that the 'China Cycle' of globalisation has been ushered in. If there were an economic slowdown in China or an increase of 1% in its growth rate, most countries in the world would be impacted greatly. Globalisation formerly dominated by the US has now run into trouble. Relational thinking, with traditional Chinese wisdom at its core, holds that informal interactions and a nonstructured web of relations among nations will help defuse the tension of the leadership dilemma within the global system. Such a dilemma arises out of the history of a hegemon acting as the world leader who constructs a rule-based system that global development relies on totally. Once this system reveals its own limitations and the hegemon lacks the will to reform, globalisation will be on a low tide. China's vision of reglobalisation is a multi-centred and relation-oriented dynamic mode, emphasising network thinking of multiple centres and diverse participation instead of an established centre or leadership role. In this view, as important as nodes are, to transcend the tunnel visions of each node, a nonhierarchical, open, and flat relationship pattern is necessary. This is a crucial distinction between Chinese- and American-style governance: the former advocates soft interactions while the latter emphasises enforcement and independence. Traditional globalisation stresses a governance system in which an actor with superior strength controls another actor through rewards and punishments. Thus, such a system implies coercion, dominance, control, violence, and other conflictual forces. In the globalised interactions of interdependence, superior strength comes from 'relational power' rather than from 'coercive power'.[30] Relational power refers to the assimilation and soft influence of power. It exists in the network of social interaction and has acquired the feature of intersubjectivity and cannot be reduced to individual attributes. The prominent liberalist international relations (IR) scholar G. John Ikenberry pointed out that the power basis of American 'international constitutional order' is the commitment of mutually beneficial relations with US allies.[31] The ways of realising power include legitimacy and resources. The concept of 'soft power' proposed by the preeminent IR scholar Joseph S. Nye clearly diverts the legitimacy of power to relational power.[32] This so-called relational power is the ability to obtain resources through relationships. The network of relations and the resources flowing within it are like blood vessels and blood, or form and content. China's diplomacy is marked by such relationality and network thinking. For instance, its foreign aid programmes have abandoned power-dominated exchanges, strived to broaden relationship channels, emphasised the effectiveness of relationship investment, which helps to overcome the temptation of short-term interests and realise the sustainability of core support.[33] China has recently upheld the principle of amity, sincerity, mutual benefit, and inclusiveness, on the basis of which it maintains healthy relationships with neighbouring countries. Initiatives such as establishing the AIIB and the BRI have been launched to construct an interconnected regional and global network. On 7 September 2013, President Xi Jinping put forward the initiative of building the Silk Road Economic Belt during his visit to the University of Nazarbayev in Kazakhstan. In October that year, the Twenty-First-Century Maritime Silk Road initiative was proposed during his state visit to Indonesia (see Figure 1.3).

In May 2017, the Leaders Roundtable of the Belt and Road Forum for International Cooperation was held in Beijing, gathering heads of state and heads of government representing more than 30 countries as well as distinguished guests from more than 100 countries. Through dialogues and close communication on trade, economy, culture, and people-to-people exchanges, these neighbouring

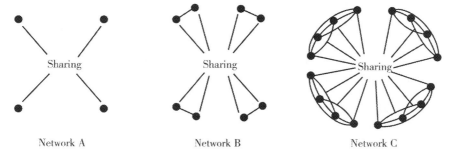

Figure 1.3 The network expansion model of the Belt and Road.

Embracing globalisation and China's narrative   21

countries and international organisations have become 'nodes' that connect the strategic network of China's diplomacy. The total trade volume generated from the Belt and Road network between 2014 and 2016 has exceeded $3 trillion. China's investment in the Belt and Road countries has surpassed $50 billion, with Chinese companies having set up 56 trade and economic zones in more than 20 countries, creating about $1.1 billion of tax revenue and 180,000 jobs. In his speech at the opening ceremony of the forum, President Xi mentioned the idea of building networks no less than five times. While talking about the achievements of the Belt and Road trade, he said,

> During the forum, a number of cooperation agreements on policy connectivity and action plans will be signed. We will also launch Belt and Road cooperation initiative on trade connectivity together with some 60 countries and international organisations. Such policy connectivity will produce a multiplying effect on cooperation among the parties involved.

The so-called 'multiplying effect' reveals the focus on network transmissions.[34] Network thinking benefits globalisation by providing information and trust and by nurturing public goods.

First, relations can transmit information and trust. Network relations can be strong and weak based on different levels of familiarity, attachment, and frequency of contact. The prominent American political scientist Robert Putnam distinguished between 'bridging' and 'bonding' networks, wherein the former is socially inclusive with open channels of access, giving rise to established connections between heterogeneous groups, while the latter is exclusive of outsiders, leading to identity circles of strong cohesion.[35] On the one hand, weak ties are the loose associations of different networks, often indicating lower levels of frequency of interaction, familiarity, closeness, mutual trust, and a shorter history of engagement. As the subject of weak ties belongs to different groups without a common identity, with longer social distances, a more convoluted chain of action and higher informational heterogeneity between them, the information transmitted by weak ties tends to be nonrepetitive and of the best value to individual actors. China has a triple identity in international society: it is a large, developing, and non-Western country. This composite identity can serve as a bridge between the Global South and the Global North. Not only can China transmit the voices of developing countries in the socioeconomic development arena, but also urge developed countries to carry out the obligations of global governance. When China stands at the 'structural hole' – connecting the two groups with either strong or weak ties – of the global network, it will enjoy the advantage of being a mediator who transmits information and resources both ways while sustaining the weak ties between developing and developed countries.[36] On the other hand, strong ties are those between parties with a long history of engagement, higher levels of emotional attachment, closeness, and reciprocity.[37] Countries in the same network can mobilise each other's resources in times of need through mutual trust; by repeated interaction, trust building, and nurturing social capital, one country's forces can be

22 *Reglobalisation*

shared by its partners. In daily life, one can borrow a friend's car to move his or her own house. In diplomatic practice countries can get things done with the strength of partners. Friendship is a form of social capital. In the same way, a positive diplomatic relationship is social capital. Sustaining social capital requires reciprocity, a mutually beneficial relationship at the fundamental level.[38] The most typical example of reciprocity between China and the US is that of US President George W. Bush attending the Opening Ceremony of the 2008 Beijing Olympic Games to reciprocate and show the importance China placed on bilateral ties. To reciprocate, then Chinese President Hu Jintao attended the 2010 Nuclear Security Summit held in Washington. Through this, China retained its bilateral ties in harmony.

Second, a network of ties nurtures social capital. The preeminent Chinese IR theorist Qin Yaqing pointed out that the logic of Chinese diplomacy is that as long as the process of cooperation is maintained, even if expected outcomes cannot be met right away, the trust will not worsen to irreversible levels.[39] The process of relations is self-executing and dynamic. China's Confucian culture advocates 'never doing unto others what one does not want to be done unto himself'. While dealing with conflicts of interest among different civilisations, Confucian culture emphasises tolerance and restraint, achieving overall order by turning conflict into harmony and hostility into friendship. Such ideas will surely find a way into China's diplomatic philosophy, orienting diplomatic decisions more toward long-term ties. When China is locked into a certain relationship with another party, in times of crisis, China would rather refrain from pursuing the maximisation of short-term utility and avoid hard bargains, in order to maintain positive long-term ties and leave some space in case of uncertain surroundings. The international society is relational, and the best way for China to influence the world is to nurture trust, norms, and reciprocity through social capital. The social capital theory has become an emerging paradigm of analysis in the West since the 1990s. The concept was first proposed by the prominent French sociologist Pierre Bourdieu, who thought that social capital is the sum of the resources, actual or virtual, by virtue of possessing a durable network of more or less institutionalised relationships.[40] This idea has been inherited and developed further in sociology, economics, and political science. The idea of social capital was introduced and increasingly drawn upon in the field of IR. Nan Lin, a leading scholar on social networks and social capital noted that '[as an] investment in social relations with expected returns in the marketplace', social capital can be defined as 'resources embedded in a social structure that are accessed and/or mobilised in purposive actions'.[41] Social capital theory advocates the sharing and mutual promotion of one's own interests and others' rather than a pure moralism or idealism in diplomacy. Social capital is a sort of regional public good instead of private property. Different forms of social capital, such as trust, norms, and networks, are mostly public goods, while traditional forms of capital are private goods. The social capital within a common network accumulates itself instead of being competitive and exclusive. When we take social capital to mean the organisational norms and the social ties of harmonious coexistence, cooperation, and trust commonly possessed by a country, a region or a group of countries, social capital as a collective resource can be a public good.[42]

Embracing globalisation and China's narrative   23

Notes

1 Sui Xiuyong, 'Zhongguo yuanyang haiyun jituan: "Zhongguo shenyun" quanqiu jingzhengli jihe?' ['China COSCO Shipping Corporation: What Is the Global Competitiveness of the "Chinese Magical Shipping Company?"'], cn156.com, 24 February 2016, http://www.cn156.com/article-65973-1.html.

2 Shanghai Shipping Exchange, http://www.sse.net.cn/indexIntro?indexName=intro.

3 Data collected by the authors from the graduation records of Yenching University, currently stored at the Archives of Peking University.

4 Zhang Baijia, 'Gaibian ziji, yingxiang shijie: 20 shiji Zhongguo waijiao jiben xiansuo chuyi' ['Change Oneself and Influence the World: On the Basic Threads of Chinese Diplomacy in the 20th Century'], *Zhongguo shehui kexue* [*Chinese Social Sciences*], No. 1, 2002, pp. 4–19.

5 Shao Yu and Qin Peijing, *Quanqiuhua 4.0: Zhongguo ruhe chonghui shijie zhidian* [*Globalisation 4.0: How Can China Bring Itself Back to the Top of the World*], Nanning, Guangxi: Guangxi Normal University Press, 2016; Shao Yu, '"Yidai yilu" kaiqi quanqiuhua 4.0 shidai' ['The "Belt and Road" Ushers in the Era of Globalisation 4.0'], *Shanghai zhengquan bao* [*Shanghai Securities News*], 1 April 2015; Zhou Ailin, 'Yatouhang: kaiqi "quanqiuhua 4.0" moshi' ['The AIIB: Starting the "Globalisation 4.0" Model'], Yicai.com, 15 April 2015, https://www.yicai.com/news/4605057.html.

6 Francis Fukuyama, *The End of History and the Last Man*, London, UK: Avon Books, 1992; Mark Sheetz, "Debating the Unipolar Moment," *International Security*, Vol. 22, No. 3, pp. 168-174.

7 Xi Jinping, 'Jointly Shoulder Responsibility of Our Times, Promote Global Growth', Keynote Speech at the Opening Session of the World Economic Forum 2017 Annual Meeting, 7 January 2017, Xinhuanet.com, http://www.xinhuanet.com/english/2017-01/18/c_135991184.htm.

8 Fu Ying, 'Quanqiu de biange yu Zhongguo de juese' ['Global Changes and China's Role'], *Cankao xiaoxi* [*Reference News*], 9 March 2017.

9 Homi Kharas, 'The Emerging Middle Class in Developing Countries', *OECD Development Centre Working Papers*, No. 285, OECD Publishing, Paris, http://dx.doi.org/10.1787/5kmmp8lncrns-en, 2010, p. 28.

10 US National Intelligence Council, *Global Trends 2030: Alternative Worlds*, December 2012, https://www.dni.gov/files/documents/GlobalTrends_2030.pdf, p. 9.

11 'Zhongguo chujing renshu he xiaofei ju shijie zhishou' ['China's Overseas Visits and Consumption Leading the World'], *Hainan ribao* [*Hainan Daily*], 30 January 2016, http://news.163.com/16/0130/07/BEIGQE7U00014Q4P.html.

12 Chang Lulu and Chen Zhimin, 'Xiyinxing jingji quanli zai Zhongguo waijiao zhong de yunyong' ['The Appeal of Economic Power and Its Use in Chinese Diplomacy'], *Waijiao pinglun* [*Foreign Affairs Review*], No. 3, 2014, pp. 1–16.

13 Eswar S. Prasad, *Gaining Currency: The Rise of the Renminbi*, Oxford, UK: Oxford University Press, 2016.

14 Li Yuqian, 'Zhongguo dui shijie jingji zengzhang de gongxianlv chaoguo 30%' ['China Has Contributed Over 30% of World Economic Growth'], Caixin.com, 13 January 2017, http://economy.caixin.com/2017-01-13/101043565.html.

15 Su Qingyi, '"Yidai yilu" jianshe tuidong jingji quanqiuhua fazhan' ['"The Belt and Road" Construction Facilitating the Development of Economic Globalisation'], Policy Brief No. 201707, The Institute of World Economic and Politics, Chinese Academy of Social Sciences, 28 March 2017, http://www.iwep.org.cn/xscg/xscg_sp/201703/W020170328861603712963.pdf.

16 Xi Jinping, 'Xieshou tuijin "yidai yilu" jianshe: zai "yidai yilu" guoji hezuo gaofeng luntan kaimushi shang de jianghua' ['Push Forward the "Belt and Road" Construction Hand in Hand: Speech at the Opening Ceremony of the Belt and Road Forum for

24 Reglobalisation

International Cooperation'], *Xinhua News Agency*, 14 May 2017, http://news.xinhuane t.com/politics/2017-05/14/c_1120969677.htm.

17 Yue Jianyong, 'Peaceful Rise of China: Myth or Reality?' *International Politics*, Vol. 45, No. 4, 2008, pp. 439–456; Bonnie S. Glaser and Evan S. Medeiros, 'The Changing Ecology of Foreign Policy-Making in China: The Ascension and Demise of the Theory of Peaceful Rise', *The China Quarterly*, No. 190, 2007, pp. 291–310.

18 Chen Zhimin and David Zweig, eds., *Guoji zhengzhi jingjixue yu Zhongguo de quanqiuhua* [*International Political Economy and China's Globalisation*], Shanghai, China: Shanghai SDX Joint Publishing, 2006, p. 238.

19 See Karl Polanyi, *The Great Transformation: The Political and Economic Origins of Our Time*, Boston, MA: Beacon Press, 2001; Liu Yang, 'Tupo xianzhi, chongxin tansuo renlei shenghuo de kenengxing: Ka'er Bolani de "Da zhuanxing"' ['Breaking Limits and Rediscovering the Possibilities of Human Life: Karl Polanyi's "The Great Transformation"'], *Shehui kexue bao* [*Chinese Social Sciences Today*], 14 December 2010, p. 10.

20 Mark Granovetter, 'Economic Action and Social Structure: The Problem of Embeddedness', *American Journal of Sociology*, Vol. 91, No. 3, November 1985, pp. 481–510.

21 Niall Ferguson and Moritz Schularick, 'Chimerica? Think Again', *The Wall Street Journal*, 5 February 2007, p. 17.

22 Xinlang Caijing, 'Zhongguo zuida maoyi hezuo huoban yuanchao Meiguo, chengwei quanqiu maoyi zhudaozhe' ['China Has Become a Dominant Player of Global Trade, Far Surpassing the US in Terms of the Number of Largest Trade Partners'], *Guancha .cn*, 17 December 2013, http://www.guancha.cn/economy/2013_12_27_195361.sh tml.

23 Granovetter, 'Economic Action and Social Structure: The Problem of Embeddedness', pp. 481–510.

24 Wang Zhengxu, '"Zai quanqiuhua" shidai de Zhongguo xuanze' ['China's Choice in the "Re-globalisation" Era'], *Zhongguo xinwen zhoukan* [*China News Weekly*], No. 2, 2014, pp. 30–32.

25 Chen Zhimin and Zhou Guorong, 'Guoji lingdao yu Zhongguo xiejinxing lingdao juese de goujian' ['International Leadership and China's Role as a Facilitative Leader'], *Shijie jingji yu zhengzhi* [*World Economics and Politics*], No. 3, 2017, pp. 15–34.

26 Chen Zhimin and Chang Lulu, 'Quanli de ziyuan yu yunyong: jianlun Zhongguo waijiao de quanli zhanlue' ['The Resources and Application of Power: A Study on China's Power Strategy'], *Shijie jingji yu zhengzhi* [*World Economics and Politics*], No. 7, 2012, pp. 4–23; Zhang Qingmin, 'Lijie shibada yilai de Zhongguo waijiao' ['Understanding China's Diplomacy Since the 18th National Congress of the Communist Party of China'], *Waijiao pinglun* [*Foreign Affairs Review*], No. 2, 2014, pp. 1–20.

27 Wang Yizhou, *Quanqiu zhengzhi yu Zhongguo waijiao: tanxun xinde shijiao yu jieshi* [*Global Politics and Chinese Diplomacy: Exploring New Perspectives and Explanations*], Beijing: World Affairs Press, 2003, pp. 7–9; Wang Yizhou, 'Lun Zhongguo waijiao zhuanxing' ['On China's Diplomatic Transformation'], *Xuexi yu tansuo* [*Study and Exploration*], No. 5, 2008, pp. 57–67.

28 Studies on the networks in international relations include: Margaret E. Keck and Kathryn Sikkink, *Activists Beyond Borders: Advocacy Networks in International Politics*, Ithaca, NY: Cornell University Press, 1998; Miles Kahler, ed., *Networked Politics: Agency, Power, and Governance*, Ithaca, NY: Cornell University Press, 2009; John M. Owen IV, *The Clash of Ideas in World Politics: Transnational Networks, States, and Regime Change, 1510–2010*, Princeton, NJ: Princeton University Press, 2010; Zeev Maoz, *Networks of Nations: The Evolution, Structure, and Impact of International Networks, 1816–2001*, Cambridge, UK: Cambridge University Press, 2011; Anne-Marie Slaughter, *A New World Order*, Princeton, NJ: Princeton University Press, 2005;

Embracing globalisation and China's narrative 25

Anne-Marie Slaughter, *The Chessboard and the Web: Strategies of Connection in a Networked World*, New Haven, CT: Yale University Press, 2017.

29 Yang Luhui, 'Heping jueqi yu Zhongguo zhoubian waijiao xinlinian he xingeju' ['The Peaceful Rise and the New Idea and Structure of China's Diplomacy with Neighboring Countries'], *Lilun tantao* [*Theoretical Discussion*], No. 6, 2014, pp. 5–10.

30 Understanding 'power' as 'a type of social relationship' is a widespread view among Chinese scholars of political science. See Yang Guangbin, *Zhengzhixue daolun* [*Introduction to Political Science*], Beijing, China: China Renmin University Press, 2000, pp. 31–46.

31 John Ikenberry, *After Victory: Institutions, Strategic Restraint, and the Rebuilding of Order after Major Wars*, Princeton, NJ: Princeton University Press, 2001; John Ikenberry, *Liberal Leviathan: The Origins, Crisis, and Transformation of the American World Order*, Princeton, NJ: Princeton University Press, 2012.

32 Joseph S. Nye, *Soft Power: The Means to Success in World Politics*, New York, NY: Public Affairs, 2004; Joseph S. Nye, *The Paradox of America Power: Why the World's Only Superpower Can't Go It Alone*, Oxford, UK: Oxford University Press, 2010; Joseph S. Nye, *The Future of Power*, New York, NY: Public Affairs, 2011; Joseph S. Nye, 'Soft Power', *Foreign Policy*, Vol. 80, 1990, pp. 153–171.

33 Cao Dejun, 'Guoji zhengzhi de "guanxi lilun:" gainian, lujing yu tiaozhan' ['A "Relational Theory" of International Politics: Concepts, Approaches and Challenges'], *Shijie jingji yu zhengzhi* [*World Economics and Politics*], No. 2, 2017, pp. 36–53.

34 Xi Jinping, 'Xieshou tuijin "yidai yilu" jianshe: zai "yidai yilu" guoji hezuo gaofeng luntan kaimushi shang de jianghua' ['Push Forward the "Belt and Road" Construction Hand in Hand: Speech at the Opening Ceremony of the Belt and Road Forum for International Cooperation'], Xinhua News Agency, 14 May 2017, http://news.xinhuane t.com/politics/2017-05/14/c_1120969677.htm.

35 Robert D. Putnam, *Making Democracy Work: Civic Traditions in Modern Italy*, Princeton, NJ: Princeton University Press, 1993.

36 Ronald S. Burt, *Structural Holes: The Social Structure of Competition*, Cambridge, MA: Harvard University Press, 1992.

37 Granovetter, 'Economic Action and Social Structure: The Problem of Embeddedness', pp. 481–510.

38 Yan Jirong, *Shehui ziben yu guojia zhili* [*Social Capital and National Governance*], Beijing: Peking University Press, 2015, pp. 86–87.

39 Qin Yaqing, *Guanxi yu gocheng: Zhongguo guojiguanxi lilun de wenhua jiangou* [*Guanxi and Process: The Cultural Construction of Chinese International Relations Theory*], Shanghai, China: Shanghai People's Publishing House, 2012, p. 151.

40 Pierre Bourdieu, 'The Forms of Capital', in John G. Richardson, ed., *Handbook of Theory and Research for the Sociology of Education*, New York, NY: Greenwood, 1986, pp. 241–258.

41 Nan Lin, *Social Capital: A Theory of Social Structure and Action*, Cambridge, UK: Cambridge University Press, 2001, pp. 19, 24–25, 40.

42 Robert Putnam, 'The Prosperous Community: Social Capital and Public Life', *The American Prospect*, Vol. 13, No. 4, 1993, pp. 35–42. For a comparison of different conceptualisations of social capital between Bourdieu and Putnam, see Martti Siisiäinen, 'Two Concepts of Social Capital: Bourdieu vs. Putnam,' paper presented at ISTR Fourth International Conference 'The Third Sector: For What and for Whom?', Trinity College, Dublin, Ireland, 5–8 July, 2000.

2 From Globalisation to Reglobalisation

There are two kinds of forces in the world: swords and ideas. In the long term, ideas will ultimately triumph over swords.

Napoleon Bonaparte

Appreciate the culture of others as you do your own, and the world will become a harmonious whole.

Fei Xiaotong, one of the foremost
sociologists in China, 1996

Globalisation traditionally refers to the internationalisation of economic activities, meaning the dissemination of capital, goods, services, labour, and information beyond domestic markets and across national borders.[1] Globalisation is dynamic and evolutionary and has now entered a new phase of expansion and reconfiguration after numerous rounds of enlargement, competition, contraction, and adjustment.[2] The year 2008 was a clear historical fault line, marking the starting point of the reglobalisation process. The immense success of the Beijing Olympic Games and the enormous destruction of the US financial crisis both took place that year and really pushed China, which had been keeping a low profile until then, into the centre of the world stage. The global financial crisis, which began in the United States, has thoroughly exposed the shortcomings of the old model of globalisation. The Western academic and policy communities have launched a heated debate on the future of globalisation. Before the outbreak of the financial crisis, most Western academics held an optimistic attitude toward globalisation. Most of the views held that globalisation was a new stage in the development of world history and an irresistible trend. Globalisation is the process of spreading different things to people in all corners of the world. By integrating different civilisations, economies, and knowledge systems, the well-being of humankind as a whole can significantly improve.[3] The free flow advocated by globalisation has greatly improved the efficiency of resource allocation. However, under the impact of the global financial crisis, the attitudes of Western societies toward globalisation have changed significantly and pessimistic views such as antiglobalisation and deglobalisation, the return of geopolitics, and the fragmentation of the world are all on

From Globalisation to Reglobalisation 27

the rise, reflecting the anxiety and insecurity of the Western world. Trump's advocacy of 'America First', Britain's exit from Europe, and the rise of populism and right-wing forces in the US and Europe are, in part, votes of no confidence toward globalisation.[4] We will now analyse two kinds of attitudes toward globalisation between the West and China.

2.1 The Western dilemma of old globalisation

The word 'globalisation' was believed to have first been proposed and subsequently popularised by American economist Theodore Levitt in 1985. However, it has no commonly accepted definition. Back then, globalisation referred to a process of the internationalisation of economic activities. People have given it a variety of definitions. One widely accepted definition is the spread of capital, goods, services, labour, and information beyond domestic markets and borders. The dividends of globalisation have not been shared fairly between developed and developing countries. Thus, a new concept of 'responsible globalisation' emerged at the 29th Annual Meeting of the World Economic Forum in Davos, Switzerland, at the end of January 1999. While discussing globalisation, scholars in the past focussed more on economic globalisation, which has been recognised the world over; however, when anthropologists focus on globalisation, they find that the close relationship between the economy and culture reflects a new problem, namely cultural globalisation. They argue that previous studies have failed to recognise the diversity of globalisation and call for the phenomenon to be seen as a politically, economically, and culturally intertwined process. As a result, not only has the study of goods, trade, capital, colonialism, imperialism, and other economic fields introduced the perspective of globalisation, but studies focussing on culture, social organisations, transnational flows, and global identity have also become a new direction of contemporary anthropology.[5]

The views constituting the long-drawn debate on what globalisation is in academic circles can be roughly divided into two categories. The first group thinks that globalisation is mainly the global linkage and flow of economic phenomena, that is, the formation of a unified economic community in the world. The second group sees globalisation as a political or cultural convergence, and thinks that scientific and technological progress has compressed the space-time distance and that this closer interaction has led to the spread of transnational identities, which has finally resulted in the integration of the international community into a '*datong shehui*' (Society of Great Harmony) or a '*datong shijie*' (World of Great Hamony).

Supporters of economic globalisation see liquidity and flattening as important features of the phenomenon. As Karl Marx envisaged in the *Communist Manifesto*, workers all over the world, because of the division of labour in international trade and their shared fate, are already in a vast proletarian network. Once workers realise that they are in this network, they can unite to fight and resist the globalised interest distribution pattern monopolised by the bourgeoisie. Global economic factors such as production, trade, commodities, capital, and market

28 *Reglobalisation*

penetrate and expand into all corners of the world, weaving an invisible network in which everyone occupies different positions. This is the economic effect of globalisation. But when different countries are integrated into a global network of rules, individual differences seem to be flattened out and local cultures in different countries become diluted. Global standards allow people in each country to pursue an imaginative, unified, globalised way of life, a model that does not simply add up the different national characteristics but presents a mixed multivariate grafting. While everyone can find familiar aspects in globalisation, they may face more unknown and unfamiliar parts as well. As a result, economic globalisation seems to integrate consumer behaviour the world over, but not people's identities. The Western societies seen today are still torn apart by polarised forces, and the entire global community is still divided into the Global South and the Global North. This kind of fault line will always exist. The question is who will become the winner and who will become the loser. The desolate factories in the Rust Belt of the north-eastern United States and the sense of loss and deprivation felt by the blue-collar class that depends on them to survive will only be heightened in a unified global market. Globalisation, in their view, is a terrible blackhole that deprives them of their job opportunities. They are not only antagonistic to the elite at home, but also to the working class in developing countries such as China and Vietnam. They seem to be at odds with every part of globalisation. They see themselves as the losers in globalisation. When Donald Trump was elected the 45th president of the United States, the unemployed blue-collar workers in the Rust Belt were thrilled that someone would speak for them at last. As soon as he took office, Trump announced the expulsion of illegal immigrants, the construction of the border wall, and threatened to launch a trade war against China to bring back 'stolen jobs'. Therefore, it can be said that the 2016 presidential election was a historic event that highlighted the self-contradictions of globalisation.

Supporters of political globalisation see polarisation and fragmentation as important features. Economists see a shrinking world of technology, ecology, communications, and commerce as reducing transaction costs and expanding overall welfare. However, many scholars who support political globalisation argue that this view only looks at the surface and ignores its essence. Karl Marx, in his *Communist Manifesto*, argued that globalisation was essentially the spread of inequality in the world, which made more and more proletarians get involved in the division of labour in the world, working without dignity in a relatively low-level economic system; therefore, Marx believed that globalisation awakened the working class, but to truly solve global inequalities, the greedy capitalist system needs to be eliminated. The question is: will the elimination of one party by another in a polarised society lead to a renewed polarisation within the victorious party? As distribution is relative under any system, there will always be some people who get more and others who get less. Robert Cox, a leading neo-Marxist, has given us a pluralistic understanding of globalisation. He believed that globalisation, as we understand it at present, has multiple meanings, including economic, spatial, ideological, and temporal dimensions, but political globalisation is its most important essence.[6] The 2008 global financial crisis is a significant node in

From Globalisation to Reglobalisation   29

a historical turn of events. The isolationist sentiments and antiglobalisation wave in the Western world are on the rise. At the critical moment when support for globalisation is most necessary in the world, developed countries (especially the hegemon, the United States) are beginning to retreat into their own and are shirking their responsibility toward global governance. A Centre for Economic Policy Research (CEPR) report, released in 2016, shows that trade protectionism is putting global free trade at peril. For example, the United States implemented trade protection measures 120 times in 2009. That number rose to 741 in 2013 and 1066 in 2016. Russia implemented trade protection measures 72 times in 2009 and 334 times in 2013. This rose to 559 in 2016. In contrast, China, as an emerging economy, opposes all forms of protectionism and advocates trade and investment liberalisation and facilitation.[7] A second question worth pondering over arises here. Why has China, which is currently at a disadvantage in the global division of labour, come to be the most active guardian of globalisation and free trade, whereas Western countries, as the biggest beneficiaries of globalisation, have gradually closed their doors? In answering this, we need to think about the political implications of globalisation, that is, any global movement will eventually need to be applied locally in order to be localised. When economic issues are localised, a reshuffling of local interests will occur, where conservatives are unwilling to lose more while radicals want to get more. Thus, when the seemingly harmonious surface of globalisation is torn off by localisation and glocalisation in the process, an embarrassing political split is left behind. In his highly influential book *The World Is Flat: A Brief History of the 21st Century*, Thomas Friedman, a prominent journalist and *New York Times* columnist, described the integrated world as an undifferentiated, equal, and flat world.[8] However, his idea of flattening here, is merely a flattening in the economic sense as a result of interconnection, and not a flattening in the political and cultural sense. In contrast, the flat economic surface leads to the deepening of political hierarchisation. The renowned literary theorist and critic Edward Said took the birth of Orientalism as an example to dissect the discursive hegemony of the West in developing Orientalism. Based on this critical theory, many scholars began to pay attention to the expansion of globalisation to China, especially the cultural expansion dominated by consumerist ideology. They pointed out how the Third World had accepted the 'consumer guidance of sales promotion' in the face of numerous advertising media, that is, the combined result of the globalisation from the 'upper' elite and the globalisation from the 'low end'. This perspective, in a sense, reflects the hierarchy of different countries in the global economic structure.[9]

Ironically, however, globalisation was once equated with Americanisation or Westernisation. However, is it a historical retrogression that the United States and Europe are now preoccupied with deglobalisation, trade protectionism, and isolationism? For a long time, the Kuznets Curve portrayed an optimistic outlook for supporters of globalisation. While the gap between the rich and the poor will widen in the early stages of economic growth, economic growth will eventually narrow the social gap between them; however, this conjecture has not been confirmed in the era of globalisation. The gap between the rich and the poor has been

30 *Reglobalisation*

expanding in most countries since the 1980s. Thomas Piketty's highly acclaimed book, *Capital in the Twenty-First Century* offers a powerful exposition for this widening gap. He pointed out that historically, the rate of return on capital has been higher than the rate of income growth, leading to widening social disparities between the rich and the poor.[10] In the era of globalisation, governments have to rely more on income tax to support welfare expenditure because of the stronger transnational tax avoidance capacity of capital. Thus identifying the winner and the loser of globalisation becomes paramount. In *Global Inequality*, Branko Milanovic, a former World Bank economist, carefully examined the changes in the incomes of different groups over the 20 years – from 1988 at the twilight of the Cold War to 2008 when the global financial crisis broke out – when globalisation was at its peak. He found that groups in the global income rankings of 40–60% profited the most, with an average income increase of 80% in 20 years. This group represented the 'global emerging middle class', mainly in emerging economies in Asia. The biggest losers were the middle and low-income classes in developed countries, whose incomes barely increased in the span of 20 years. As a result, the gap between the middle- and low-income classes of the United States (the bottom 20% of the income group) and the upper and middle classes of China (the top 20% of the income group) narrowed down from 6.5 times in 1988 to 1.3 times in 2011.[11] If emerging countries such as China and India continue to narrow the gap with developed countries, global inequality will be mainly reflected in the domestic gaps between the rich and the poor by 2050.[12]

The social split in the 2016 US presidential election was a result of a long period of accumulation. The elite enjoyed higher wages and investment incomes, richer commodity choices, and more international lifestyles, while the underprivileged had to lose jobs and endure poverty owing to offshore production and outsourcing by multinational companies while facing increasingly fierce competition from immigrants. This double split in the global society, that is, domestic and international polarisation, eventually led to the plight of traditional globalisation, embodied in three aspects.

First, as the core engine of old globalisation, the United States and its global hegemony were caught in a dilemma of 'involution'. The 9/11 terrorist attacks in 2001 were an important watershed in the history of American hegemony. On the one hand, 9/11 directly led to the Afghanistan War and the Iraq War, both started by the United States, which dealt a heavy blow to the erstwhile international order. On the other hand, under the influence of the incident, more and more terrorist organisations began to imitate Al-Qaeda, so suicide terrorist attacks became a trending tactic. For example, according to the University of Maryland's Global Terrorism Database (GTD), 2,456 suicide terrorist attacks occurred worldwide from 1972 to 2012, resulting in 24,840 deaths and 56,448 injuries (including those of terrorists).[13] Since then, the global financial crisis originating in the United States in 2008 has caused tremendous economic losses and psychological trauma to the Western world. It reveals the fundamental weaknesses of the Western political system, undermines the inherent self-confidence of Westerners, and exposes the 'Washington Consensus' to more and more criticism and reflection. Many

From Globalisation to Reglobalisation   31

Westerners no longer have illusions about their own political system, especially when bankers make big bonuses for themselves and governments use taxpayers' money to bail out banks and big corporations. The global financial crisis has made the strength and international influence of emerging economies rise steadily, while those of the United States have declined relatively. In particular, the gap between China and the United States seems to be closing. Former US Treasury Secretary and former Harvard University President Larry Summers observed that living standards in the United States have doubled every 30 years, while those in China have doubled every 10 years over the past 30 years. After the outbreak of the global financial crisis in 2008, many large companies were on the verge of bankruptcy, and this led to economic depression and sustained high unemployment in many countries such as the United States.[14] The Occupy Wall Street protests in October 2011 were escalated, with thousands of protesters marching in Washington DC, and they gradually turned into a mass social movement all over America. The slogan of the movement was 'We are the 99%', which profoundly revealed the deeper meaning of Occupy Wall Street: the US financial crisis was rooted in greed on Wall Street, corruption in the banking sector, and corporate interference in politics. The movement hoped to create a world where everyone was equal, instead of the rich 1% owning everything. Faced with internal and external difficulties, then US President Barack Obama, who came into office in the wake of the 2008 financial crisis, held high the banner of change. The United States became more concerned about its domestic development, and more reluctant to carry a burden outside its territory. On 20 January 2017, Donald Trump was officially inaugurated as the President of the United States. He pursued the so-called 'principled realism' and advocated and adhered to 'America First'. The Trump administration rolled out many controversial policies, including withdrawing from the Trans-Pacific Partnership (TPP) agreements, building a wall on the US-Mexican border, and putting up an immigration ban on people of Muslim origin. The United States and Europe, as the core of the Western world, experienced unprecedented uncertainty in their own development that had not been seen since World War II. International public opinion also lamented about the 'Trump shocks'.

Second, the disadvantages of old globalisation are gaining prominence, but it is difficult for the Western world to come up with practical solutions. The 2008 global financial crisis has thoroughly exposed the shortcomings of the old model of globalisation, and pessimistic voices such as deglobalisation, return of geopolitics, and the fragmentation of the world are on the rise. However, some scholars believe that the development and evolution of the international configuration in the post-Cold War era seems to be neither globalisation nor deglobalisation but nonpolarised and disorderly transformation.[15] Viewed in this light, the post-Cold War world is a system in which the polarised structure of the old great powers is disintegrating and fragmenting, with international forces being more diffused. Richard Hass, President of the Council on Foreign Relations, first put forward the idea of the 'nonpolar world', pointing out that 'the principal characteristic of twenty-first-century international relations is turning out to be nonpolarity: a

32   *Reglobalisation*

world dominated not by one or two or even several states but rather by dozens of actors possessing and exercising various kinds of power'.[16] Echoing Hass, Ian Bremmer, President of the Eurasia Group, described the fragmentation of world power after the Cold War as the 'Group of Zero' (G-Zero). G-Zero refers to a world in which no country or coalition of nations is willing to sustain global leadership; nor is it capable of doing so.[17] The nonpolar world emphasises that the traditional great power politics have begun to shift to nonmajor powers. In addition, the development mode under old globalisation thinking shows a lack of inclusiveness. For a long time, the world economy has made great progress under the impetus of economic globalisation, and all countries have shared the positive results of it; however, owing to the lack of inclusiveness in the economic development model, the development of the world economy is seriously imbalanced. Developed economies play a central role in international economic relations by virtue of their strong advantages in capital, technology, and management, while developing countries are in peripheral and dependent positions. The relationship between the centre and the periphery is an unequal relationship between domination and being dominated as well as between exploitation and being exploited, both of which seriously restrict the progress of developing countries. The lack of inclusiveness in the economic development model has led to serious imbalances in the economic development of developed and developing countries, leading to a halt and reversal of economic globalisation. In the five years after 2008, the speed of growth of global trade remained slower than that of global gross domestic product (GDP). Statistics show that global cross-border capital flows in 2016 amounted to $4.3 trillion, which was only one-third of the peak at $12.4 trillion in 2007.[18] It is the first time that this has happened since World War II, or it could be considered as a turning point in the global economy.

Third, the uncertainty around the world order is increasing, and the anxiety of people from all over the world is rising, too. The global financial crisis has led many to question the legitimacy, effectiveness, and durability of the US global leadership. Although the existing international order was established by the United States after World War II, it is rather difficult for the US to fully dominate the international system today. Instead, it is more passively coping with the rapid changes in the world, and it has neither the will nor the ability to promote a new world order. Fareed Zakaria, a prominent American political commentator, argued in his book *The Post-American World* that the world is moving away from American economic domination into a post-American world supported by multiple forces.[19] As the oldest, largest, and most influential security and defence conference in the world, the Munich Security Conference designated its 2017 theme as 'Post-truth, post-West, and post-order'. Delegates at the conference clearly sensed that the existing international order was undergoing serious crises and challenges. It was, however, difficult for them to agree where the world is heading, and there was a palpable air of alarm and soul-searching both inside and outside the venue. This uncertainty is reflected in two aspects. On the one hand, the voice of deglobalisation is on the rise. The inequality of globalisation rules creates the opposition between losers and winners. Disadvantaged people actively stir up nationalist sentiments and try to use fear and uncertainty to pursue their own interests. Deglobalisation refers to the regression process of the interdependence and economic integration that has been brought by globalisation. This concept was caused by 9/11, which dealt a blow to globalisation. Since then, views of deglobalisation have been growing, such as 'globalism is dead', 'sinking globalisation', and 'globalisation has ended unexpectedly'.[20] The 2008 global financial crisis popularised the concept of 'deglobalisation' as put forward by Walden Bello.[21] On the other hand, geopolitical risks are intensifying. Since 2008, distrust among major powers has risen sharply. Traditional geopolitical issues such as the Ukrainian, Crimean, and North Korean nuclear crises, as well as the US 'pivot' to Asia and the terrorist attacks in the Middle East have taken place one after another. A new Cold War seems to be starting.[22] Some local wars or terrorist attacks, nationalist xenophobic incidents, street riots, and cases of immigrant discrimination are also increasing in number.[23] As Kissinger warned: one of the fundamental causes of 'an international order's crisis is when it proves unable to accommodate a major change in power relations'.[24]

2.2 The definition of reglobalisation

With the rising isolationism in the West, the process of globalisation has been frustrated, but the temporary low tide does not mean the end of globalisation. Among the emerging forces of globalisation comprising emerging countries, China has undoubtedly personified the new momentum that can support and promote globalisation. Globalisation has not stopped or been reversed, but has changed its form and has begun to take the emerging countries to the centre and to consider the economic and social embeddedness from the standpoint of developing countries. For a long time, China, India, Brazil, Russia, South Africa, and other emerging economies have been carrying out domestic reforms to integrate into the Western economic order. When the Western economic system was in crisis, these countries began to reshape and reform the rules set by the West, a situation that had never happened in the last 500 years. Globalisation began to shift from developed to developing countries, especially the emerging ones. This is one of the reasons why the BRICS (Brazil, Russia, India, China, and South Africa) and G20 meetings have attracted so much attention from the rest of the world. Although the West is still at the core of the international system, it is not these core countries that have led the reforms, but those emerging powers that were once on the periphery of the system now taking the lead, which reflects the transformation of the momentum of globalisation from developed to developing countries.

The reglobalisation proposed in this book refers to the reforms in the process of globalisation by emerging countries represented by China and the mode upgrade and expansion effect produced by such reforms. Traditional globalisation is based on the centre/periphery economic structure. The 'scissors gap' caused by the trade of manufactured goods and raw materials between developed and peripheral countries constitutes one of the root causes of the inequity of

34 Reglobalisation

globalisation. When emerging countries rise in a full-fledged manner and China becomes the largest trading partner of developed and developing countries, the dual pattern of globalisation will evolve into a tripartite pattern, that is, the interconnection of developed, emerging, and peripheral countries. This interconnection of the Three Worlds will transcend the opposition between 'high-level' and 'low-level' globalisation and narrow the hierarchical gap between the centre and the periphery. The reason the current globalisation process is defined by 're' rather than 'new' is that the expansion of globalisation promoted by emerging countries such as China is not entirely new but rather undergoes internal reforms to upgrade the existing international architecture, which is part of China's embedded-style rise.

First, the reglobalisation pattern moves from economic- to political-oriented globalisation and from high- to low-level globalisation. Since 2008, the form of globalisation has changed from the former economic to the mutual shaping stage of economic and political globalisation. In other words, the power of globalisation cannot be understood solely by the theoretical models of economists because, behind every increase in trade figures, there are conflicts of interest among many actors. These hidden political latitudes that are now completely exposed under the spotlight are important reasons for Trump's election as the president of the United States, for the British referendum to exit the European Union, and for the election of France's young President Emmanuel Macron. Western societies torn apart by economic globalisation have led to a self-revolution of the underprivileged, with most of the population telling the traditional high-level beneficiaries of globalisation through their votes that they are angry because the world of low-level globalisation is being destroyed. As a result, the contradiction between high- (big capitalists, consortia, and the highly educated elite) and low-level globalisation (small traders, ordinary immigrants, blue-collar workers, the unemployed) is revealed openly. People at the low end of the economic and social ladders shout that they are the 99% harmed by globalisation, while those at the high level are the so-called elite 1% that reaps the dividends of globalisation. The outbreak of the global financial crisis exacerbated the confrontation between high- and low-level globalisation. When one looks back at the 2016 US election, they will not forget the 75-year-old candidate, Bernie Sanders. As an atypical Democratic presidential candidate, Sanders had no qualms indicating that it was time for the Democrats to make some changes. The fact that the Democrats could not effectively talk to American wage-earners made this grassroots Democrat feel deeply ashamed. Sanders was considered as completely different from Hilary Clinton, another Democratic presidential candidate. With a social democratic platform, Sanders opposed elite rule and advocated a radical transformation of high-level globalisation. During his campaign, he resisted the influence of money on politics and the monopoly of democracy by the rich, so he never accepted campaign donations from big consortia but received small donations from ordinary supporters. Campaign donations averaged $34 per person and, by the end of the campaign, the US senator had raised $218 million, which was in sharp contrast to Hillary Clinton's $2,700 per person, setting off a genuine grassroots movement.[25]

Sanders urged that public universities be free of tuition fees and reduce student debts, which has been widely welcome by young voters. At the same time, he advocated wider universal health care, increased minimum wage, and trade union influence. The core logic of Trump's economic policy is to guide industries to relocate and increase employment through tax cuts and trade protection. Both the Democratic grassroots representative Sanders and the Republican candidate Trump represented the voices of the middle and lower classes who had long felt deprived. The common ground of Sanders and Trump's policy agendas was to safeguard the interests of the grassroots classes and transform globalisation from being completely economically led to being politically led. As a result, the tendency of trade protectionism in the United States is becoming more and more prominent, and ethnic conflicts and conservative ideas in the United States are also becoming more and more serious. In short, reglobalisation is not intended at overthrowing globalisation but rather to turn globalisation on its head, to turn the pattern of economic globalisation dominated by big capitalists into political globalisation dominated by grassroots people. The chaos that we now see in the Western world is the game between these two forces of globalisation. If we use a mental diagram, it is that 99% of us want to change the global structure of the distribution of benefits dominated by 1%. The simple word "change" can propel a Black man to the presidency of the United States for the first time in history. However, unfortunately, Obama's plan for change was blocked by vested interests and an upgraded, more antiestablishment, nonmainstream President Trump emerged and took the helm, trying to 'make America great again'. What he really meant was to 'make the bottom people strong again' and make low-level globalisation strong again (see Figure 2.1).

Second, the willingness and ability of the Western powers to participate in globalisation have declined, and the momentum of globalisation has shifted from the traditional Western powers to emerging ones. After the 2008 global financial crisis, the Western countries led by the United States were preoccupied

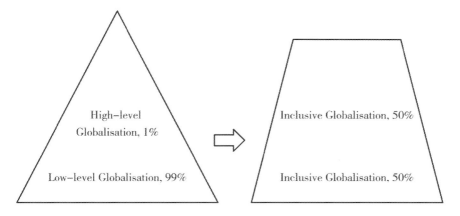

Figure 2.1 The transformation of reglobalisation: from verticalisation to flattening.

36 *Reglobalisation*

with fighting recession and, to various degrees, retreated into isolationism. The emerging countries represented by China were increasingly involved in global governance, and this injected new impetus into globalisation. Emerging economies experienced a remarkable rise around 2008. These countries were once on the periphery or semiperiphery of globalisation for a long time and began moving to the centre. Unlike the high-level globalisation that the West dominated over, these emerging countries represent the interests of developing countries as a whole and are, therefore, a reflection of low-level globalisation in international relations. In 2001, Jim O'Neill, chief economist at Goldman Sachs, coined the term 'BRIC' countries, an acronym for four emerging markets that attracted global attention, namely Brazil, Russia, India, and China. In 2009, leaders of these four countries met in Russia, and the BRIC cooperation mechanism was officially launched. In 2010, BRIC incorporated South Africa and went from BRIC to BRICS. BRICS made remarkable achievements in economic, financial, security, environmental protection, and other aspects of global governance, effectively promoting the development of a more equitable and reasonable global governance system. Statistics show that from 2010 to 2016, global trade grew at an average annual rate of 4.2%, while China's foreign trade grew at a rate of 8.4%, the United States' at 5.2%, India's at 7.3%, Russia's at 5.6%, Brazil's at 3.7%, and South Africa's at 3.5%. In 2016, the total trade volume of BRICS reached \$5.2 trillion, accounting for 17.7% of total world trade. Their status in the world trade structure is constantly on the rise. This is because of the steady increase in the share of BRICS trade in global trade. China's foreign trade in 2016 accounted for 12.4% of the world's total trade, exceeding that of the United States (12.3%), while that of India accounted for 2.1%, Russia 1.6%, Brazil 1.1%, and South Africa 0.5%. With the economic transformation of BRICS in the future, their foreign trade is expected to grow steadily.[26] Forecasts show that the trade volume of BRICS countries will reach \$12.8 trillion in 2026, accounting for 24.8% of the global trade volume, with an average annual growth rate of 9.1% over the next 10 years, which will still be higher than the average growth rate of 6.0% of global trade. BRICS will continue to play the role of an engine in global trade growth.

The weight of BRICS in the world is mainly reflected in two aspects. First, the total population of the five countries accounts for 41.2% of the world (see Figure 2.2), which constitutes huge labour markets and vast emerging consumer markets. At present, China has become one of the main driving forces of the global middle-class population growth. If China's economic growth maintains its current trend, the number of middle-class people in China will have reached 75% of the total domestic population by 2030. The US National Intelligence Council predicts that the global middle-class population will grow to 3.2 billion by 2020, and that the number will reach about 4.9 billion by 2030.[27] In this rapid growth trend, emerging markets such as China and India will account for most of the growth. China and India are expected to account for 66% of the world's middle class by 2020, and 59% of the world's consumption will be driven by them, when compared with 23% in 2009.[28]

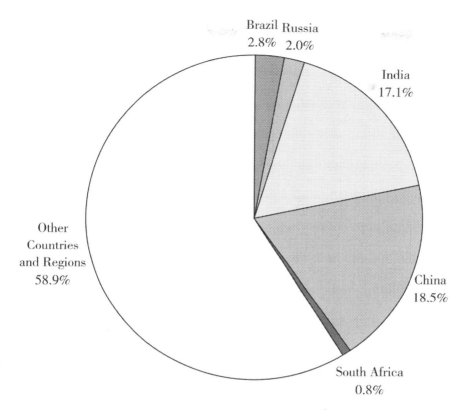

Figure 2.2 BRICS countries' share of world population in 2016.

The release of consumer demand from the middle class will be in line with China's economy going global, and the power of Chinese consumers will explode in the next 10 years, making it an important force supporting the global economy. Once these seemingly enormous potentials in the business sector begin to influence global consumption patterns and preferences, they will also have a profound impact on global governance. China's demographic dividend will become a force that cannot be ignored in global economic governance. Second, there is great potential for economic interaction and growth among BRICS countries.[29] Against the background of the rise of international trade protectionism, the trade networks among the BRICS and between the BRICS and other countries are deepening and expanding further. The volume of trade is growing rapidly again. Trade relations are becoming closer and closer. The interactions between BRICS and the global trade network are increasing rapidly. China has always played the role of a navigator in this trade network.

Finally, emerging countries can bridge the gap between low- and high-level globalisation by providing public goods on their own initiative. In the era of

38   *Reglobalisation*

reglobalisation, the way the world transfers power will become more and more peaceful, and the way to acquire world leadership will be to supply public goods rather than wage major wars.[30] When emerging powers take the initiative to welcome smaller and weaker countries to be 'free riders', they open up a new governance path for the supply of public goods in addition to the old system dominated by hegemonic powers. This is a model of coexistence and cooperation between old and new governance structures. The world will compete for and benefit from the supply of public goods with a transfer of power. This is a change in the theme of the times, that is, rising and hegemonic powers govern together and coexist peacefully, rather than conquer each other by force. In recent years, China has become a defender of the international order and an active supporter of economic globalisation. At the time of writing, China is the second largest economy in the world, the largest trading country, the largest buyer of many primary products, and the largest trade partner of more than 120 countries in the world. In 2016, China's contribution to Asia's economic growth exceeded 50% and reached 33.2% of the world's economic growth, exceeding the combined contribution rate of the United States, Europe, and Japan, and thus ranking first in the world.[31] In international relations (IR) theories, the theory of hegemonic stability describes the hegemonic powers and their group of partners as the cornerstone of world stability. It holds true that only the hegemonic powers have the ability and willingness to supply global public goods voluntarily in the face of world crises.[32] Charles P. Kindleberger, who developed the hegemonic stability theory, considers hegemony as a substitute for world government.[33] However, this logic does not discuss the impact of a power transition on the supply of global public goods, especially underestimating the governance capacity and willingness of emerging countries. During his visit to Mongolia in August 2014, Chinese President Xi Jinping made it clear that 'we welcome everyone to take the train of China's development, whether as an express or a free ride'.[34] At the subsequent Asia-Pacific Economic Cooperation (APEC) Beijing Summit, President Xi said, 'China is willing to provide more public goods to its Asian neighbours through interconnection. Welcome aboard the train for China's development'.[35] Klaus Schwab, Chairman of the World Economic Forum, remarked in early 2017 that 'China brings sunshine to us … and makes us more confident about the future',[36] whereas the United States and its partners were busy building walls to keep out globalisation. China's commitment to supply international public goods in the shadow of the financial crisis is particularly rare. Throughout history, there are several examples of emerging powers supplying global public goods, but the mainstream Western academic circles tend to focus on hegemonic powers, ignoring the supply capacity and willingness of potential emerging countries. Today, the United States is still the world's most powerful country, and China is still a developing one. Why is the world's strongest hegemony increasingly reluctant to assume responsibilities, whereas emerging powers like China have become active participants in global governance? From China's perspective, welcoming other countries to take a free ride is not only an important measure to defend Chinese interests, but also an important means to help promote globalisation. It is also a positive action for China to share the dividend of its rise with the world.

2.3 Four types of globalisation

Karl Polanyi, a famous British philosopher, believed that political behaviour is inseparable from the social system and is embedded in it. The political dimension of interactions in the era of globalisation will be deeply embedded in the economic dimension.[37] However, if the economic development that was originally embedded in the political framework is too detached, there will be a disembedding crisis, that will certainly deal serious damage to the social structure. Therefore, from this perspective, the fundamental problem of the political order after the 2008 global financial crisis lies in the disconnect between political and economic globalisation. From the perspective of embeddedness, the transformation of the old and new systems can be summarised as two continuous processes of disembeddedness and reembeddedness. In other words, after the old globalisation system is in trouble, through active reform, the relationship between politics and economy can be reconstructed to realise reembeddedness on the new grounds. The political-economic binary relationship model helps us to understand why globalisation is off track and how to initiate reforms. When the old engine of globalisation is in trouble, the burden of global economic growth and globalisation shifts to the emerging countries represented by China. In the process of reglobalisation led by China, the rules of globalisation will undergo readjustments and different actors will reconstruct the process in line with their own preferences.

Logically, according to the degrees of openness of the global economy and harmony in global politics, the pattern of globalisation can be divided into four types, each of which has a wide range of dynamic mechanisms (see Figure 2.3).

Type I is 'closed globalisation'. It is an extreme situation in which actors in the global economy are separated from each other and there is no necessary political coordination. As a result, the whole world is divided into fragmented nation-states that are bent on mercantilism. In terms of liquidity, this process is in a low-speed mode. This form of globalisation cannot be considered globalisation in the complete sense of the term. Historically, the Cold War can be seen as a typical case of closed globalisation. The two camps confronted each other and neither opened its market for the other. The world economic fault line of coexistence of both economic systems was initially delineated by the military fault lines, which soon became political. This was particularly evident in the division of Europe and Germany. In addition, the Soviet Union, China, and other socialist bloc countries boycotted US-led multilateral economic institutions, such as the IMF and

Figure 2.3 Four types of globalisation.

40   *Reglobalisation*

the World Bank, and did not participate in the General Agreement on Tariffs and Trade (GATT). The world was split into two halves according to ideological fault lines, and the political and economic interactions between both sides lacked sufficient coordination, so much so, that the process of globalisation was almost stalled. In 1938, exports from Eastern European to Western European countries accounted for 68.4% of their total exports, yet this number dropped to 14.4% in 1953. The fragmented world market increased the weakness of world economic development in the early 1950s. When the Cold War unfolded, the drawbacks of the highly centralised planned economic system led by the Soviet model emerged gradually, seriously affecting the competitiveness of the socialist bloc in the world market.[38] However, the closed globalisation during the Cold War also brought about an unexpected result, that is, the division of the two markets contributed to regional integration within each. The two parallel markets prompted the two rival camps to strengthen their internal economic cooperation, and this laid the foundation for the integration of the future world market while separating the world. Paradoxically, while the world was divided into two camps because of the Cold War, it was also condensed into two regions, that is, two plates only a step away from being merged into one.

Type II is 'involuted globalisation'. The concept of 'involution' was proposed by Clifford Geertz, a prominent American anthropologist. It refers to the phenomenon in which a social or cultural pattern, after reaching a certain form at a certain stage of development, stagnates, or cannot be transformed into another advanced pattern, and is replaced by a greater degree of internal complexity, involving a process of internal refinement and complexity against the background in which the external expansional conditions are strictly constrained.[39] The crisis of involuted globalisation refers to the fact that global interaction is in a state of undeveloped growth. The 20 years between the two World Wars were like this. The United States was superior in terms of strength and the British Empire had begun to decline, but the rising United States did not take on the responsibility of global governance until after World War II. This era of no hegemonic power politically with a relatively open economy is what we call involution. In the words of the poet Matthew Arnold, the British Empire began to show signs of being much like a weary giant in 1914; the United Kingdom's attention was distracted by old and new tasks in Asia and Africa as the 'world police' burdened with too expansive a jurisdictional area.[40] Similarly, the exceptional expansionism of US foreign policy after the Cold War, in the eyes of some scholars, is also causing the steady decline of the United States. They pointed out that 9/11 not only ushered in the decline of US power, but also showed that the more the United States tries to dominate the world and establish a new empire, the faster was its decline. Immanuel Wallerstein, a prominent sociologist, for example, presented a vivid metaphor: 'the eagle has fallen'.[41] Charles Kupchan, a leading IR scholar at Georgetown University, focussed on the decline of the United States and the rise of Europe from the perspective of US-European relations. He argued that a multipolar transformation was inevitable and that America's world dominance could last another decade. If American politicians are aware of this trend,

From Globalisation to Reglobalisation   41

Kupchan argued, it would be wise to design an order to accommodate the rise of forces such as the European Union and China, rather than insist on sustaining US global dominance.[42] September 11 symbolised the decline of the hegemonic position of the United States to some extent, but until 2008, a few emerging powers in the world took the initiative to assume responsibility for global governance. In this period, China continued to adhere to the dictum of *'taoguang yanghui'* (keeping a low profile and biding time), concentrating its efforts on domestic economic growth, while espousing a relatively detached attitude toward the external world.

Type III is 'disembedded globalisation', in which global political and economic imbalance unfolds in an era of hegemony, political coordination, and increasing global power diffusion. The strategic relationship between the traditional hegemon and the emerging powers changed dramatically between 2008 and 2013. The most typical example was the significant change in strategic trust between the two great powers China and the United States. In September 2009, US Deputy Secretary of State James Steinberg advocated 'strategic reassurance' between China and the United States, arguing that the United States should not only protect its interests, but should also adapt to China's rise. Strategic reassurance, according to Steinberg, must seek to highlight the common interests between Beijing and Washington DC, while addressing the root causes of mistrust directly. The United States and its allies should not seek to contain China. The United States welcomes China's rise as a prosperous power. However, Beijing should also try to reassure other countries that China's rise does not come at the cost of the security and well-being of other countries.[43] The Obama administration's policy toward China went through two stages: from 2008 to the first half of 2010, it focussed on promoting US-China cooperation, with the aim of establishing stable strategic relations in exchange for China's cooperation on many issues of concern for the United States, such as battling the global economic recession. From 2010 onward, Obama's China policy shifted to emphasise on the 'pivot to Asia' politically, economically, and militarily. US-China relations continued to worsen after a lot of friction between both powers, including the Copenhagen Climate Summit, the Google incident, the US arms sales to Taiwan, Obama's meeting with the Dalai Lama, and the South China Sea issue. The 2014 US *Quadrennial Defense Review* stated that the US military had prioritised 'Rebalancing to the Asia-Pacific' and had taken a series of measures to bolster its military presence in the Asia-Pacific region, with 60% of US naval warships to be deployed in the region by 2020.[44] The strategic mutual suspicion between China and the United States indicated the heightened tension over relative gains brought about by globalisation, which made the cooperation between the two great powers increasingly difficult to obtain and sustain.

Type IV is 'inclusive globalisation'. In the wake of the global financial crisis, the impetus for globalisation gradually shifted from advanced economies to emerging powers such as China. Since 2012, the Chinese new leadership advocated a foreign policy of *'fenfa youwei'* (striving to accomplish something) and actively promoted its call for economic globalisation to be more open, inclusive, balanced, beneficial, and promising to all parties when the globalisation process

42 *Reglobalisation*

faces challenges. The reglobalisation of inclusiveness focusses on the unique functions of each role. The power of the world is no longer monopolised by a single centre but constructs a symbiotic and interlocking new and old power structure. The inclusiveness of reglobalisation is reflected in the interweaving relationship between low-level globalisation led by emerging countries and high-level globalisation represented by developed countries. It not only pays more attention to equality and sustainability economically, but also emphasises coordination and consultation politically. Joseph Nye, a prominent IR scholar and former dean of Havard Kennedy School, likened the existing structure of world politics to a 'complex three-dimensional chessboard game' with three levels of chessboards: the top level represents military power, which is largely unipolar and will remain so for years to come; the middle level represents multipolar economic power structure; and the bottom level represents transnational activities. Non-state actors, such as global social movements and terrorist groups, operate largely outside government control.[45] We can consider the reglobalised world as a decentralised multidimensional system. Amitav Acharya, a preeminent IR scholar, called the existing world order a 'multiplex order' that can be likened to a 'multiplex cinema'—a complex that houses several movie theatres and one that gives its audience a choice of watching a variety of movies with different plots, actors, and directors; therefore, this is not a vertical hierarchical structure, but a multidimensional parallel 'composite world' – a more regionalised (like different movies) and more diversified order – a diversified and decentralised world that is linked together by networks and institutions.[46]

The classification of four types of globalisation, focussing on the economic and political logic involved, suggests that in order to understand the nature of globalisation, we need to examine both political and economic factors. The traditional literature on globalisation either focusses on the integration and flattening trends at the economic dimension (as represented by Thomas Friedman's *The World Is Flat: A Brief History of the 21st Century*), or worries heavily about the political conflicts and global fault lines that interact with globalisation (as represented by Samuel Huntington's *Clash of Civilizations*)[47]. However, this book advocates an eclectic analytical framework that focusses on the interactions between politics and the economy. When both politics and the economy are on a downward trend, globalisation will inevitably be at a low point or even risk breaking down; when political and economic factors are not in harmony, that is, one dimension is strong and the other is weak, globalisation encounters more and more governance problems, and, unsurprisingly, there will be calls for reform. September 11 exposed a huge political crisis hidden beneath the superficial prosperity of neoliberal globalisation. The fact that the world has become flat may have widened rather than narrowed the schism between civilisations. We generalise the paradox into two: the involutional and the disembedded forms of globalisation. The outbreak of the 2008 global financial crisis worsened the worldwide political paralysis and economic recession, thus inviting global disorder. Fortunately, when the hegemonic power increasingly embraced retrenchment and isolationism, China, along with other emerging powers, began to actively assume responsibility for global governance, making both material and ideational contributions to global stability. Committed to in-depth adjustment of the structure and dynamics of globalisation, what China envisions is different from the liberal international order. The process of adjustment is long, just like prescriptions in traditional Chinese medicine which may not be as quick as Western medicine to take effect but can affect the body systems' fundamental conditions by regulating meridians and consolidating the foundation. Presently, rather than advocating replacing the old form of globalisation, China has presented a progressive view of a limited and gradual reform of globalisation. For a long time, China's reforms have mainly focussed on the domestic realm. The focus of the reform and opening up policy was reform. Opening up is an important means of serving the larger goal of reform. China influenced the world by reforming itself. However, while China's domestic reforms have achieved remarkable feats, the world order is in crisis. If China wants to make major breakthroughs in both domestic and global governance, it needs to take the lead in the process of reglobalisation, expand, and upgrade the existing international order by bringing more voices of emerging powers, and achieve effective integration of old and new mechanisms. In short, for the purpose of achieving a network of multicentred governance, China should be committed to coordinating political and economic globalisation and promoting inclusive coexistence of low- and high-level globalisation.

Notes

1 David Held, Anthony McGrew, David Goldblatt, and Jonathan Perraton, *Global Transformations: Politics, Economics and Culture*, Stanford, CA: Stanford University Press, 1999, pp. 14–15.
2 For important works on globalisation, see Ulirich Beck, *What is Globalization?* London, UK: Polity Press, 2000; Randal D. Germain, ed., *Globalization and Its Critics: Perspectives from Political Economy*, New York, NY: ST. Martin's Press, INC., 2000; Anthony Giddens, *Runaway World: How Globalization is Reshaping Our Lives*, New York, NY: Routledge, 2002; Manfred Steger, *Globalization: A Very Short Introduction*, Oxford, UK: Oxford University Press, 2003; Anthony McGrew and David Held, *Globalization Theory: Approaches and Controversies*, New York, NY: Polity Press, 2007; Dani Rodrik, *The Globalization Paradox: Democracy and the Future of the World Economy*, New York, NY: W. W. Norton & Company, 2011; Jopseh Stiglitz, *Globalization and Its Discontents Revisited: Anti-Globalization in the Era of Trump*, New York, NY: W. W. Norton & Company, 2017.
3 Oliver Reiser and Blodwen Davies, *Planetary Democracy: An Introduction to Scientific Humanism*, New York, NY: Creative Age Press, 1994.
4 Rodrik, *The Globalization Paradox*, 2011; Walden Bello, *Capitalism's Last Stand: Deglobalization in the Age of Austerity*, London, UK: Zed Books, 2013; Stiglitz, *Globalization and Its Discontents Revisited*, 2017; Manfred B. Steger, *Globalisms: Facing the Populist Challenges*, New York, NY: Rowman & Littlefield Publishers, 2019; Leila Simona Talani and Roberto Roccu, eds., *The Dark Side of Globalisation*, London, UK: Palgrave Macmillan, 2019; Peter A. G. van Bergeijk, *Deglobalization 2.0: Trade and Openness during the Great Depression and the Great Recession*, Cheltonham, UK: Edward Elgar Publishing Ltd., 2020.
5 Arjun Appadurai, *Modernity at Large: Cultural Dimensions of Globalisation*, Minneapolis, MN: University of Minnesota Press, 1996.

44 *Reglobalisation*

6 Robert Cox, *Production, Power and World Order: Social Forces in the Making of History*, New York, NY: Columbia University Press; Leslie Sklair, 'Competing Conceptions of Globalisation', *Journal of World-System Research*, Vol. 5, No. 2, 1999, pp. 142–163.

7 The number of trade restrictions adopted by China in 2016 was only 241. This was less than those of India (562) and Brazil (299). China is one of the countries with the least number of trade restrictions among the world's major economies. See Simon J. Evenett and Johannes Fritz, *FDI Recover? The 20th Global Trade Alert Report*, 30 August 2016, http://www.globaltradealert.org/reports/download/15.

8 Thomas Friedman, *The World Is Flat: A Brief History of the 21st Century*, New York, NY: Farrar, Straus and Giroux, 2005.

9 Edward Said, *Orientalism*, New York, NY: Vintage, 1979.

10 Thomas Piketty, *Capital in the Twenty-First Century*, translated by Arthur Goldhammer, Cambridge, UK: Belknap Press of Harvard University Press, 2017.

11 Branko Milanovic, *Global Inequality: A New Approach for the Age of Globalisation*, Cambridge, UK: Belknap Press of Harvard University Press, 2016, pp. 15–30.

12 Zheng Yu, 'Quanqiuhua Jincheng bingwei nizhuan' ['The Process of Globalisation Has Not been Reversed'], *Wenhua zongheng [Beijing Cultural Review]*, No. 6, 2016, pp. 42–50.

13 See database at http://www.start.umd.edu/gtd.

14 Chase Foster, 'Inequality, Occupy Wall Street and the New Economic Paradigm: A Conversation with Larry Summers', *Kennedy School Review*, Vol. 12, 2012, pp. 94–97.

15 Liu Jianfei, 'Lun shijie geju zhong de 'feijihua' qushi' ['On the Trend of Non-polarization in the International Configuration'], *Xiandai guoji guanxi [Contemporary International Relations]*, No. 4, 2008, pp. 1–5.

16 Richard Hass, 'The Age of Nonpolarity', *Foreign Affairs*, Vol. 87, No. 3, May/June 2008, pp. 44–56.

17 Ian Bremmer, 'From G8 to G20 to G-Zero: Why No One Wants to Take Charge in the New Global Order', *New Statesman*, 11 June 2013, https://www.newstatesman.com/politics/politics/2013/06/g8-g20-g-zero-why-no-one-wants-take-charge-new-global-order.

18 Tang Nan, 'Jinrong quanqiuhua de tuichao: kuajing ziben liudong jianshao' ['The Recession of Financial Globalisation: A Decrease in Cross-border Capital Flows'], FTChinese.com, 28 August 2017, http://www.ftchinese.com/story/001074001#adch annell D = 2000.

19 Fareed Zakaria, *The Post-American World*, New York, NY: W. W. Norton & Company, 2008, p. 2.

20 Jayshree Bajoria, 'The Dangers of "Deglobalization"', *Council on Foreign Relations*, 16 March 2009, http://www.cfr.org/immigration/dangers - deglobalization/p18768.

21 Walden Bello, *Deglobalization: New Ideas for Running the World Economy*, Cape Town, South Africa: David Philip Publishers, 2003.

22 Robert Legvold, *Return to Cold War*, Cambridge, UK: Polity Press, 2016.

23 Xu Biao, Pang Qinghui et al., 'Cengjing fengguan wuxian de quanqiuhua tuise: ququanqiuhua qiaoran kaishi' ['The Color of the Once Glorious Globalisation Begins to Fade with the Silent Commencement of Deglobalisation'], Hexun.com, http://opinion,hexun.com/2016-08-14/185502326.html.

24 Henry A. Kissinger, *World Order*, London, UK: Penguin Books, p. 366.

25 David Fahrenthold, 'How Bernie Sanders' "Political Revolution" Would Change the Nation?' *The Washington Post*, 18 January 2016, https://www.washingtonpost.com/politics/how-bernie-sanderss-political-revolution-would-change-the-nation/2016/01/18/4c1c13fa-bde4-11e5-9443-7074c3645405_story.html; Sam Stein and Jason Cherkis, 'The Inside Story of How Bernie Sanders Became the Greatest Online Fundraiser', *The Huffington Post*, 28 June 2017, https://www.huffpost.com/entry/bernie-sanders-fundraising_n_59527587e4b02734df2d92c1.

From Globalisation to Reglobalisation   45

26 Tang Xinhua, "Jinzhuan guojia' maoyi dashuju fenxi' ['Big Data Analysis of BRICS Trade'], *Kaifaxing jinrong yanjiu* [*Developmental Finance Research*], No. 5, 2017, pp. 86-96.
27 US National Intelligence Council, *Global Trends 2030: Alternative Worlds*, December 2012, https://www.dni.gov/files/documents/GlobalTrends_2030.pdf, p. 9.
28 Homi Kharas, *The Emerging Middle Class in Developing Countries*, Brookings Report, 31 January 2010, https://www.brookings.edu/research/the-emerging-middle-class-in-d eveloping-countries/, p. 28.
29 National Bureau of Statistics, *Jinzhuan guojia lianhe tongji shouce 2015* [*The 2015 Joint Statistical Handbook of BRICS Countries*], Beijing, China: China Statistics Press, 2015.
30 Marie T. Henehan and John Vasquez, 'The Changing Probability of International War, 1816-1992', in Raimo Vayrynen, ed., *The Waning of Major War: Theories and Debates*, London, UK: Routledge, 2006, p. 288.
31 Xu Huixi, 'Shuju xianshi: jinsinian Zhongguo dui shijie jingji gongxianlv chao Ou Mei Ri zonghe' ['Statistics Show China's Contribution to the World Economy in the Last Four Years has Exceeded that of the United States, Europe and Japan Combined'], *Jingji ribao* [*Economic Daily*], 2 September 2017, http://www.ce.cn/xwzx/gnsz/gdxw /201709/25/t20170925_26260741.shtml.
32 Mancur Olson Jr. and Richard Zeckhauser, 'An Economic Theory of Alliances', *The Review of Economics and Statistics*, Vol. 48, No. 3, 1971, pp. 266–279.
33 Charles Kindelberg, *The World in Depression, 1929–1939*, Berkeley, CA: University of California Press, 2013.
34 Xi Jinping, 'Huangying dacheng Zhongguo fazhan de lieche' ['Welcome Onboard China's Development Train'], Xinhuanet.com, 22 August 2014, http://news.xinhuanet .com/world/2014-08/22/c126905369.htm.
35 Xi Jinping, 'Zhongguo yuanwei guoji shehui tigong gengduo gonggong chanping' ['China Is Willing to Provide More Public Goods to the International Community'], People.com.cn, 3 September 2016, http: //politics.people.com.cn/nl/2016/0903/c1001 -28689064.html.
36 Chen Zhi and Huo Xiaoguang, 'Shijie jingji luntan zhuxi Shiwabu: Xi zhuxi de jianghua wei women dailai le yangguang' ['World Economic Forum Chairman Schwab: President Xi's Speech has Brought Us Sunshine'], Xinhuanet.com, 17 January 2017, http://www.xinhuanet.com/world/2017-01/17/c_129451023.htm.
37 Polanyi, *The Great Transformation: The Political and Economic Origins of Our Time*; Liu Yang, 'Tupo xianzhi, chongxin tansuo renlei shenghuo de kenengxing: Ka'er Bolani de "Da zhuanxing"' ['Breaking Limits and Rediscovering the Possibilities of Human Life: Karl Polanyi's "The Great Transformation"'], *Shehui kexue bao* [*Chinese Social Sciences Today*], 14 December 2010, p. 10.
38 Ye Jiang, *Dabianju: Quanqiuhua, lengzhan yu dangdai guoji zhengzhi jingji guanxi* ['*Great Change: Globalisation, the Cold War and Contemporary International Political and Economic Relations*'], Shanghai, China: Shanghai SDX Publishing, 2004, p. 107.
39 Clifford Geertz, *Agricultural Involution: The Processes of Ecological Change in Indonesia*, Los Angeles, CA: University of California Press, 1969.
40 Aaron L. Friedberg, *The Weary Titan: Britain and the Experience of Relative Decline, 1895–1905*, Princeton, NJ: Princeton University Press, 1989; Niall Ferguson, 'Sinking Globalization', *Foreign Affairs*, Vol. 84, No. 2, 2005, pp. 64–77.
41 Immanuel Wallerstein, 'The Eagle Has Crash Landed', *Foreign Policy*, July/August 2002, pp. 60–68; Immanuel Wallerstein, 'Shock and Awe?' Fernand and Braudel Center, *Binghamton University Commentary*, No. 111, 15 April 2003, https://www.bin ghamton.edu/fbc/archive/111en.htm.
42 Charles Kupchan, *The End of the American Era: US Foreign Policy and the Geopolitics of the Twenty-first Century*, New York, NY: Alfred A. Knopf, 2002.

46 *Reglobalisation*

43 Kelly Currie, 'The Doctrine of Strategic Reassurance', *The Wall Street Journal*, 22 October 2009; James Steinberg and Michael O'Hanlon, *Strategic Reassurance and Resolve: US-China Relations in the Twenty-First Century*, Princeton, NJ: Princeton University Press, 2014.
44 US Department of Defense, *Quadrennial Defense Review 2014*, Washington, DC, 4 March 2014, p. 34.
45 Joseph S. Nye, Jr., *The Paradox of American Power: Why the World's Only Superpower Can't Go It Alone*, Oxford, UK: Oxford University Press, 2003.
46 Amitav Acharya, *The End of American World Order*, Malden, MA: Polity, 2014, pp. 6–8.
47 See Friedman, *The World is Flat*, 2005; Samuel Huntington, *The Clash of Civilizations and the Remaking of World Order*, New York, NY: Simon & Schuster, 1996.

3 Inclusive development and interconnected thinking

To govern the town as if it were one's house, the town cannot be governed well. To govern the country as if it were one's town, the country cannot be governed well. To govern the world as if it were one's country, the world cannot be governed well. One ought to govern one's house as it is, one's town as it is, one's country as it is, and the world as it is.

Guanzi: Herdsman

A single flower does not make spring, while one hundred flowers in full blossom bring spring to the garden.

President Xi Jinping quoting this ancient
Chinese poem in 'The Keynote Speech at the
2013 Annual Boao Forum for Asia'

A new round of reglobalisation driven by emerging economies including China is unfolding slowly. The 2008 global financial crisis exposed the challenge of the old version of globalisation and the inner weakness of the Western liberal order. Against this background, China, along with other emerging powers, has taken the lead in actively promoting a new round of reglobalisation, which is not to overthrow the existing international order but to reform and upgrade it from within. It is like an off-road car that used to run in the wilderness and is now turning old, which the driver cannot drive smoothly. There is bound to be a new voice questioning and reflecting on the current dilemma that leads to open discussion on whether to keep on with the old car on a hopeless road or to get out of the car together and bring tools to repair it, lubricate it, remove the rust and dust and, even, if necessary, to improve the power and performance of the engine. Through joint participation in its transformation, the 'car' of globalisation can be revitalised again and can race toward new goals. The drivers can continue to be former or new ones, or old and new drivers can take turns to drive. This metaphor indicates that humankind should try to adjust its thinking to adapt to the new environment and the new wave of re-globalisation.[1]

3.1 The inclusive philosophy of China's rise

Chinese traditional thinking contains a profound philosophy of tolerance and inclusiveness, in that only when all things are in harmony and form one family

48 *Reglobalisation*

can world harmony be achieved. Confucianism emphasises the difference in order between close and distant relationships and that even strangers on the periphery of the relationship network should be accommodated and accepted as far as possible.[2] Within and outside the family, the highest guiding principle of interpersonal communication is that 'harmony is most precious', and individuals must try their best to maintain a harmonious and good relationship with acquaintances. 'Benevolence' (*ren*) is the principle of communication between two people, but if, based on benevolence, one also adheres to the principle of 'being close to one's relatives' (*qin qin*),[3] they can extend the harmony between two people to the entire community and come up with the idea of 'one's own people'.[4] The Confucian relationalism (guangxi zhuyi), when projected into the area of international relations (IR), holds that the best world order is one in which 'the four seas are one family and the whole world is in harmony'. It treats a sort of family-like emotional connection as an analogy for social and international relations. This *tianxia* (all under heaven) system, or cosmopolitanism, is also a kind of world political design of 'taking the person as the person, the home as the home, the town as the town, the country as the country, and the world as the world'.[5] Therefore, unlike Western scholarship, which often likens the international system to a 'market', Confucianism likens the world to a 'family' with relationships of interests and kin; when conflicts arise, one ought to try to 'reduce big issues to small ones' and seek common ground while reserving differences, and to pursue overall harmony as the fundamental interest of the family.[6] China's inclusive thinking on reglobalisation helps transcend the so-called liberal order dominated by the West. For example, the logo used in the Belt and Road Forum for International Cooperation held in Beijing in May 2017, like the pattern of yin and yang in Chinese traditional culture, is a circular logo without edges and corners, in which blue represents the ocean, yellow represents land, and the two embrace each other, conveying the inclusive spirit of the world marching forward together, hand-in-hand (see Figure 3.1). The inclusive philosophy of China's rise will provide a philosophical and value basis for reglobalisation in two ways.

First, adhering to the 'harmony being the most precious' concept, rather than to the 'winning as paramount' concept, helps to reconcile the political and economic contradictions of globalisation as well as tensions at the domestic and international levels. Economic freedom is the weapon of the strong, while political protest is the weapon of the weak. At present, the globalisation process dominated by the so-called liberal order seems fair and free on the surface, but it is actually a competitive game in which the strong win and the weak lose, separating the high-level 'winners' from the low-level 'losers'. Under conditions of resource scarcity, the winners of globalisation are bound to protect their gains by taking advantage of rules. However, owing to the long-term stability of the system, such a class gap will be fixed for a long time, and it will be extremely difficult for the 'losers' of globalisation to change their disadvantageous positions because they would have to go against large and systematic international institutions. For neoliberals, while international institutions help to reduce transaction costs, promote the flow of information, and avoid violent competition, virtually any institution itself is

Inclusive development and interconnected thinking 49

(a) (b)

Figure 3.1 The inclusive spirit conveyed by the Belt and Road Forum for International Cooperation.

nonneutral.[7] Thus, there is a structural contradiction between high- and low-level globalisation in the current process. Developed countries that have had the power of international rule-making will inevitably integrate their preferences into the international system. This invisible rule control has led to the long-term disadvantage of developing countries in the distribution of global dividends. Therefore, despite the existence of a large number of hard-working actors in the world, they often find it difficult to obtain fair treatment and results. The resulting resentment against increasing inequality has now spread into Europe and the United States and has fuelled the global protests against the political and economic establishment. More and more emerging countries unite to demand a fairer and more equitable international political and economic order from developed countries. In the face of seemingly irreconcilable zero-sum competition, the resilience of Chinese wisdom has emerged gradually. In the early 1950s, China, together with India and Myanmar, jointly advocated the Five Principles of Peaceful Coexistence, which won wide approval in the international community, namely mutual respect for sovereignty and territorial integrity, mutual nonaggression, noninterference in each other's internal affairs, equality and mutual benefit, and peaceful coexistence. The Five Principles of Peaceful Coexistence is a valuable international norm initiated by China and other partners during the zero-sum, highly competitive atmosphere of the Cold War, which still hold sway to this day. Of course, in today's increasingly interdependent era of globalisation, the principle of noninterference in each other's internal affairs has been repeatedly violated as new norms such as the 'responsibility to protect' or R2P have evolved. Nevertheless, the spirit of inclusiveness embodied in the Five Principles of Peaceful Coexistence can provide impetus for a new round of reforms in the international system.

Second, the inclusive philosophy opposes the zero-sum and hierarchical competition in IR and strives to bring the strengths of each country into play

50 Reglobalisation

while stimulating enthusiasm for active cooperation. The Confucian view of inclusiveness is a mixture of long-term holistic interests. As Confucianism believes that 'friendship cannot stand always on one side', reciprocity has persisted for thousands of years in the Chinese people's practices of 'friendship' and 'mutual exchange'. As China was the epicentre of the East Asian Confucian cultural circle, the concepts of 'courtesy and reciprocity' naturally permeated most parts of East Asia with the spread of Confucian culture. Agrarian civilisations tend to produce a relatively closed social network (where people meet frequently) in which members form interdependent behavioural characteristics and psychological patterns. With strong cohesion and group identity, this closed network can break through time and space, create generational continuity, and maintain the mutual trust and benefits of members of the network. With time, the relationship network will also generate inertia and expansibility.[8] In the twenty-first century, hegemonic powers will no longer simply try to win by strength or pursue simple coercive logic. In the *Global Trend 2030* report published in 2012, the National Intelligence Council of the United States explicitly declared that

> By 2030, no country—whether the US, China, or any other large country—will be a hegemonic power. The empowerment of individuals and diffusion of power among states and from states to informal networks will have a dramatic impact, largely reversing the historic rise of the West since 1750, restoring Asia's weight in the global economy, and ushering in a new era of 'democratisation' at the international and domestic level.[9]

China's reform proposal for the old and imperfect international system advocates openness and tolerance. Since the new leadership took power in 2012, China's approach to the international order has changed from passive to active participation. Against this background, the BRI, the new Asian security concept, and the idea of a 'community of shared future for humankind' (*renlei mingyun gongtongti*) put forward by China all contain inclusive Confucianism as the foundation, showcasing the openness, flexibility, and practicality of China's approach to reglobalisation. Ancient Chinese people considered 'the Earth being square and Heaven being round' and the interplay between yin and yang as symbols of harmony. Confucian inclusive philosophy holds that one's life is incomplete and can only manifest through contact with others. Without others, the attributes of oneself will lose meaning.[10] To promote inclusive reglobalisation, we need a new mode of relational interaction. The goal of connectivity is limited, and the strategic posture is restrained. The emphasis is on giving full play to China's real advantages. It is 'Oriental wisdom' that manifests as inclusiveness, integration, convergence, and the dissolution of closure, exclusion, and opposition. In stark contrast, China actively promoted connectivity when the United States began to build walls. Although China is not a global leading power yet, it has the ability to take the initiative to act and promote connectivity in its neighbouring region.

3.2 The symbiotic wisdom of heaven and earth

The pattern of IR in ancient East Asia embodies Confucian thinking around 'attaching more importance to relations rather than entities'.[11] Dating back to the tributary system of the Western Zhou Dynasty, with the Chinese civilisation at the centre, the orderly difference pattern originated from the Central Plains to the border, from the suzerain state to the vassal states. In Confucian culture, the principle of respect advocates the order of superiority and inferiority based on the differentiation of roles, while the principle of kinship advocates courtesy, tolerance, and harmony in horizontal interactions. Therefore, according to the differences in affinity between countries, the interaction within different sets of countries in the East Asian Confucian cultural circle is different.[12] The studies on the tributary order in East Asia and the *tianxia* idea have brought many kinds of inspiration to the analyses of relationality. More and more scholars have realised that international relations in the Chinese and Western contexts are essentially different. At least until modern times, the logic of international interactions in East Asia was quite different from the sovereignty structure of the Western Westphalian system. Zhao Tingyang criticised the individualistic hypothesis of Western IR theory from a philosophical level. He pointed out that the dualist thinking of separating actors and rationalising them and rendering them utilitarian was incompatible with traditional East Asian thinking.[13] Zhang Feng also advocated that China's longstanding relational thinking should be fully tapped into and applied to today's diplomatic analysis. However, unlike process-oriented relations, he analysed East Asian international relations from the structural dimension and considered the Ming Dynasty East Asian history as a special relational international structure.[14] Relational thinking focuses on dynamic and situational interactions rather than on fixed or mechanical attributes. As a product of social construction, there are significant differences between relational and substantive thinking. The former considers the relationship factor as the basis of order and that the actors are inseparably linked with each other. The actors tend to maintain long-term relations and moderately concede short-term interests. The latter pertains to the substantive factors as a basis of order, rational self-interest as the only reason for action, and the unit attribute determines interactive results. Generally speaking, there are ostensible differences between relationalism and substantivism in the view of order, theoretical metaphors, and diplomatic revelations. Western society generally prefers substantive thinking, while Chinese Confucianism puts a premium on the relational approach, the cultural contextualisation of which is reflected in the following aspects.

First, Confucian relational thinking emphasises tolerance and harmony. This Confucian essence is deeply influenced by the yin and yang concepts of *Zhouyi* or the *Book of Change*. The so-called 'harmony generates and sameness stifles vitality', 'gentlemen seek harmony but not uniformity, while petty individuals seek uniformity but not harmony', 'harmony is most precious', and 'seeking common ground while reserving differences' all reveal the 'peace and harmony' thinking in Chinese culture. Under the influence of Confucian culture, the Chinese people

52 Reglobalisation

have formed a way of thinking that puts a premium on groups rather than on individuals, emphasising relationships rather than entities. In the IR community in China, the preeminent IR theorist Qin Yaqing was among the first to propose that the zero-sum logic in Western discourses could not explain China's longstanding practice of peaceful development and that China's pacifist preference could be understood only by returning to the Confucian relational tradition.[15] In view of Confucianism, the existence of an individual is incomplete; without connection with others, the individual will lose his or her meaning. This idea of relationality has been embedded in the mode of interactions between China and other East Asian countries. For China, the priority of foreign policy-making oftentimes is not short-term interests but how to maintain long-term harmonious relations with the outside world. In contrast, Western rational thinking is atomically oriented and essentially materialistic, emphasising the independence and competition of interests.

Second, Confucian relational thinking holds that both sentiments and reason should be considered while making decisions. In dealing with international crises, China's projection of power is embedded in the relationship network, including moral considerations. China often avoids interfering in other countries' affairs in order to maintain overall harmony. This is similar to the moral principles of the Chinese people in dealing with everyday disputes such as 'business is never personal' and 'harmony makes money'. Maintaining a balance of relations is already a constitutive principle of the daily behaviour of the Chinese people, and this mode of thinking will prompt Chinese diplomacy to pursue a kind of relational security that maintains harmony between countries, rather than substantial security advocated by the West.[16] For instance, in the North Korean nuclear crisis, in the Myanmar issue, and the Darfur crisis in Sudan, China did not rely on its own strength to pressure one side. Instead, it guided the so-called 'troublemaker' into a just environment of dialogue and consultation by utilising traditional relations, informal channels, nongovernmental networks, and multilateral mechanisms. China seeks to play the role of a mediator, to bring out the advantages of the circumstances and not coercively interfere in the internal affairs of all parties concerned and seeks to adhere to the principle of turning rigidity into flexibility and conflict into harmony through 'consultative involvement'.[17]

Third, Confucian relational thinking emphasises mutual benefit and reciprocity. Different from the logic of rational transactions, relational thinking emphasises reciprocal logic. In the Chinese context, reciprocity includes altruistic aid and instrumental exchange. 'Helpers help themselves', in that one who helps others can expect feedback and reciprocity from others and, together, form a mutually supportive network and reduce the risks and uncertainty of survival.[18] As the reciprocal mechanism ensures that we are not only resource givers, but also beneficiaries when in need, the benefits are different from those of the tit-for-tat strategy. Although rational self-interest behaviour will initially lead to advantages in the form of resource accumulation, and opportunistic strategies will maximise returns in the short term, in the long run, however, Confucian relational thinking holds that reciprocity and human relations are the best strategies to secure and

Inclusive development and interconnected thinking 53

sustain success. In the Chinese society of human relations, the host can see what he or she gets from the basket filled with gifts from the guest and the long-term benefits from an empty basket. He or she never lets the guest take an empty basket home. The pursuit of personal interests in a world of mutual benefit is mixed with moral obligations. The best winning strategy is to maintain the long-term social order rather than simply pursuing short-term personal interest.[19]

3.3 Connectivity is power

In 2013, Chinese President Xi Jinping formally put forward the BRI. Over the past few years, this initiative has been supported by more than 100 countries and international organisations. China issued a joint document with 56 countries and regional cooperation organisations to promote the BRI, signed a free-trade area agreement with 11 countries along the routes, and signed bilateral investment agreements with 56 other countries along the routes. By the end of 2016, China's companies built 38 large-scale transportation infrastructure projects along 26 Belt and Road countries. China's investment in the Belt and Road countries has totalled $51.1 billion, and 52 economic- and trade-cooperation zones have been completed in 18 countries along the routes, with a total investment of $15.6 billion. The Asian Infrastructure Investment Bank (AIIB), proposed by China, attracted 57 founding members since its launch in January 2016, with a total of $1.73 billion in loans to support nine infrastructure projects in seven countries. On May 2017, at the Belt and Road Forum for International Cooperation held in Beijing, China and other countries discussed ways to promote the BRI to comple- ment each other's advantages and drive regional economic growth.

Historically, successful emerging powers realised the organic integration of internal and external support. The British Empire of the nineteenth century, for example, built its splendour on colonial systems throughout the world, the East India Company's business networks, and overseas military bases. America's global hegemony today stems not only from its own superior physical resources (such as GDP, science and technology, education, industrial systems, and advanced governance systems), but also lies in its longstanding support network with the outside world, especially its global military alliance system. Throughout the major international operations of the United States, its allies have offered it strong support in the form of political statements, military dispatches, logistical supplies, intelligence sharing, cost sharing, and other forms. For a rising power, the global extension of overseas interests will depend on the support of strategic networks. In the twenty-first century, China's rise involves the continuous inte- gration into the world and building increasingly close ties with the outside world. China, which is heading toward the centre of the world stage, should not only evaluate its own strengths, but also learn to examine the relationship between itself and the world beyond it.[20] From the perspective of the relationship network, the rise of a great power is a process of mobilising and absorbing internal and external resources with domestic resources as its backing and external links as its grasp.[21] China is currently experiencing a diplomatic transformation from

54 *Reglobalisation*

'keeping a low profile and biding time' to 'striving for accomplishing something' with a greater emphasis on the initiative in shaping the external environment and leading the trend of reglobalisation.

On the one hand, China is more active in shaping and building the global network. When China resumed its legitimate seat in the United Nations in 1971, the number of its diplomatic relationships was only 64, less than half of the total membership of the United Nations at that time.[22] By the end of 2019, China had established diplomatic relations with 180 countries, and the Ministry of Foreign Affairs of China had overtaken the United States to have the largest diplomatic network of 276 embassies and consulates around the world.[23] China has followed the unique strategy of nonalignment in partnership as its long-term diplomatic strategy. President Xi Jinping made it clear at the Central Foreign Affairs Work Conference in November 2014 that 'on the premise of adhering to the principle of non-alignment, we should make friends and form a global partnership network'.[24] In addition, cultural exchanges, city diplomacy, and economic and trade networks have been expanding. The network of diplomatic relations intertwined with countless relations and nodes constitutes the field of China's rise. It can be said that China's diplomacy in the new era pays more attention to the relationship between its own destiny and that of the outside world. Words such as 'nonaligned partnership', 'Belt and Road', 'interconnection network', and 'global partnership network', which are actively advocated in China's diplomatic discourse, fully highlight the diplomatic orientation of China's active weaving of the community network of shared future, which is a positive response to global relevance. It can be said that the process of China's rise is a history of continuous integration with the world and the ever-expanding network of external contacts.

On the other hand, China is actively weaving its partnership network. The long-term accumulation of history and culture makes the relationship ethics of Chinese Confucian culture exert a subtle influence on diplomacy. As the Chinese sayings go, 'just as a fence needs the support of three stakes, an able fellow needs the help of three other people', and 'distant relatives are inferior to the nearest neighbours'.[25] Based on their different degrees of closeness with relatives and acquaintances, Chinese people tend to interact with each other according to the difference pattern of family members, acquaintances, half acquaintances and strangers.[26] Unlike formal alliances, China's partnership system is not a mandatory exchange of rights and obligations, but a platform for the development of bilateral and multilateral relations. Thus, it has more of a rallying effect and is more conducive to winning the recognition and support of most countries with its open, flexible, and nonmandatory characteristics. As President Xi pointed out, 'partnership means a good man doing good and great things together with others'.[27] In the established and upgraded partnerships, the words 'comprehensive' and 'friendly' also indicate the difference in the order of China's diplomatic relations. According to statistics, as of April 2016, 84 countries and regional integration organisations had established partnerships with China, including 79 countries and 5 regional integration organisations (see Table 3.1).[28] Unlike the United States and other Western countries that emphasised exclusive alliances, China is

Table 3.1 China's partnership network

Differential Pattern, Partnership, and Nonalignment, Mainly Bilateral	
Highlighting Strategic Cooperation	**Highlighting Strategic Relations**
(1) Comprehensive Strategic Cooperative Partnership: Russia (2011); (2) All-weather Strategic Partnership: Pakistan (2015); (3) Comprehensive Strategic Partnership: Vietnam (2008), Laos (2009), Cambodia (2010), Myanmar (2011), and Thailand (2012); (4) Strategic Partnership: India (2015), Korea (2008), Turkey (2010), Afghanistan (2012), and Sri Lanka (2013).	(1) Strategic Partnership: Canada (2005), Nigeria (2006), Serbia (2009), Angola (2010), Poland (2011), Ireland (2012), United Arab Emirates (2012), Chile (2012), Uzbekistan (2012), Kyrgyzstan (2013), Tajikistan (2013), Turkmenistan (2008), Ukraine (2013), Qatar (2014), Costa Rica (2015), Ecuador (2015), Sudan (2015), Jordan (2015), Czech Republic (2016), Association of Southeast Asian Nations (2003), and African Union (2004); (2) Innovative Strategic Partnership: Switzerland (2016).
Highlighting Comprehensive Relations	**Highlighting Friendly Relations**
(1) All-round Strategic Partnership: Germany (2014); (2) Comprehensive Strategic Partnership: EU (2003), Britain (2004), France (2004), Italy (2004), Spain (2005), Portugal (2005), Greece (2006), Denmark (2008), South Africa (2010), Kazakhstan (2011), Brazil (2012), Peru (2013), Mexico (2013), Malaysia (2013), Indonesia (2013), Belarus (2013), Algeria (2014), Argentina (2014), Venezuela (2014), Australia (2014), New Zealand (2014), Mongolia (2014), Egypt (2016), Saudi Arabia (2016), and Iran (2016).	(1) A Closer Comprehensive Partnership: Bangladesh (2010); (2) All-round Friendly Partnership: Belgium (2014); (3) All-round Partnership in Keeping with the Times: Singapore (2015); (4) Comprehensive Friendly Partnership: Romania (2004), Bulgaria (2014), Maldives (2014); (5) Comprehensive Partnership: Ethiopia (2003), Croatia (2005), Nepal (2009), Tanzania (2013), Kenya (2013), Republic of the Congo (2013), Netherlands (2014), Timor-Leste (2014); (6) Friendly Cooperative Partnership: Hungary (2004) and Senegal (2014); (7) Cooperative Partnership: Fiji (2006), Albania (2009), Trinidad and Tobago (2013), Antigua and Barbuda (2013), and Finland (2013) (8) Friendly Partnership: Jamaica.

Note: Table compiled by the authors.

one of the few countries in the world that has adhered to the principles of nonalignment for long. It is also one of the countries with the most intensive partnership networks in the world. This is also an important manifestation of the peaceful, inclusive, and networked nature of China's rise. At different levels, China's strategic partnership presents three basic characteristics: equality, peace, and inclusiveness.

56 *Reglobalisation*

3.4 Building a community of shared future

'A community of shared future for humankind' has become a cornerstone concept in China's diplomatic relations in recent years.[29] As early as 2011, in a white paper titled 'Peaceful Development of China', China proposed the concept of a 'community of shared future'. Later, this concept was advocated by several top leaders in China. In April 2013, President Xi, while delivering a keynote speech at the Boao Forum for Asia, urged the region and the world to foster a sense of a 'community of shared future'. During his visit to Indonesia in October 2013, President Xi proposed to build a 'China-ASEAN community of shared future'. That same month, while speaking at a meeting on relations with neighbouring countries, he pointed out that 'the sense of a community of shared future should take root in the neighbouring countries'. At the Central Foreign Affairs Work Conference held in November 2014, one of the largest gatherings of the senior-most leaders and top diplomats, President Xi mapped out China's diplomatic strategies and emphasised that it should endeavour to build a 'community of shared future with neighbouring countries'. In March 2015, President Xi made it clear that an Asian community of shared future should be built. Thus far, Chinese officials and academics have put forward a variety of 'communities of shared future', including a 'community of shared future for humankind', a 'Asia-Pacific community of shared future', an 'Asian community of shared future', a 'community of shared future for neighbouring countries', a 'China-ASEAN community of shared future', a 'China-Africa community of shared future', and a 'China-Pakistan community of shared future'. In a sense, the idea of a 'community of shared future for humankind' comes from a profound understanding of the contemporary world by the Chinese people. It embodies the unique perspective and mode of thinking of the Chinese civilisation and the unique Chinese way of dealing with foreign affairs. It is the product of Chinese wisdom and an important intellectual contribution of China to humankind. Indeed, it can become a public good in the world's marketplace of ideas.

As a manifestation of idealist thinking in China's vision of the world, the concept of a community of shared future serves China's interests well. Only when China has a peaceful environment can it extend the 'period of strategic opportunities' (*zhanlue jiyuqi*), rest assured of its peaceful development, and realise the great rejuvenation of the nation. The idea of a community of shared future also serves the interests of the world. Only when the world is better off can China also be better off. As the Chinese saying goes, 'a single flower does not signify spring, but a garden full of colourful flowers does'. China's development is not a threat but an opportunity for the whole world. Its economic growth has entered into the 'new normal', and China will continue to provide markets, growth, and investment opportunities for all countries. In 2015, China set the goal of lifting its entire population of people who live under the poverty line, amounting to over 70 million in all, out of poverty by the end of 2020, a goal that it is set to realise. Achieving this ambitious and inspiring goal will not only reduce the burden of global economic growth, but also add valuable experience to the cause of

Inclusive development and interconnected thinking 57

international poverty reduction. As a promoter of a community of shared future for humankind, China should emphasise sharing development achievements and promoting security cooperation with its neighbouring countries, while actively making goodwill gestures to countries with doubts about its strategic intentions, exercise strategic restraint and make concessions when necessary, and ultimately earn other countries' support for its leadership in building a community of shared future for humankind and their willingness to integrate into such a community. The greatest magic and charm of the idea of a community of shared future for humankind lies in its vision of breaking the wall between 'in-groups' and 'out-groups' by transforming the competing 'Self' and 'Other' into an inclusive 'We'. In the long histories of the Yellow and the Yangtze River basins, the Indus and Ganges River basins, the Euphrates and Tigris River basins in Asia, as well as the history of Southeast Asia, many ancient civilisations were bred, reflecting and complementing each other and making important contributions to the progress of human civilisation. Today's Asia is still characterised by diversity. Different civilisations, nationalities, and religions converge and blend to form a colourful Asian family. We should promote exchanges and dialogues among different civilisations and different modes of development, learn from each other's strengths and weaknesses, develop together through exchanges and mutual learning, and make civilised exchanges and mutual learning a bridge to enhance friendship among people of all countries as a driving force for the progress of human societies and as a link to safeguard world peace. Its essence highlights the following keywords: 'wide consultation', 'joint contributions', 'shared benefits', and 'win-win' in order to build a community of shared future.

First, wide consultation implies discussing a development plan together. The BRI covers more than 60 countries and regions in the world, with a total population of more than 4.4 billion, about 63% of the world's total, and a combined economy of more than $20 trillion, accounting for 29% of the world's economy. All these countries and regions together play an important role in the global economy. From the inception, the BRI aimed at achieving the linked development of land and maritime economy and trade along with social culture. Wide consultation aims to establish a new mechanism across the countries and regions so that people can jointly discuss and plan the future direction of development and unify their development goals. Only when the goals and plans of development are a result of joint discussions can we form a consensus, combine into one force, and work toward common development goals. Behind the old version of globalisation is a strong Western civilisation. The highly influential narratives of the 'end of history'[30] or 'the world is flat' indeed highlight the discursive hegemony of the West. Today, in the course of bridging the gap the rich and the poor and seeking common development, the BRI emphasises the need to promote the revival, prosperity, and innovation of civilisations and transcend the expansionist idea of Western civilisation that has been popularised in the old version of globalisation. The BRI has also promoted global cooperation through regional cooperation. Globalisation and regional integration are mutually reinforcing. The BRI aims to promote global cooperation through regional and wider intercontinental

58   *Reglobalisation*

cooperation. The six major economic corridors under the BRI framework are an industrial chain layout, expanding to the whole world through continuous extension, and putting the whole world into a layout of a new global industrial chain, as well as a new type of industrialisation and urbanisation. This goes beyond the contradiction between regional integration and globalisation and improves connectivity between different regions. For example, the China-Pakistan Economic Corridor not only links China and Pakistan together, but will also extend to the Indian Ocean, the Persian Gulf, and Europe in the future. Therefore, it is a truly global strategic layout of regional integration and globalisation.

Second, coconstruction implies joint development. The BRI is based on the joint development of the Belt and Road countries and regions. China has taken the lead in setting an example and has also provided operational and sustainable development plans and structures for the BRI, such as the establishment of the Silk Road Fund and its advocacy in favour of establishing the AIIB. The idea of coconstruction is also reflected in two old Chinese sayings: 'Let those with money contribute money; and let those with strength contribute strength', and 'when everybody adds fuel, the flames rise high'. That is, no matter the amount of capital, it can only be combined to promote the development of the BRI. Although the development of the BRI focusses on the countries and regions along the routes, its success is related to the recovery and development of the global economy. Its achievements will undoubtedly benefit all countries and people the world over. Only with the capital (including private capital) of all countries along the routes and the joint venture of global capital, can the BRI be steadily promoted under the premise of coconstruction. The BRI is a big pattern of land and sea links. Originally, globalisation was maritime, with 90% of trade transported by sea. The BRI literally means 'one belt and one road' in Chinese, implying maritime and land integration. Take the China-Pakistan Economic Corridor as an example: as one of the six corridors along the Belt and Road, it links the coastal areas of Pakistan and the areas in the north. Together, the six corridors of the BRI can help change the layout of the North and South of the global economy and reduce the wealth gap between the rich and the poor countries. Therefore, the BRI will help make globalisation more balanced and inclusive, bringing benefits and prosperity to more people.

Third, sharing refers to sharing the fruits of development with all countries participating in the BRI. Data show that from 2013 to 2015, the average growth rate of the countries along the Belt and Road has increased by 5.3%, which is 2 percentage points higher than the world average in the same period, and the proportion of their GDP in the world has increased from 29.1% to 30.3%. In the next 30 years, the GDP growth rate of the countries along the routes is estimated to reach an average of 3–5 percentage points per year, the GDP of these countries will double, and the living standard of 60% of the world's population will double at the present level, and this will bring about at least 3 percentage points of global economic growth. The BRI, which advocates an equal, open, balanced, and inclusive cooperation framework, is going to upend the global division of labour under the conditions of the old version of globalisation with Western economies at the

Inclusive development and interconnected thinking   59

centre, reaping profits, and developing countries at the periphery, supplying cheap raw materials, labour, and resources.[31]

Finally, wide consultation, joint contributions, and shared benefits are the key parameters of the BRI. Indeed, with the ultimate goal of facilitating the development of a community of shared future for humankind, the BRI aims to deliver win-win outcomes for all participants, jointly winning the future of global economic growth. The idea has been welcomed by the international community. In February 2017, the United Nations, for the first time, included the concept of building a community of shared future for humankind in one of its resolutions. In today's world of reglobalisation, we prosper or fall together. No country can deal with global challenges affecting world peace and development such as infectious diseases, climate change, terrorism, piracy, illegal immigration, environmental degradation, and so on, by itself. No matter where people live, what their beliefs are, or whether or not they are willing, they are actually already in a community of shared future for humankind. Therefore, all countries should set aside their disputes and work together to provide institutional arrangements and more public goods to build a peaceful, stable, prosperous, and harmonious world.

Notes

1 Zhang Yuyan, 'Zaiquanqiuhua langchao zhengzai yonglai' ['The Wave of Re-globalisation is Coming'], *Shijie jingji yu zhengzhi* [*World Economy and Politics*], Vol. 1, 2012, p. 1.

2 Fei Xiaotong, *Xiangtu Zhongguo, shengyu zhidu* [*Rural China, Fertility System*], Beijing, China: Peking University Press, 1998, pp. 29–30.

3 *Shuowen Jiezi: Renbu* [*Explaining Graphs and Analyzing Characters: The Human Radical*] says that 'to be benevolent (*Ren*) is to be close'. *Mengzi: Jinxin I* [*Mencius: Dedication and Goodness Part I*] says that 'to be benevolent is to be human; to combine one's humanity and benevolence is to follow the Way'. 'Benevolence' (*Ren*) connotes politics; good politics is 'to be close to one's relatives'. There are two ways for a benevolent person to love another person: a positive way, by which 'one establishes others in order to establish himself, and facilitate others in order to facilitate himself'; and a passive way, by which 'one does not do unto others what one does not wish done to himself'. See Xu Jianxin, 'Tianxia tixi yu shijie zhidu: ping *Tianxia tixi: shijie zhidu zhexue daolun*' ['The Tianxia System and World Institutions: A Review of *The Tianxia System: An Introduction to the Philosophy of World Institution*'], *Guoji zhengzhi kexue* [*Quarterly Journal of International Politics*], Vol. 2, 2007, p. 124; Xu Yufei, 'Zhongguo zhengzhi zhexue zhongde "tiandao renli" yu Zhongguo waijiao zhanlue' ['The Chinese Political Philosophy of the 'Heavenly Rites' and Chinese Diplomatic Strategy'], *Dangdai yatai* [*Journal of Contemporary Asia-Pacific Studies*], Vol. 1, 2004, pp. 124–153.

4 David L. Hall and Roger T. Ames, *Thinking through Confucius*, Albany, NY: State University of New York, 1987; Hung-Ming Ku, *Spirit of the Chinese People: With an Essay on 'The War and the Way Out'*, Peking, China: Peking Daily News, 1915.

5 *Analects of Confucius* says that 'There is government, when the prince is prince, and the minister is minister; when the father is father, and the son is son', i.e. when the hierarchy is in order (see *Analects of Confucius: Yan Yuan*). See Zhang Qixiong, 'Zhonghua shijie zhixu yuanli de yuanqi: jindai Zhongguo waijiao fenzheng zhong de gudian wen-

60 *Reglobalisation*

hua jiazhi' ['The Sources of Chinese Principles of World Order: The Classical Cultural Values of China's Diplomatic Disputes in Modern Times'], in Wu Zhipan et al., eds. *Dongya de jiazhi* [*The Values of East Asia*], Beijing, China: Peking University Press, 2010, p. 115.

6 Qin Yaqin, *Guanxi yu guocheng: Zhongguo guoji guanxi lilun de wenhua jiangou* [*Guanxi and Process: Cultural Construction of Chinese International Relations Theory*], Shanghai, Chian: Shanghai People's Publishing House, 2012; Chiung-Chiu Huang and Chih-yu Shih, *Harmonious Intervention: China's Quest for Relational Security*, Farnham, UK: Ashgate, 2014.

7 Zhang Yuyan, 'Liyi jituan yu zhidu fei zhongxing' ['Interest Groups and Institutional Non-Neutrality'], *Gaige* [*Reform*], Vol. 2, 1994, pp. 97–105.

8 Literature on 'the workings of "*Guanxi*"' abounds in sociological and anthropological studies, which proves valuable for the study of the '*Guanxi*' doctrine in international relations. Major works include Mayfair Mei-Hui Yang, *Gifts, Favors, and Banquets: The Art of Social Relationships in China*, Ithaca, NY: Cornell University Press, 1994; Yunxiang Yan, *The Flow of Gifts: Reciprocity and Social Networks in a Chinese Village*, Stanford, CA: Stanford University Press, 1996; Xiangqun Chang, *Guanxi yihuo lishang wanglai: Jiangcun huhui, shehui zhichiwang he shehui chuangzao de yanjiu* [Guanxi or Li Shang Wanglai? Reciprocity, Social Support Networks and Social Creativity in a Chinese Village], Shenyang, Liaoning: Liaoning People's Publishing House, 2009.

9 US National Intelligence Council, *Global Trends 2030: Alternative Worlds*, 2012, p. iii.

10 Qin Yaqing, 'Rule, Rules, and Relations: Towards a Synthetic Approach to Governance', *The Chinese Journal of International Relations*, Vol. 4, No. 2, 2011, pp. 117–145.

11 John King Fairbank, ed., *The Chinese World Order: Traditional China's Foreign Relations*, Cambridge, MA: Harvard University Press, 1968.

12 Yongjin Zhang, 'System, Empire and State in Chinese International Relations', in Michael Cox, Tim Dunne and Ken Booth, eds., *Empire, Systems and States: Great Transformation in International Politics*, Princeton, NJ: Princeton University Press, 1999, p. 53.

13 Zhao Tingyang, *Tianxia tixi: shijie zhidu zhexue daolun* [*The Tianxia System: Introduction to the Philosophy of World Institution*], Nanjing, China: Jiangsu Education Publishing House, 2005, pp. 52–56.

14 Feng Zhang, *Chinese Hegemony: Grand Strategy and International Institutions in East Asian History*, Stanford, CA: Stanford University Press, 2015, pp. 26–77.

15 Qin Yaqing, 'Shijie zhengzhi de wenhua lilun: wenhua jiegou, wenhua danwei yu wenhuali' ['A Cultural Theory of World Politics: Cultural Structure, Cultural Units and Cultural Power'], *Shijie jingji yu zhengzhi* [*World Economy and Politics*], No. 4, 2003, p. 4–9; Qin Yaqing and Wei Ling, 'Jiegou, jincheng yu quanli de shehuihua: Zhongguo yu dongya diqu hezuo' ['Socialization of Structure, Process and Power: Cooperation between China and East Asia'], *Shijie jingji yu zhengzhi* [*World Economy and Politics*], No. 3, 2007, pp. 7–13.

16 Chiung-Chiu Huang and Chih-yu Shih, *Harmonious Intervention: China's Quest for Relational Security*, pp. 170–171.

17 Li Zhiyong, 'Guifan zhenglun yu xieshang jieru: Zhongguo dui buganshe neizheng de chongsu' ['Normative Debate and Consultative Intervention: China's Remodeling of the Norm of Non-Interference in Internal Affairs'], *Dangdai yatai* [*Contemporary Asia-Pacific Studies*], No. 3, 2015, pp. 130–155.

18 Gao Qiqi, 'Shequn shijie zhuyi: quanqiu zhili yu guojia zhili hudong de fenxi kuangjia' ['Community Cosmopolitanism: An Analytical Framework for the Interaction between Global Governance and National Governance'], *Shijie jingji yu zhengzhi* [*World Economy and Politics*], No. 11, 2016, pp. 25–39.

Inclusive development and interconnected thinking 61

19 Xiangqun Chang, *Guanxi or Li Shang Wanglai? Reciprocity, Social Support Networks and Social Creativity in a Chinese Village.*

20 Anne Marie Slaughter, *New World Order*, Princeton, NJ: Princeton University Press, 2010; Qin Yaqing, *Guanxi yu guocheng: Zhongguo guoji guanxi lilun de wenhua jiangou* [Guanxi and Process: The Cultural Construction of Chinese International Relations Theories], Shanghai, China: Shanghai People's Publishing House, 2012.

21 Brian Hocking, et al., *Futures for Diplomacy: Integrative Diplomacy in the 21st Century*, Netherlands Institute of International Relations, 2012, p. 9.

22 Wu Jianmin, 'Zhongguo: cong bianyuan zouxiang wutai zhongxin' ['China: From the Periphery to the Center Stage'], in The Editorial Department of the People's Daily, ed., *Renmin ribao pinglun nianbian* [*Annual Review of the People's Daily 2009*], Beijing, China: Red Flag Publishing House, 2010, p. 121.

23 'Zhonghua renmin gongheguo yu geguo jianli waijiao guanxi riqi jianbiao' ['List of the Dates of the Establishment of Diplomatic Relationships between the PRC and Various Countries'], The Ministry of Foreign Affairs of the PRC, http://infogate.fmprc.gov.cn/web/ziliao_674904/2193_674977/; 'Global Diplomacy Index: 2019 Country Ranking', The Lowy Institute, https://globaldiplomacyindex.lowyinstitute.org/country_rank.html.

24 Xinhua News Agency, 'Zhongyang waishi gongzuo huiyi zaijing juxing' ['The Central Foreign Affairs Conference was Held in Beijing'], *Renmin ribao* [*People's Daily*], 30 November 2014, http://politics.people.com.cn/n/2014/1130/c1024-26118788.html.

25 Francis Lang Kuang Hsu, *Clan, Castes and Club*, Princeton, NJ: D. Van Nostrand Company, 1963; Yang Guoshu, 'Zhongguoren de shehui quxiang: shehui hudong de guandian' ['The Social Orientation of the Chinese People: A Perspective of Social Interaction'], in Yang Guoshu, ed., *Zhongguoren de xinli yu xingwei* [*Psychology and Behaviour of the Chinese People: A Study of Localization*], Beijing, China: China Renmin University Press, 2004; Huang Guangguo, *Mianzi: Zhongguoren de quanli youxi* [*Face: Power Game of the Chinese People*], Beijing, China: China Renmin University Press, 2004; Jin Yaoji, 'Rujia xueshuo zhong de geti he qunti ['An Interpretation of Individuals and Groups in Confucianism from a Relational Perspective'], in Jin Yaoji, ed., *Zhongguo shehui yu wenhua* [*Chinese Society and Culture*], Hong Kong, China: Oxford University Press, 1993.

26 David L. Hall and Roger T. Ames, Thinking through Confucius; Hung-Ming Ku, *Spirit of the Chinese People: With an Essay on 'The War and the Way Out'*.

27 Xi Jinping, 'Gongjian mianxiang weilai de yatai huoban guanxi: zai yatai jinghe zuzhi di ershi'er ci lingdaoren feizhengshi huiyi shang de kaimuci' ['Building a Future-Oriented Asia-Pacific Partnership: Opening Speech at the 22nd Informal Meeting of APEC Leaders'], *Renmin ribao* [*People's Daily*], 12 November 2014.

28 Men Honghua and Liu Xiaoyang, 'Zhongguo huoban guanxi zhanlue pinggu yu zhanwang' ['China's Partnership Strategy Evaluation and Prospect'], *Shijie jingji yu zhengzhi* [*World Economy and Politics*], No. 2, 2015, p. 68; Tang Jian, 'Huoban zhanlue yu huoban guanxi: lilun kuangjia, xiaoyong pinggu he weilai qushi' ['Partnership Strategy and Partnerships: Theoretical Framework, Utility Assessment and Future Trends'], *Guoji guanxi yanjiu* [*International Relations Study*], No. 1, 2016, pp. 50–78; Liu Bowen and Fang Changping, 'Zhoubian huoban guanxi wangluo yu Zhongguo zhoubian anquan huanjing' ['Neighboring Partnership Network and China's Neighboring Security Environment'], *Dangdai yatai* [*Contemporary Asia-Pacific Studies*], No. 3, 2016, pp. 68–100.

29 For a critical review of the concept, see Geremie Barmé, Linda Jaivin, and Jeremy Goldkorn, eds., *Shared Destiny*. Acton, Australia: The Australian National University Press, 2015; Phillipa Brant, 'One Belt, One Road? China's Community of Common Destiny', The Lowy Institute, March 31, 2015, https://www.lowyinstitute.org/the-interpreter/one-belt-one-road-chinas-community-common-destiny; Nadège Rolland,

62 *Reglobalisation*

'Eurasian Integration "a la Chinese": Deciphering Beijing's Vision for the Regionasa "Community of Common Destiny"', *The Asan Forum*, June 5, 2017, http://www.thea sanforum.org/eurasian-integration-a-la-chinese-deciphering-beijings-vision-for-the-re gion-as-a-community-of-common-destiny/; Fu Ying, 'China's Vision for the World: A Community of Shred Future', *The Diplomat*, June 22, 2017, https://thediplomat.com /2017/06/chinas-vision-for-the-world-a-community-of-shared-future/; Jacob Mardell, 'The "Community of Common Destiny" in Xi Jinping's New Era', *The Diplomat*, October 25, 2017, https://thediplomat.com/2017/10/the-community-of-common-dest iny-in-xi-jinpings-new-era/.

30 Francis Fukuyama, *The End of History and the Last Man*, London, UK: Avon Books, 1992; Thomas Friedman, *The World is Flat: A Brief History of the 21st Century*, New York, NY: Farrar, Straus and Giroux, 2005.

31 Li Chaodong, '"Yidai yilu" tuijin goujian renlei mingyu gongtongti' ['The "Belt and Road" Initiative Promotes the Construction of the Community of Shared Future for Humankind'], *Renmin ribao* [*People's Daily*], 17 May 2017.

4 The Belt and Road Initiative and global governance

Let China sleep. For when she wakes, the world will tremble.

Napoleon Bonaparte

Napoleon said that China is a sleeping lion. When the sleeping lion wakes up, the world will tremble. The lion in China has woken up, but it is a peaceful, amiable and civilised lion.

Speech by Xi Jinping at the 50th Anniversary Conference of the Establishment of China-French Diplomatic Relations on 27 March 2014

Imbalanced globalisation needs to be fixed. Reglobalisation, a new stage of globalisation with balanced and inclusive development, is what the world badly needs. Taking the lead in promoting reglobalisation, China put forward the Belt and Road Initiative (BRI), which adheres to the concept of inclusive development, emphasises the promotion of a more inclusive and balanced development of globalisation, and seeks for China to develop and progress with all other countries in the world. The BRI is committed to weaving an open network linking China, Central Asia, Southeast Asia, South Asia, Africa, and Europe. The network is neither a formal alliance nor an international institution. It is an interconnected community covering 65% of the world's population, a third of the world's gross domestic product (GDP), and a quarter of the world's trade volume. The BRI has promoted the diversity of globalisation, has eliminated the simple and comprehensive mode of replicating Western developed countries, and has stimulated the energy of low-level globalisation while also opening up a more diversified mode of economic development and civilisational progress. The old model of globalisation is too dependent on the West and lacks the contributions and elements of emerging countries. Faced with strong economic and cultural dominance by the West, globalisation has become a one-way street, with capital and technology flow from developed to developing countries, while talent and dividends converge from all over the world into developed countries. This unequal payoff structure makes it difficult for developing countries to leverage on their comparative advantages. The BRI, through 'wide consultation, joint contributions and shared benefits', enables every country to have the opportunity and platform to participate in the enterprise, giving full play to their comparative advantages.[1]

As of the end of March 2019, more than 100 countries had expressed their willingness to endorse and participate in building the BRI. China signed 173 cooperation agreements with 125 countries and 29 international organisations, covering areas of connectivity, manufacturing capacity, investment, trade, finance, science and technology, and people-to-people exchange.[2] Through the establishment of the 'Five Links' of the BRI, namely policy coordination, infrastructure development, investment and trade facilitation, financial integration, and cultural and social exchange, China will also provide a large number of international public goods in infrastructure and regional financing for countries along the routes.[3] In terms of trade performance, the bilateral trade volume between China and the countries along the Belt and Road economic corridors increased from $57.79 billion in 2000 to $866.39 billion in 2014, with an average annual growth rate of 21.3%, which was 4.2 percentage points higher than that of China's foreign trade in the same period and 13.4 percentage points higher than that of global trade in the same period (see Figure 4.1).[4]

On 17 March 2017, the UN Security Council unanimously adopted Resolution 2344, calling on the international community to strengthen regional economic cooperation through the BRI. China has actively fulfilled its international responsibilities and has deepened cooperation with relevant international organisations under the framework of the BRI. It has signed a cooperation document with the United Nations Development Program (UNDP), the United Nations Economic

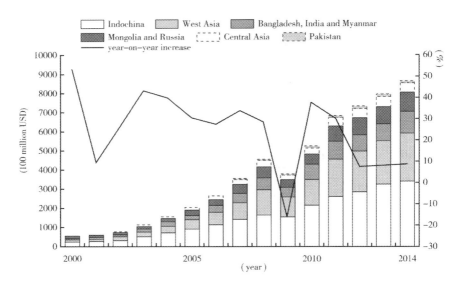

Figure 4.1 Bilateral trade between China and the countries along the Belt and Road economic corridor.

and Social Commission for Asia and the Pacific (ESCAP), and the World Health Organization (WHO). One of the key points for China, as a responsible stakeholder, to promote reglobalisation is the strategic layout of the BRI.

4.1 Shaping the new order of the Silk Road

In 2013, during his visits to Kazakhstan and Indonesia, President Xi Jinping put forward the proposals of the Silk Road Economic Belt and the Twenty-First-Century Maritime Silk Road, respectively. On 28 March 2015, the National Development and Reform Commission (NDRC), the Ministry of Foreign Affairs (MOFA), and the Ministry of Commerce (MOFCOM), authorised by the State Council, jointly issued the *Vision and Actions on Jointly Building Silk Road Economic Belt and 21st Century Maritime Silk Road*. The document details the background, principles, framework, cooperation mechanisms, and the direction and tasks of building the Belt and Road.[5] From a historical perspective, the BRI is the revitalisation of the spirit of the ancient Silk Road and the legacy of Admiral Zheng He's voyages, with the aim of breaking through the institutional barriers and unfair structures of the old form of globalisation by improving connectivity. The BRI covers the Asian and European continents as well as the Western Pacific and the Indian Ocean, encompassing 65 countries along the routes. The 64 other countries include Mongolia, 11 in Southeast Asia, 8 in South Asia, 5 in Central Asia, 19 in West Asia and North Africa, and 20 in Central and Eastern Europe (see Table 4.1). Data show that the total GDP in 2016 of the 64 countries along the Belt and Road was estimated at $12 trillion, accounting for 16% of the world's GDP. Their combined population was 3.21 billion, accounting for 43.4% of the world's total. The total foreign trade volume in 2016 was $7.189 trillion, accounting for 21.7% of global trade.[6] In 2016, the total trade volume between China and other countries along the routes was $953.5 billion, accounting for 25.7% of China's global trade volume, up 0.3 percentage points from 25.4% in 2015.[7] The Belt and Road development plan initiated by China has become a major international public good and has attracted attention worldwide. Its new models and new features have provided a distinctive new plan for global governance and development. Its new logic is embodied in three aspects.

The BRI is an open, loose network with a 'zero threshold'. Unlike the traditional closed 'club'-type of cooperation mechanism, it advocates free participation, does not limit the number of participants or apply any restrictions in terms of the participants' ideology, political system, or development path and is committed to dispersing geopolitical risks, promoting regional integration, and opposing the traditional powers' zero-sum, geostrategic thinking. China believes that countries along the routes can feel free to respond positively as long as there is an interest or need to participate in the BRI. Cooperation can be based on mutual goodwill and interest, and there are no fixed or exclusive membership constraints. This is wide consultation, joint contributions, and shared benefits in a true sense. Even if there are differences and frictions between some Belt and Road countries, they can temporarily shelve these differences for mutually beneficial cooperation under

66 *Reglobalisation*

Table 4.1 The national conditions of the 65 countries along the Belt and Road in 2016

Region	Country	Population	GDP	Import Volume	Export Volume	Import and Export Volume
1 East Asian Country	Mongolia	301.4	116.5	38.7	45.0	83.7
11 Southeast Asian Countries	Singapore	558.4	2945.6	2968.9	3468.1	6436.9
	Thailand	6898.1	4097.2	1957.4	2136.1	4093.5
	Vietnam	9263.7	2013.6	1909.5	1865.0	3774.5
	Malaysia	3152.3	3092.6	1685.4	1895.7	3581.1
	Indonesia	25880.2	9369.6	1426.9	1502.8	2929.8
	The Philippines	10419.5	3103.1	859.4	563.1	1422.5
	Myanmar	5225.4	740.1	219.1	131.1	350.2
	Cambodia	1577.6	194.8	141.7	135.4	277.1
	Brunei	42.3	91.0	32.4	63.4	95.8
	Laos	716.3	133.6	60.4	34.4	94.8
	Timor-Leste	118.7	21.0	6.1	3.4	9.5
8 South Asian Countries	India	130971.3	22887.2	3566.8	2610.1	6176.9
	Bangladesh	16151.3	2262.6	392.3	354.5	746.8
	Pakistan	18987.0	2699.7	439.9	220.9	660.8
	Sri Lanka	2125.2	848.1	189.7	104.4	294.1
	Nepal	2875.8	218.7	66.1	6.6	72.7
	Afghanistan	3273.9	172.8	45.0	8.2	53.2
	Maldives	35.4	32.8	19.1	1.4	20.6
	Bhutan	79.1	24.8	5.1	2.3	7.5
5 Central Asian Countries	Kazakhstan	1794.7	1161.5	194.4	418.5	612.9
	Uzbekistan	3134.3	616.5	99.3	56.5	155.8
	Turkmenistan	546.3	354.0	55.0	92.7	147.7
	Kyrgyzstan	605.9	60.3	39.2	15.4	54.6
	Tajikistan	865.5	62.5	34.9	7.5	42.5
19 West Asian or North African Countries	UAE	985.6	3251.4	2221.8	1533.8	3755.6
	Saudi Arabia	3201.3	6182.7	1638.2	2014.9	3653.1
	Turkey	7855.9	7511.9	1986.0	1426.1	3412.1
	Israel	852.8	3061.9	620.7	640.6	1261.3
	Qatar	257.8	1708.6	326.1	779.7	1105.8
	Egypt	9020.3	3307.7	659.4	211.9	871.3
	Kuwait	422.5	1062.1	319.1	551.6	870.7
	Iraq	3606.7	1484.1	314.6	531.0	845.6
	Iran	8046.0	3861.2	438.6	383.2	821.8
	Oman	395.7	516.8	290.1	319.3	609.3
	Bahrain	131.9	300.8	163.4	136.8	300.2
	Jordan	697.6	398.0	200.4	78.6	279.0
	Azerbaijan	949.2	351.4	100.8	160.6	261.4
	Lebanon	459.7	528.0	161.6	21.4	183.0
	Georgia	367.8	139.4	87.8	18.2	106.0
	Yemen	2913.2	373.1	62.6	19.5	82.1
	Armenia	299.1	107.7	32.3	17.8	50.1
	Syria	341.8	1850.2	44.5	4.6	49.1
	Palestine	2699.7	470.5	7.5	1.1	8.6

(*Continued*)

Table 4.1 (Continued)

Region	Country	Population	GDP	Import Volume	Export Volume	Import and Export Volume
20 Central or East European Countries	Russia	14630.0	11327.4	1827.8	3439.1	5266.9
	Poland	3800.3	4735.0	1885.2	1964.6	3849.7
	Czech	1056.1	1852.7	1422.0	1628.3	3050.3
	Hungary	983.5	1177.3	877.9	961.0	1838.8
	Slovakia	541.8	898.0	702.1	726.8	1429.0
	Romania	1986.9	1819.4	698.5	598.5	1297.0
	Ukraine	4250.1	835.5	351.1	384.4	735.4
	Slovenia	206.5	437.9	284.5	309.8	594.2
	Lithuania	287.5	430.2	271.9	249.4	521.3
	Belarus	945.1	458.9	274.6	234.1	508.8
	Bulgaria	712.6	493.6	268.2	234.5	502.7
	Serbia	713.2	373.8	192.2	148.4	340.6
	Croatia	420.4	499.3	202.0	129.6	331.6
	Estonia	131.2	238.5	149.5	131.7	281.3
	Latvia	197.6	281.8	130.7	113.0	243.6
	Bosnia and Herzegovina	385.4	163.2	67.6	47.8	115.4
	Macedonia	207.6	104.2	64.0	44.9	108.9
	Albania	288.5	122.7	43.2	19.3	62.5
	Moldova	355.3	60.8	39.9	19.7	59.5
	Montenegro	62.3	41.8	22.6	3.5	26.2
64 Countries in All		**321266.1**	**120139.6**	**35903.7**	**35981.8**	**71885.5**
China				**15883.1**	**21138.4**	**37021.6**

Source: The World Bank and the United Nations Statistics Division, 2016; part of the statistics drawn from forecasts of the WTO, the UN, and the IMF.
Note: Owing to the differences in the data update cycles of each country, the GDP of Yemen is from 2013, the GDPs of Iran and Syria are from 2014, and some other countries' data are from 2015.

this initiative. China is committed to achieving an open, inclusive, widely beneficial, and win-win platform that is set up jointly by China and other partners. The BRI is not a solo act, but a chorus with all countries and regions along the routes. The BRI does not evade competition, but avoids intensifying it. It advocates virtuous competition based on comparative advantage over complementary areas of production. The influence of the BRI reaches far more than the core area of the Eurasian continent. It also includes many transcontinental regions such as Japan and South Korea in Asia, Britain in Europe, Ethiopia and Kenya in Africa, and Brazil and Venezuela in South America.[8] It is precisely because of the openness of the BRI that the participating countries, unrestricted by rigid constraints, can carry out practical cooperation with China based on specific projects. Chinese culture holds that even if cooperation does not go smoothly, making friends is an important result in itself. As the Chinese proverb goes, 'benevolence and justice exist despite the lack of business deals'

68 Reglobalisation

(*shengyi bucheng renyi zai*). Such a globalisation model focusses on the process of interaction rather than on the outcome per se.

Second, the BRI is decentralised and encourages the bottom-up empowerment style of leadership. Such leadership is based on sovereign equality and diversity. It advocates that priorities and choices of the countries concerned should be respected. However, the traditional rules of globalisation are based on rationality. The logic of the competition to win is implicit, that is, in order to occupy a favourable position in the tide of globalisation, a country must expand its interests through competition without considering the impact on other countries. As early as in 2003, China announced that it would not follow the path of the rise of traditional great powers through force. Rather, it would adhere to the strategy of peaceful development. The key to peaceful development is to avoid zero-sum competition for development. While developing itself, China needs to promote world development and contribute to the international community.[9] In 2013, China held the Conference on the Diplomatic Work of Neighbouring Countries and put forward the principles guiding its relations with neighbouring countries, namely, amity, sincerity, mutual benefit, and inclusiveness. China believes that the BRI needs to remain open, inclusive, and beneficial to others. Inclusiveness refers to the pooling of different forces, opposing all forms of protectionism, abolishing barriers to globalisation, and sharing risks and opportunities together.[10] Based on this, the Belt and Road advocates the new norms and values of common development and sharing prosperity. In the interconnected community of shared future for humankind, countries must remain open, inclusive, and cooperative, thus providing an experimental field for the troubled global governance in Asia and Europe, from which a model of inclusive and symbiotic globalisation, that is reglobalisation, can be conceived.[11] According to British expert Shantanu Mitra's estimate, by 2020, the BRI will benefit 63% of the world's population and contribute $2.1 trillion to the global GDP.[12] By unleashing the dividends of China's rise, reglobalisation has realised the inclusive and win-win coexistence of multiple interests (see Figure 4.2).

Finally, in terms of the cooperation strategy, China advocates that each participant should engage in infrastructure development based on comparative advantage. Undoubtedly, the construction of infrastructure projects such as roads, railway, bridges, canals, and ports will serve as an important basis for the prosperity and development of the Asian economy in the future. China enjoys important comparative advantages in infrastructure development. On the one hand, it boasts of cutting-edge technology and deep experience in managing large-scale infrastructure development across the world.[13] For example, China is the world's largest producer of renewable energy and its hydropower technology is very mature. Statistics from the International Hydropower Association show that by 2018, China's hydropower sector had grown to a total capacity of 352 GW, representing over a quarter of the world's installed capacity, ranking first globally.[14] China has the longest high-speed railway network in the world. By the end of 2016, its high-speed railway operation mileage had exceeded 20,000 kilometres, accounting for about 65% of the world's total.[15] On the other hand, China's technology and labour costs are

The Belt and Road Initiative and global governance 69

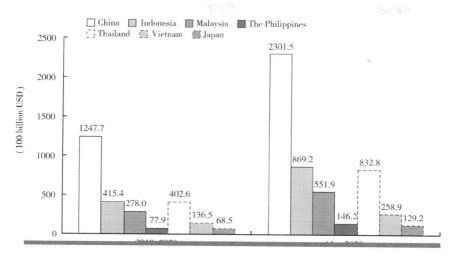

Figure 4.2 The macro economic benefits of Asian interconnectivity (transportation, communications, and energy).

relatively low and the comparative advantage of exporting its large-scale infrastructure construction model is obvious.[16] It has actively tried to promote the development of connectivity through institutional buildup. The Shanghai Cooperation Organisation (SCO), China-Association of Southeast Asian Nations (ASEAN) Free Trade Area, China-ASEAN Dialogue Relations, the Bangladesh-China-India-Myanmar Economic Corridor, the China-Pakistan Economic Corridor, and other mechanisms provide institution-based consultation frameworks for regional development.[17] On 27 March 2017, New Zealand became the first Western developed country to sign a cooperation agreement with China on the BRI. The groundbreaking agreement will broadly demonstrate the effect of this initiative for the international community and bode well for the promotion of the BRI.

Infrastructure networks are 'club goods', that is, the number of actors benefiting from the external effects is fixed. Cross-border liquidity can be enhanced significantly by expanding and improving infrastructure such as transport networks and communications facilities. China has played an important role in regional infrastructure development through the promotion of the BRI. Relying on international financial platforms, trade service networks, and data coconstruction and experience sharing, the BRI has generated positive network externalities, allowing all participants along the routes to interact with each other and to reap the benefits. On the one hand, regional infrastructure connectivity can help smaller and weaker economies participate more effectively in the process of reglobalisation and achieve economic growth. Infrastructure can help to improve productivity, promote trade, reduce transaction costs, provide basic elements for economic development, and serve as an important driving force for the improvement of

70 *Reglobalisation*

living standards of countries along the routes.[18] Antonio Istash, an expert of the World Bank Institute, found that China's infrastructure connectivity initiative can effectively improve regional productivity and alleviate poverty. This approach is being translated into a shared experience in the Asia-Pacific region. According to statistics, the rate of return on infrastructure investments of the BRI has increased significantly, ranging from 20% to 200%.[19] On the other hand, infrastructure connectivity is conducive to disseminating China's experience and philosophy of development. 'If you want to be rich, build roads first' is a popular slogan for development in China. This simple expression conveys a profound economic law, which is that infrastructure and industrial planning are among the core elements of promoting economic development in leaps and bounds. Therefore, for countries that are currently in extreme poverty, the urgent need is to improve their infrastructure. Most countries along the routes of the Belt and Road are developing countries that face problems such as the obsolescence of infrastructure, poor road conditions, inadequate power supply, and lack of telecommunication facilities. The promotion of the BRI can help address these challenges by improving infrastructure connectivity in these countries.[20] From Table 4.2, we can see that the proportion of investment in China's construction projects along the Belt and Road has increased rapidly. In 2015, the total value of contracted projects in China and the total value of completed projects accounted for 44.12% and 44.96% of the total, respectively. Both numbers increased in 2016, far surpassing the proportion of China's outward direct investment in the same period.[21]

4.2 Building a sharing platform of reglobalisation

Compared with the traditional mode of globalisation, the BRI shows that the core feature of the process of reglobalisation is to promote the establishment of a new cross-regional networked international relations through enhancing connectivity. The BRI will connect each nation's domestic infrastructure network with the

Table 4.2 China's investments and construction contracts in countries along the Belt and Road

Year	China's FDI		China's Construction Contracts		China's Finished Construction Contracts	
	Total	*Percentage of Belt and Road*	*Total*	*Percentage of Belt and Road*	*Total*	*Percentage of Belt and Road*
2013	901.7	–	1716.3	–	1371.4	–
2014	1028.9	13.28%	1917.6	–	1424.1	–
2015	1180.2	12.56%	2100.7	44.12%	1540.7	44.96%
2016	1701.1	8.6%	2440.1	51.65%	1594.2	47.64%

(Unit: $100 million; %)
Source: Lei Cong, 'Zhongguo-zhongnan bandao jingji zoulang jianshe yu fazhan' ['Construction and Development of the China-Indochina Economic Corridor'], pp. 155–214.

The Belt and Road Initiative and global governance   71

regional network based on mutual willingness to promote the formation of an interconnected network of all things. Owing to the rapid development of internet technology, this interconnection has covered four channels: the land, sea, air, and the internet. The integrated network structure promotes closer links between the global economy and society and brings more countries and regions into a smooth and orderly coconstruction and sharing system. The more intensive, perfect, and smooth the network of a country, a city, or a field, the stronger the integration and distribution, the more intensive functions it produces, and the greater the opportunities and degree of sharing development.[22] The inclusive reglobalisation promoted by the BRI will enable more equal distribution of the globalisation dividends, fill the gap between the Global South and North, and encourage multinational corporations, social organisations, and local governments to participate in shaping the process of reglobalisation. As an important attempt for China to promote the transformation of global governance, the BRI has an inherent logic to build a platform for sharing interests that has three aspects.

First, through the diffusion effects of networks, China would build a cooperation circle with neighbouring countries. There is a growth triangle theory in economics that says that countries in different stages of economic development can set up cross-border economic cooperation zones in adjacent regions, which helps to strengthen the complementary relationship between factors of production and markets, promote trade and investment, and achieve regional political stability and economic development.[23] This is typical network thinking, which integrates many heterogeneous actors through the network linking principle of two points connecting a line and three points linking a surface to produce systematic effects. From the perspective of relational networks, a country can easily bring its former relationship into a new relational network and expand it. The basic framework of the network model of interstate interaction is that of a triad that comprises three points (actors) and possible relationships among them to form a subnetwork. Tripartite relationships are of great significance. The establishment, cancellation, expansion, and contraction of network relationships are all based on the triad as the smallest unit. In real life, one can see that if A and C have a lot of contact, and B and C also have a lot of contact, then we can expect a lot of contact between A and B. In relational sociology, this situation is theorised as the 'Forbidden Triad' hypothesis, that is, if A and C have a strong relationship and B has a strong relationship with C, then it is impossible for A and B to have no relationship, in that they will at the minimum have a weak relationship.[24] It can also profoundly clarify the transitivity of interstate relations: when Country A in the international system is connected with Country B because of various factors such as interests or threats, their original partnership network is indirectly linked, and their respective allies, E and D, are in a potential triad. Under the hypothesis of the Forbidden Triad, E and D will finally establish a direct relationship, so that the original small network can be expanded. By analogy, with the passage of time and under normal circumstances, the partners of E and D that have no former relationship will most likely form a partnership because of the direct links between E and D. With time, the network evolves from different regions to a whole system. With more and more triad systems at the

72 Reglobalisation

regional level, the relationship transfer and synergy effect between triad systems will promote the formation of the whole network. In a fully connected system, no country can derive any more benefits from unilateral disruption of relations than it already enjoys so that the system becomes balanced.[25]

From this point of view, the Belt and Road is a typical extended network of tripartite relations (see Figure 4.3). Small-scale economic cooperation among some countries within the region takes place first through the provision of preferential policies to each other. By giving full play to complementarity in economic and trade structure and geographical convenience, such cooperation will eventually lead to the establishment of bilateral economic cooperation zones.[26] When small-scale cooperation achieves early harvests, its demonstrative effect can attract other countries in and outside the region to participate gradually like a coral reef accumulating continuously, so as to form a huge cooperative 'island chain', in which the participating countries are the nodes. The ever-expanding 'island chain' surrounds and distinguishes other countries that are not involved in it, so these uninvolved countries can be identified as the 'blank spots' in the entire network. As a whole, the interest-sharing relationship between countries that have established cooperative networks has become closer and closer. Countries that have not participated in the networks have become isolated nodes. Under the burden of the demonstrative effect and peer pressure, they will have the motivation to tentatively understand and participate in the networks. In the early development stage of the BRI, the 'N–X' cooperation mechanism can best reflect this network expansion mode. The 'N–X' cooperation mechanism means that, based on equal consultation, friendly cooperation, and future-oriented perspectives, the N member states participating in regional or subregional cooperation choose other X member states to take the lead in bilateral or multilateral cooperation while temporarily excluding the member states with immature conditions that are unwilling to participate in cooperation projects. As a result, the cooperation with the latter group of member states will be carried out at a smaller level and in a flexible manner in order to reduce the time and opportunity costs caused by too many differences. Thus, substantive cooperation results can be accumulated incrementally, which will form demonstrative effects and attract more countries in the region to participate and develop together.[27] For example, while establishing the economic corridor among China, Bangladesh, India, and Myanmar, China advocates beginning with areas that involve low politics and low sensitivity, progressing gradually from the easiest to the most difficult, finding the right entry point, and starting from the areas and projects in which the four countries have the strongest degrees of complementarity, the most urgent desire for cooperation, and the greatest potential for breakthroughs. By promoting the overall activity through small steps, we can eventually form a wide and multilevel communication channel and coordination network.

Second, we should transform differences into advantages of cooperation, advocate common development, and form a ladder-like complementary pattern. In the realm of reglobalisation, complementarity is more important than homogeneity, as differences lead to connectivity. The BRI has been able to receive positive responses from most countries along the routes because China, as the 'world factory' and 'trade engine', has provided an opportunity for countries with different factor endowments to play to their comparative advantages, and the complementary system built through relationships of interdependence is more sustainable. According to the data standards provided by the World Bank, the development of the 65 countries involved in the BRI is not synchronous, and there is a clear time lag in development. From the perspective of development stages, the proportion of high-income countries and middle- to high-income countries in the total number of countries along the routes is low. There are about 20 high-income countries, with a total population of 195 million, accounting for 16.4% of the high-level countries in the world. The number of middle- to high-income countries is 21, with an aggregate population of approximately 529 million, accounting for 20.4% of the upper-middle-income countries' total population, while the number of low- to middle-income countries is 19, with a combined population of 2.4 billion, accounting for 82% of the world's low-income countries' total.[28] Specifically, from the perspective of competitiveness ranking, per capita income and development modes, we can see the diversity of the countries along the Belt and Road. Almost all countries and development models in the world are included here (see Table 4.3). For example, among the participants, Singapore ranks second in competitiveness in the world, while Myanmar ranks 134th; China is the second largest economy, Qatar has the third biggest per capita GDP, and Laos, Myanmar, Cambodia, and Bangladesh have a per capita GDP of around $1,000. All these are underdeveloped countries as defined by the UN. There are innovation-driven countries (such as Singapore and Qatar), efficiency-driven countries (such as China and Thailand), and countries in transition from efficiency- to innovation-driven modes (such as Russia, Turkey, and the United Arab Emirates), as well as factor-driven countries (such as India and Pakistan) and countries in transition from factor- to efficiency-driven modes (such as Saudi Arabia and Kuwait). The hierarchical nature of such a difference is not a barrier to regional cooperation, but an important advantage of coagulation as a driving force. Mutual dependence and complementary advantages are fundamental to achieving win-win cooperation in all countries along the routes. For example, the 65 countries also have great potential for industrial cooperation. Specifically, the Singaporean and Turkish economies are mainly based on the tertiary industry, with service industries accounting for 75% and 65% of their GDP, respectively, while the economic structure of Oman, Kuwait, the United Arab Emirates, Saudi Arabia, and other Middle Eastern oil-producing countries, as well as of China, the biggest manufacturer in the world, is dominated by industrial production, with industrial output accounting for 69%, 67%, 59%, 57%, and 43% of each one's GDP, respectively. Myanmar, Cambodia, Laos, Tajikistan, and Pakistan among many other preindustrial countries have a high proportion of agriculture in their economic structure, accounting for 57%, 30%, 28%, 27%, and 25% of their GDP, respectively. Each of these countries has its own strengths and needs. Through free trade, they can highlight their own advantages and promote domestic and international economic development.[29] Facing extremely diverse economic and social development levels, different religious and cultural traditions, and different

74 *Reglobalisation*

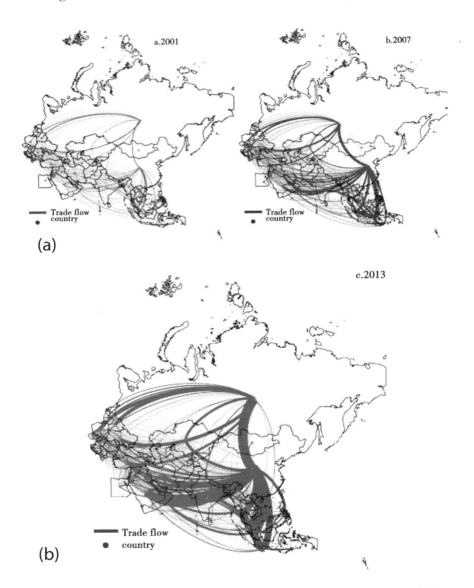

Figure 4.3 Illustration of the trade flow along the Belt and Road: From 2001 to 2007 to 2014.

national development modes of 65 countries, we need to leverage the inclusive, diverse, and relevant characteristics of reglobalisation.

Dialectically speaking, it is also the differences that make common development more meaningful. As the biggest trader in goods, the largest manufacturing power, and the second largest economy in the world, China's Belt and Road

Table 4.3 The national competitiveness and stages of development of countries along the Belt and Road economic corridor

Countries	World Ranking	Competitiveness Index	Composition of the Index			Stage of Development
			Basic Conditions	Efficiency	Innovation	
Singapore	2	5.6	6.3	5.7	5.1	5
UAE	12	5.3	6.2	5.2	4.8	4
Qatar	16	5.2	6.1	5.0	5.1	5
Malaysia	20	5.2	5.5	4.9	5.0	4
Saudi Arabia	24	5.1	5.7	4.6	4.2	2
China	28	4.9	5.3	4.7	4.1	3
Thailand	31	4.7	5.0	4.5	3.8	3
Kuwait	40	4.5	5.2	3.9	3.4	2
Bahrain	44	4.5	5.3	4.5	3.8	4
Turkey	45	4.5	4.8	4.4	3.9	4
Oman	46	4.5	5.7	4.3	3.8	4
Kazakhstan	50	4.4	4.8	4.3	3.5	4
Russia	53	4.4	4.9	4.5	3.5	4
Vietnam	68	4.2	4.4	4.0	3.4	1
India	71	4.2	4.2	4.2	3.9	1
Tajikistan	91	3.9	4.2	3.5	3.5	1
Laos	93	3.9	4.1	3.6	3.5	1
Cambodia	95	3.9	4.1	3.6	3.2	1
Mongolia	98	3.8	4.0	3.8	3.2	2
Bangladesh	109	3.7	3.8	3.6	3.0	1
Kyrgyzstan	108	3.7	3.9	3.6	3.0	1
Pakistan	129	3.4	3.3	3.6	3.5	1
Myanmar	134	3.2	3.4	3.1	2.6	1

Note: Of the stages of development, 1 represents the factor-driven stage, 2 the transformation from factor- to efficiency-driven stages, 3 the efficiency-driven stage, 4 the transformation from efficiency-driven to innovation-driven stages, and 5 the innovation-driven stage.
Source: World Economic Forum, *The Global Competitiveness Report (2014-2015)*. Re-cited from Wang Jinbo, '*Yidai yilu' jingji zoulang yu quyu jingji yitihua: xingcheng jili yu gongneng yanjin* [*The 'Belt and Road' Economic Corridors and Regional Economic Integration: Formation Mechanism and Function Evolution*], p. 14.

development has included the Three Worlds of developing, emerging, and developed countries. It is a typical experiment of the reglobalisation mode in Asia and Europe. When such complementary cooperation promotes countries along the routes to narrow their gap, it will also contribute toward narrowing the gap between the Global North and South, thus filling the gap between 'high-level' and 'low-level' globalisation. The additional consolidation of the overall strength of developing countries and emerging economies will help bolster their voices and representation in global governance and promote the balanced development of reglobalisation. The strategy of promoting industrial cooperation must also vary from country to country, according to local conditions: for countries with

76 *Reglobalisation*

relatively low levels of industrialisation, the BRI will make it more convenient to access the global value chain and will help expand employment through commodity trade, enrich the types of consumer products, and enhance the welfare of local consumers. Economic cooperation with different economies can create conditions and accumulate experience for industrial transformation. Medium-size industrialised countries can connect with China's complete industrial system, take on China's extraordinary capacity in labour-intensive industries, and make up for shortcomings in technology, manpower, and management modes. In the face of highly developed industrialised countries or postindustrialised countries, China is committed to taking advantage of its broad market and cooperating with these countries in innovation, talent, and high-level management. For example, they can cooperate in setting up a global innovation base, in environmental protection, emerging technology standards, and intellectual property protection.[30] At present, the pattern of interdependent development in Eurasia is taking shape. Some studies have pointed out that China has surpassed the United States as the main source of primary products and capital supply for Asia and Europe. For example, measured by the index of primary products supply, China provided a large quantity of primary products in the countries along the Belt and Road in 2015, with the index being over 20 in Mongolia, Thailand, Philippines, and Vietnam, indicating a high level of dependence on the Chinese primary market by these countries. The primary product market supply index of the United States in countries along the routes has begun to weaken, suggesting a decline in their involvement in the industrial division of labour in these areas. Between 2010 and 2015, China became the largest primary commodity trader in these regions.[31]

Third, we should build a 'point to axis to network' economic system, with domestic and international linkages, in a step-by-step manner. The content of the reglobalisation cooperation advocated by China has grown from simple to complex. The field of such cooperation has spilled over from the economy to politics and security, and the mode of cooperation has evolved from a low to a high level.[32] It is worth noting that, in terms of development levels, the Belt and Road is not only interconnected internationally, but it also links China's prosperous eastern coastal areas and the western regions to the process of reglobalisation. By enabling the eastern region to drive the western one and the international market to drive the domestic one, the Belt and Road has established a multilevel interaction pattern from the node to the axis and from the axis to the network. It has effectively realised the two major links of China's domestic and international development with other countries. From the perspective of regional economics, the 'economic corridor' is a belt-shaped spatial and regional complex formed by major and cross-border transportation lines as the axis, and surrounding urban areas, as well as the subregional economic cooperation zones such as the hinterland, in areas such as industrial connection, logistics, and commerce. It is multilevel in nature.[33] Under the framework of the BRI, China has actively proposed the six major economic corridors plan, which can help the countries along the routes to improve their infrastructure and promote the integration of eastern and western China. Through the multilevel opening of local, national, regional, and

The Belt and Road Initiative and global governance   77

global elements, industrial division of labour and transport links can be combined at multiple levels to form an efficient production community.[34] The new pattern of regional cooperation explored by the BRI can help less developed countries to get rid of 'development marshes' and help to solve the current problems of globalisation, such as the gap between the rich and the poor, unbalanced regional development, and unfair distribution of interests. At present, the New Eurasian Land Bridge Economic Corridor, the China-Mongolia-Russia Economic Corridor, the China-Central Asia-West Asia Economic Corridor, the China-Indochina Peninsula Economic Corridor, the Bangladesh-China-India-Myanmar Economic Corridor, and the China-Pakistan Economic Corridor, which the BRI advocates, connect points of regional economic cooperation from the north, west, and south, achieving radiation effects.

The six economic corridors embed major countries and cities in the global value chain. In the north, the New Eurasian Land Bridge Economic Corridor, and the China-Mongolian-Russian Economic Corridor pass through the central and eastern parts of the Eurasian continent. Among these, the New Eurasian Land Bridge Economic Corridor departs from the city of Alashankou in Xinjiang, passes through Kazakhstan, Russia, Belarus, Ukraine, Poland, Germany, and finally reaches Rotterdam Port in the Netherlands. The New Eurasian Land Bridge has changed the horizontal pattern of world logistics. Compared with the Siberia Continental Bridge, the New Eurasian Land Bridge has shortened the distance of land transportation by an estimate of 2,000 to 2,500 kilometres. The advantages of the New Eurasian Land Bridge in Central and West Asia are more prominent. The eastern and western ends of the New Eurasian Land Bridge connect both major global economic centres of the Pacific and Atlantic Oceans. Along the New Eurasian Land Bridge are hundreds of varieties of mineral and rich energy resources, along with more than 200 billion tonnes of coal reserves, about 150 billion tonnes of oil reserves, and nearly 750 billion cubic metres of natural gas reserves. Broad prospects exist for cooperation.[35] The economic corridor between China, Mongolia, and Russia, taking advantage of the geographical benefits of the land connection of the three countries, connects the industrial restructuring of the three countries with the extended network of economic corridors, links the economically vibrant East Asian economic circle with the developed European economic circle, and connects the cooperation channels of the Persian Gulf, the Mediterranean Sea, and the Baltic Sea.[36] These economic corridors are not only based on expanding common interests, but will also create a new benefit-sharing model, in which the creation, overlapping, and rational distribution of interests will give rise to signs of economic prosperity on the northern line of the once marginalised Eurasian continent. Through open and inclusive cooperation, not only can the 'cake' be made bigger, but also upgrade the level and quality of the cake. On 11 September 2014, President Xi Jinping proposed that the Silk Road Economic Belt should be linked with the Eurasian Economic Union and Mongolia's Grasslands Route to build an economic corridor linking China, Mongolia, and Russia. On 23 June 2016, the heads of state of the three countries jointly witnessed the signing of the Outline of Planning for

78 *Reglobalisation*

the Construction of the China-Mongolia-Russia Economic Corridor, which was the first multilateral cooperation plan under the framework of the BRI. Mongolia is a completely inland country, without seaports. Owing to distance, 92% of its goods are exported through China and 73% of its goods are imported through Russia. Mongolia relies entirely on China and Russia for transportation. There are obvious differences among China, Russia, and Mongolia in resource endowment, industrial structure, and technological level. China mainly exports manufactured consumer goods, Mongolia mainly exports raw materials and agricultural products, and Russia has obvious technological advantages in nuclear power, aviation, aerospace, electronics, and other fields.[37] Within the framework of the China-Mongolian-Russian Economic Corridor, the three parties are committed to integrating their development plans and establishing long-term stable cooperative relations in areas such as promoting the interconnection of transport infrastructure and cross-border transport.[38]

In the westbound direction, the BRI advocates the development of the China-Central Asia-West Asia Economic Corridor. The economic corridor is a transnational economic corridor staring from Aksu City in Xinjiang that passes countries such as Kyrgyzstan, Uzbekistan, Turkmenistan, Iran, Turkey, all the way to Romania, and Rotterdam Port in the Netherlands. In history, the mission of Zhang Qian – the imperial envoy and renowned explorer of the Han Dynasty – to the West in 119 BC opened up the Silk Road. The countries along the economic corridor are rich in energy and resources, especially oil, natural gas, and mineral resources. However, owing to lagging economic development and the lack of funds, the region needs China's experience in infrastructure investment and industrialisation. In this regard, the Sixth Ministerial Conference of the China-Arab Cooperation Forum in June 2014 proposed to build a '1+2+3' cooperation pattern between China and Arab countries, with energy cooperation as the main axis, infrastructure development, trade, and investment facilitation as the wings, and nuclear energy, space satellite, and new energy as the breakthrough points. In the G20 Hangzhou Summit in September 2016, the heads of state of China and Kazakhstan witnessed the signing of the China-Kazakhstan Silk Road Economic Belt Construction and the 'Bright Road' New Economic Policy Cooperative Plan. China signed cooperation documents with Tajikistan, Kyrgyzstan, and Uzbekistan to jointly build the Silk Road Economic Belt. China also signed memorandums of understanding with Turkey, Iran, Saudi Arabia, Qatar, Kuwait, and other countries to build the Belt and Road.[39]

To the south, the China-Indochina Peninsula Economic Corridor, the Bangladesh-China-India-Myanmar Economic Corridor, and the China-Pakistan Economic Corridor go hand-in-hand. The China-Pakistan and Bangladesh-China-India-Myanmar economic corridors pass through East and South Asia, the most densely populated region in the world, linking major cities along the corridors and densely populated and industrialised areas. The Bangladesh-China-India-Myanmar Economic Corridor is built across the main cities such as Kunming, Mandalay, Dhaka and Kolkata, linking railways, highways, aviation, waterways, electric power, telecommunications, and oil and gas pipelines to integrate the

The Belt and Road Initiative and global governance 79

economies of the four countries. With the completion of the China-Myanmar oil and gas pipeline, the fourth largest energy import channel in China, the process of integrating China's southwest, northern Myanmar, northeastern India, and eastern Bangladesh into economic globalisation has been accelerated. In May 2013, the idea of China and India jointly sponsoring the construction of the Bangladesh-China-India-Myanmar Economic Corridor was written into the joint statement. In July 2014, President Xi Jinping proposed the initiative of promoting the construction of the Bangladesh-China-India-Myanmar Economic Corridor. The three major economic corridors connect South and East Asia from the southwest, southeast, and south, respectively. On 20 April 2015, the leaders of China and Pakistan attended the commencement ceremony of several major projects of the China-Pakistan Economic Corridor and signed 51 cooperation agreements and memorandums, of which nearly 40 were related to the construction of the China-Pakistan Economic Corridor. The China-Pakistan Economic Corridor, which connects the Silk Road Economic Belt to the north and the Maritime Silk Road to the south, runs through the hubs of the southern and northern Silk Roads. It starts from Gwadar Port in the south and goes north to Kashi in Xinjiang, China. It is a trade corridor that includes highways, railways, oil and gas pipelines, telecommunication optical cables, and is also a flagship project of connectivity between China and its surrounding areas. As a major infrastructure project, Gwadar Port has become the top priority in over 20 cooperation agreements signed by China and Pakistan. In addition, in May 2016, the Ninth Pan-Beibu Gulf Economic Cooperation Forum and the China-Indochina Peninsula Economic Corridor Development Forum issued the China-Indochina Peninsula Economic Corridor Initiative to promote the new model of regional economic integration.[40] The development of the above economic corridors emphasise not only the interconnection of hardware, but also of software. For example, the facilitation of customs clearance of personnel and goods is one of the key points of cooperation through the economic corridor. Of course, the operational environment of the above economic corridors is rather complex and faces competition and challenges from all sides (see Table 4.4).

4.3 Geopolitical misunderstandings and clarifications

The BRI covers a vast area and inevitably faces geopolitical competition. From the perspective of zero-sum thinking, some great powers worry that the BRI will diminish their influence in the region. Therefore, they not only reject it, but also actively try to prevent their allies and partners from taking part in it. For example, the United States, Japan, and India have doubts about China's initiative. Western media circles have repeatedly described the BRI as China's strategic plot to dominate Asia. Apart from disputes among major powers, regional cooperation itself cannot be smooth sailing. Resolving or reducing conflicts properly in the process of cooperation, such as territorial issues between China and some of its neighbours, economic and trade cooperation negotiations between different neighbouring countries, refugee issues, and religious conflicts, also pose enormous challenges. Major security problems encountered in the China-Pakistan Economic

Table 4.4 Analysis of the factors influencing China's surrounding economic corridors

Name of Corridor	Related Countries	Political Factors	Security Factors	Religious Factors	Cultural Factors
New Eurasian Land Bridge	China, Kazakhstan, Russia, Belarus, Ukraine, Poland, and Germany	These countries do not consider China a rival for dominance, so the political risk is low.	Some Central Asian countries are worried about China dominating the Central Asian security situation, but security cooperation like the SCO is growing fast.	Mainly Eastern Orthodox and Catholic. The Islam practiced in Kazakhstan is quite secular, so, the religious risk is low.	Differences in culture and development models. No exchange of cultural values. Unfamiliarity among general public. Difficulty in cultural communication.
China, Mongolia, and Russia	China, Mongolia, and Russia	Russia and Mongolia are not allies of the US, so the political risk is low.	Wary of China's rise. The risk of security competition is medium.	The three countries do not have religious conflicts, so the religious risk is low.	Cultural differences between China and Russia. Cultural similarities and shared historical traditions between China and Mongolia.
China – Central Asia — West Asia	China, Kyrgyzstan, Uzbekistan, Turkmenistan, Iran, Turkey, Romania, and the Netherlands	Without the will to compete for regional leadership, the risk of geoconflict is low.	Terrorist and extremist forces are spreading, and the security environment is facing serious challenges.	Most countries along the routes are Islamic countries whose doctrines do not fully accept secularised countries, which poses great religious risks.	Great cultural differences, communication barriers, and risks.

(Continued)

Table 4.4 (*Continued*)

Name of Corridor	Related Countries	Political Factors	Security Factors	Religious Factors	Cultural Factors
China–Pakistan	China and Pakistan	Geopolitical pressure from India.	Covering disputed areas between India and Pakistan.	Pakistan's tribal and sectarian disputes are frequent, and religious risks are high.	Great cultural differences and risks.
Bangladesh, China, India, and Myanmar	Bangladesh, China, India, and Myanmar	India is sensitive to geocompetition in preventing China from competing for control over South Asia.	India is vigilant that a rising China will put forward more territorial and security buffer-zone demands.	Mainly Buddhism and Hinduism; religious risks are low.	Great cultural differences and medium cultural risks.
China–Indochina	China and 10 ASEAN countries	Most ASEAN countries have few geopolitical differences with China and have low geopolitical risks.	The ASEAN economy depends on China, and its security depends on the United States. There are many security differences on the South China Sea at issue with China.	Islamic countries in the ASEAN are mostly island countries, while other countries are more secular and have low religious risks.	Southeast Asian countries and China have the same deep cultural origin and a high degree of common aspirations.

Source: Adapted from Li Xihui, 'Jiyu diyuan zhengzhi shijiao de Zhongguo zhoubian jingji zoulang yanjiu', in Li Xihui and Deng Guangqi eds., *Zhongguo minzu diqu jingji fazhan baogao (2017)* [*Economic Development Report of China's Ethnic Minority Areas (2017)*], Beijing: Social Sciences Academic Press, 2017, pp. 13–14.

82 *Reglobalisation*

Corridor involve the proper handling of the China-India border and the India-Pakistan Kashmir disputes, the problem of Indian-Bangladeshi foreigners, and the Indus River dispute. China has repeatedly stated that it is necessary to make the Belt and Road a road of peace and opening up and has advocated the abandoning of geopolitical thinking. All countries must respect each other's sovereignty and territorial integrity, respect each other's core interests and major concerns, and no regional cooperative partnership should be directed against a third party. The reglobalisation championed by China in an open and inclusive spirit welcomes all countries to participate actively and share development opportunities. However, it is unavoidable that the supply of the BRI as a global public good is competitive.

To enhance their international influence, great powers will usually launch various programmes in global governance with the aim of providing public goods.[41] In an era of globalisation, competition among international institutions has become an important vehicle. Aiming to gain an advantage in competition, rising and hegemonic powers try their best to meet consumers' needs to defend or enhance their international status.[42] Such competition in supply is intensified when the characteristics of the goods supplied share commonality. In the race for global recognition and influence, great powers often take the initiative to supply public goods to the international community, exchanging concessions for recognition.[43] Great powers are fighting for the right to supply global public goods. This is a fire without smoke, and this competition can be intensified easily in overlapping areas of supply. Especially in the critical period of global power transition, the rising powers grow rapidly and hegemonic powers decline relatively. The competition regarding both power status and international prestige will become increasingly fierce. To expand influence, rising countries need to provide better public goods than hegemonic countries in order to gain advantages in the competition for leadership. Logic on the supply side points out that each supplier should strive for consumers, but they also face competition pressure from other suppliers at the same time. Balancing both aspects is the key to providing high-quality goods. As the number of consumers is fixed, if players face the same consumers in the same field, there must be competition, especially when the content and mode of supply also tends to be the same, the intensity of competition will increase further. In contrast, functional differentiation within fields can reduce the intensity of competition.

First, the power competition behind supply will lead to geopolitical competition. In the critical period of the transformation of international order, the great power competition will also trigger the supply competition of public goods and even a war of institutions.[44] Against the background of interdependence and competition among great powers, if China wants to supply public goods with its own characteristics, it must fully evaluate the possible risks and pressures that it faces. Against the backdrop of deficits in global governance and a low tide of globalisation, China's active supply of global public goods is confronted with many misunderstandings and distortions. Many Western scholars are worried that the 'soft power' competition over the BRI, the Asian Infrastructure Investment Bank (AIIB), and rules of the internet overlap with traditional geopolitical competition.

The existing international order was established by the US in the wake of WWII. The efforts to reform the international order and rules by China and other emerging countries, however, can easily arouse doubts and mistrust in the hegemonic power. For the US, the more global public goods and initiatives China offers, and the greater the degree of international acceptance, the more obvious the potential threat is to the United States' leadership. In particular, the substitution of Chinese public goods for traditional public goods offered by the United States will undermine the credibility of United States' hegemony. It is partly out of concern over this 'spillover effect' or the 'domino effect' that the United States resists China's global influence with the Rebalance to Asia Strategy.[45] It is also for this reason that the BRI and AIIB are often interpreted by some Western analysts as a geopolitical ambition of China, aiming at paving the way for China's regional hegemony. There are many European and American analysts who believe that the Belt and Road is the contemporary Chinese version of the Marshall Plan.[46] For a relatively declining hegemonic country, whether it provides international public goods or produces 'international public bads', the rising country will always touch sensitive nerves.[47]

Second, in the field of institutions, if there are overlapping functions of public goods, they will face the possibility of competition in the supply of public goods. As the power gap between China and the United States continues to shrink, the so-called dual pattern of 'economic dependence on China, and security dependence on the United States' is taking shape in the Asia-Pacific region.[48] This narrowing gap does not necessarily lead to competition in the supply of public goods: only when the public goods supplied by the two great powers are homogeneous will the competition for dominance become increasingly fierce. For example, some scholars believe that the outbreak of the global financial crisis in 2008 was such a turning point, allowing China's influence in the economic sphere to begin expanding to the political, institutional, and even security spheres, which alarmed the United States and led to the high-profile 'Pivot to Asia' policy of the Obama administration.[49] With the spillover of China's economic influence into institutional creativity, political appeal, and security capabilities, the homogeneity of public goods between China and the United States is progressively rising, and, as a consequence, the pressure of competition is also growing. When such competition exceeds the controllable scope, it will lead to a decline in the efficiency of public goods supply, and even the negative consequences of 'excessive institutions'.[50] In economic and trade institutions, although the high-standards of free-trade agreements, such as the Comprehensive and Progressive Agreement for Trans-Pacific Partnership (CPTTP), have endured twists and turns, their intention to exclude China and seize the new rule-making power deepens China's doubts.[51] In the Asia-Pacific region, the BRI, the CPTTP, and the Regional Comprehensive Economic Partnership (RCEP) are all attempts to shape the new round of international trade rules.[52] The New Silk Road initiative of the United States, the Russia-led Eurasian Economic Union, Japan's Partnership for Quality Infrastructure, the India-led Act East Policy and Project Mausam, the trans-Eurasian transport corridors promoted by Kazakhstan and many other countries, as well as the Modern Silk Road project

84 *Reglobalisation*

launched by Turkey are all actually overlapping and more or less competing with China's BRI.[53] Among them, the Partnership for Quality Infrastructure proposed by the Japanese government in 2015 advocated giving full play to its advantage in the field of quality infrastructure development and more than 50 years of international development experience to compete against China's 'inexpensive and efficient' model.[54] Although new public goods such as the BRI and the AIIB help innovate and improve international rules and solve inefficiencies and inequities in existing global governance systems, these public goods will inevitably face competition (Table 4.5). As a result, abandoning zero-sum thinking and adhering to the principle of wide consultation, joint contributions and shared benefits is the fundamental approach to opening up space for common development.

In view of the geopolitical misunderstandings of the BRI in the West, China has voiced its opposition to the black-and-white thinking in understanding the role of the BRI in promoting globalisation. President Xi Jinping noted at the Brazil, Russia, India, China, and South Africa (BRICS) Industrial and Commercial Forum in September 2017 that

> the co-construction of the 'Belt and Road' Initiative is not a geopolitical tool, but a platform for practical cooperation. It is not a new perspective of the interaction between China and the world. It is not about foreign aid, but a joint development initiative to build and share. The co-construction of the 'Belt and Road' Initiative will set up a new platform for all countries to achieve win-win cooperation and create new opportunities for the implementation of the 2030 Sustainable Development Agenda.[55]

Observers who use the term 'Chinese version of the Marshall Plan' to refer to China's BRI do not clearly understand the fundamental differences between the two: judging from the historical background, the strategic objectives, the mode of operation, national strengths, or the final outcome, the BRI is by no means China's 'Marshall Plan', which can be illustrated in the following three ways.

First, the background and purpose of the BRI are different from those of the Marshall Plan. The Marshall Plan originated in the early stages of the Cold War and was adapted to suit the policy needs of the United States to pursue global hegemony. At the end of World War II, European countries suffered greatly and were in a state of complete disrepair. They were faced with serious economic and political crises. At the same time, fundamental changes took place in the global balance of power. While Europe's position and role as the world's political and economic centre had been significantly weakened, the United States emerged as an unrivalled superpower. In the twenty-first century, in contrast, peace and development has become the theme of the times. The world is developing in the direction of political multipolarisation, economic globalisation, and cultural diversity. No country or group of countries can dominate world affairs alone. The global correlation of power is advancing in the direction of peace and development. Although China has become the second largest economy, it still lags behind some Western countries in terms of quality of economic growth, people's living

The Belt and Road Initiative and global governance 85

Table 4.5 Potential projects of cooperation and competition of the Belt and Road Initiative

Regional Strategy	Countries Concerned	Evaluation of Potential
Eurasian Economic Union	Russia, Belarus, Kazakhstan, Armenia, and Kyrgyzstan	By 2025, free movement of goods, services, capital, and labour will be realised, thus forming a unified market of 170 million people.
Trans-Eurasian Railway	Russia, Kazakhstan, Belarus, Poland, Germany, and the Netherlands	Starting from Vladivostok, it crosses Siberia and leads to Moscow, connecting Poland and Germany, and finally gets to Rotterdam Port in the Netherlands.
Amber Route	Estonia, Poland, Czech Republic, Austria, Germany, Italy, Greece, Switzerland, Netherlands, Belgium, France, and Spain	Transport to Italy, Greece, and Egypt via the Vistula and Dnieper rivers, from the North Sea and the Baltic Sea in northern Europe to the Mediterranean Sea in southern Europe.
New Silk Road	United States, Afghanistan, India, and Pakistan	Afghanistan is a link and central country connecting Central and South Asia, thus Central and South Asia will form a network of close regional transportation and economic links and promote regional economic integration.
ASEAN Free Trade Area	Ten countries including the Philippines, Thailand, Myanmar, Malaysia, Indonesia, and Vietnam	Advocating the spirit of equality and cooperation to work together to promote economic growth, social progress, and cultural development in Southeast Asia.
Monsoon Plan	India, Egypt, Sudan, Saudi Arabia, Yemen, Oman, Sri Lanka, Thailand, Malaysia, Singapore, Indonesia, Philippines, etc.	The Monsoon Plan falls in the broad Indian Ocean world, from East Africa, the Arabian Peninsula, the Indian Subcontinent, Sri Lanka to the Southeast Asian Islands, and India regains close ties with the Indian Ocean countries.
The Union for the Mediterranean	France, Algeria, Morocco, Tunisia, Cyprus, Egypt, Israel, Jordan, Lebanon, Malta, Syria, and Turkey, expanded to 43 countries	Former French President Nicolas Sarkozy proposed the establishment of economic, energy, immigration, democracy, and other cooperative relations, and the establishment of free-trade relations with the European Union.
The Juncker Plan	Germany, France, Netherlands, Italy, Poland, Spain, Luxembourg, Belgium, and other EU countries	The Investment Plan for Europe, the so-called Juncker Plan, introduced in November 2014, aims to promote investment within the EU, and economic growth, industrial transformation, and competitiveness of the EU.

(Continued)

86   *Reglobalisation*

Table 4.5 (Continued)

Regional Strategy	Countries Concerned	Evaluation of Potential
Japan's High-Quality Infrastructure Partnership Program	It is not confined to Asia, but covers Central and South America, Africa, Siberia and the Far East of Russia, the United States, etc.	In 2015, Japanese Prime Minister Shinzo Abe put forward a new strategy of export of foreign infrastructure mainly aimed at Asia, expanding investment areas and increasing the number of institutions involved in the implementation of the strategy.
Asia-Africa Growth Corridor	Led by Japan and India	The Asia-Africa Growth Corridor initiative was launched in September 2017 to develop high-quality infrastructure in Africa through India-Japan cooperation, supplemented by digital connectivity.
Bright Road Initiative	Kazakhstan	The plan is to build transportation networks, such as roads, railways, and airlines that radiate from Astana, the capital, to all parts of the country.
Marine Highway Plan	Indonesia	Including the expansion of five major hub ports in North Sumatra, Jakarta, East Java, South Sulawesi, Brazil, and Papua, improving logistics efficiency and developing industrial parks, etc.
Prairie Road Program	Mongolia	It comprises five projects, including the 997 km highway connecting China and Russia, the 1100 km electric railway, and the expansion of the trans-Mongolian railway and natural gas and oil pipelines.
Sustainable Development Strategy: Egypt Vision 2030	Egypt	Long-term development strategy covering three development dimensions: economic, social, and environmental.

Note: Table compiled by the authors.

standards, national defence capability, and soft power. China is only a participant in and a defender and reformer of international rules.

Second, being essentially a reflection of the will of the United States, the Marshall Plan had a strong political significance and deliberately excluded the Soviet Union from the beginning. In terms of aid conditionality in the Marshall Plan, recipient countries must accept and fulfil commitments made to the United States under the *Foreign Assistance Act of 1948*, including cooperating with other countries, facilitating the purchase of raw materials by the United States for strategic purposes, pledging not to undermine the economic stability of the United States, and accepting fiscal supervision of the United States as well as provisions set by the Administrator of the Economic Cooperation Administration of the right to impose additional conditions on aid provisionality. Such conditional assistance was able to realise the dual control of the European economy and politics to curb the development of communism in Western Europe and to establish the dominant position of the United States in Western Europe and beyond. In comparison, the BRI mainly emphasises common development. It is characterised by openness and inclusiveness. It is nonexclusive and is not directed against a third party. Among the founding members of the AIIB, developed and developing countries and big and small powers coexist. The BRI offers but does not expect to pursue Chinese values and has no ideological goals. Therefore, regardless of the implementation background, purposes, principles, and methods, China's advocacy of the BRI is by no means a replica of the Marshall Plan. The interstate relations in the BRI are equal and mutually beneficial. China does not seek to occupy a dominant position. Its aim is to achieve mutual economic benefits and win-win results. It remains to be seen whether China can really make the countries along the routes transcend religious, cultural, and ideological prejudices and arrive at a broad consensus on promoting the BRI; however, China neither expects, nor can it achieve, a China-centred hierarchical order through the BRI. In contrast, in a broader historical perspective, the proposals of the Silk Road Economic Belt and the Twenty-first-Century Maritime Silk Road are precisely the crystallisation of China's new global and regional cooperation agenda based on compatible universalism.

Third, the BRI aims to narrow the gap between developing and developed countries and avoid polarisation caused by traditional globalisation. For a long time, there has been a dual structure of 'centre–periphery' in the economic structure of globalisation. The gap caused by the trade in manufactured goods and raw materials between developed countries and peripheral countries is among the root causes of the inequity of globalisation. China, as an emerging economy, has begun to move from the periphery to the centre of the world stage, and has become the largest trading partner with both developed and developing countries. Therefore, in a sense, the structure of globalisation has evolved from a dual structure into a new 'Three Worlds' pattern: the state of interconnection among developed, emerging, and peripheral countries. The new pattern of Three Worlds is different from the original concept coined by Mao Zedong, Chairman of the Communist Party of China Central Committee (CPCCC), in the 1970s. Against the backdrop of the Cold War, Chairman Mao Zedong believed that the United States and the Soviet Union represented the First World in the hegemonic group, and Europe, Japan, Canada, and Australia were the traditional developed countries constituting the Second World, while all the remaining underdeveloped countries belonged to the Third World. The concept of the Three Worlds was still a binary division in that it reflected the thinking of the dual pattern of the Cold War. Today, reglobalisation has begun to transcend the opposition between high- and low-level globalisation,

88 *Reglobalisation*

and China, as a leading force in the process of reglobalisation, is actively playing the role of a bridge between emerging countries, narrowing the hierarchical gap between the centre and the periphery and striving to promote a more inclusive and pluralistic world. In light of this, one of the biggest merits of the BRI is that by taking into account the basic characteristics of the new Three Worlds as contextualised in the process of reglobalisation, the BRI has established time–pace and domestic–international linkages that can bring huge development dividends to the participating countries and avoid the formation of a new core–periphery structure.[56]

Notes

1 Xu Kangning, '"Yidai yilu" yinling jingji qunqiuhua jiankang fazhan' ['The "Belt and Road" Initiative Leads the Healthy Development of Economic Globalisation'], *Renmin ribao* [*People's Daily*], 15 May 2017.

2 Office of the Leading Group for Promoting the Belt and Road Initiative, *The Belt and Road Initiative: Progress, Contributions and Prospects*, Beijing, China: Foreign Language Press, 2019, pp. 1–3.

3 Huang He, 'Gonggong chanpin shijiao xia de "yidai yilu"' ['The "Belt and Road" Initiative from the Perspective of Public Goods'], *Shijie jingji yu zhengzhi* [*World Economy and Politics*], Vol. 6, 2015, pp. 138–155.

4 Wang Jinbo, '*Yidai yilu' jingji zoulang yu quyu jingji yitihua: xingcheng jili yu gongneng yanjin* [*The 'Belt and Road' Economic Corridors and Regional Economic Integration: Formation Mechanism and Function Evolution*], Beijing, China: Social Sciences Academic Press, 2016, p. 17.

5 The National Development and Reform Commission, the Ministry of Foreign Affairs (MOFA) and the Ministry of Commerce, *Vision and Actions on Jointly Building the Silk Road Economic Belt and 21st Century Maritime Silk Road*, The MOFA, 28 March 2015, https://www.fmprc.gov.cn/mfa_eng/zxxx_662805/t1249618.shtml.

6 The 'Belt and Road' Big Data Center under China National Information Center, '*Yidai yilu maoyi hezuo dashuju baogao 2017 (jianban)*' ['*The "Belt and Road" Trade Cooperation Big Data Report 2017 (Simplified Edition)*'], March 2017, p. 1.

7 Ibid., p. 8.

8 Xue Li, 'Zhongguo xuyao zhiding "zhoubian waijiao fanglue"' ['China Needs to Formulate "Peripheral Diplomacy Strategy"'], *Shijie zhishi* [*World Affairs*], No. 5, 2017, p. 73.

9 James Jungbok Lee, 'Will China's Rise Be Peaceful? A Social Psychological Perspective',
Asian Security, Vol. 12, No. 1, 2016, pp. 29–52.

10 Yang Luhui, 'Heping jueqi yu Zhongguo zhoubian waijiao xinlinian he xingeju' ['The Peaceful Rise and the New Idea and Structure of China's Diplomacy with Neighboring Countries'], *Lilun tantao* [*Theoretical Discussion*], No. 6, 2014, pp. 5–10.

11 Li Junru, 'Zhongguo yu shijie guanxi de xinjieduan' ['A New Stage of Relationship between China and the World'], *Wenhua zongheng* [*Beijing Cultural Review*], No. 2, 2013, pp. 20–22.

12 Anthea Mulakala, 'China's Development Policy and the West: Convergence or Parallel Play?' Asia Foundation, 17 June 2015, https://asiafoundation.org/2015/06/17/chinas-development-policy-and-the-west-convergence-or-parallel-play/.

13 KPMG, *Infrastructure in China: Sustaining Quality Growth*, Hong Kong, China: KPMG International, 2014, https://home.kmpg.com/cn/cn/home.html.

14 International Hydropower Association, 'China Statistics', May 2019, https://www.hyd ropower.org/country-profiles/china.

15 Xin Wen, 'Zhongguo gaotie lichen da 2 wan gongli, zhan quanshijie gaotie zongliang 65% zuoyou' ['China's High-Speed Rail Mileage Has Exceeded 20,000 Kilometers, Accounting for 65% of the World's Total'], China.com.cn, 29 December 2016, http://www.china.com.cn/news/2016-12/29/content-4005460.htm.

16 China's high-speed railway has the highest speed at 350 kilometers per hour, and its standard basic unit cost is $17 million–$21 million. The developed countries in Europe have a speed of up to 300 kilometers per hour, with an estimated cost of $25 million–$39 million per kilometer, while the construction cost of high-speed railway in the United States and Japan is even higher, reaching almost $52 million per kilometre. See statistics from International Transport Forum, December 2013, http://www.itf-oecd.org /search/statistics-and-data?f=field-publication-type%#A648&f=field-publication-type %3A657.

17 Ren Jingjing, '"Shuangchong zhuanxing:" shibada yilai Zhongguo jingji waijiao de linian chuangxin yu zhanlue buju' ['"Dual Transition:" Ideational Innovation and Strategic Layout of China's Economic Diplomacy since the 18th National Congress of the CPC'], in Liu Debin, ed., *Zhongguo yu shijie* [*China and the World*], Beijing, China: China Social Sciences Press, 2015, pp. 17–26.

18 Paul Collier, et al., 'The Cost of Road Infrastructure in Low- and Middle-Income Countries', Policy Research Working Paper 7408, the World Bank, September 2015, http://documents.worldbank.org/curated/en/124841468185354669/pdf/WPS7408.pdf.

19 Research Team of China Development Assistance Committee, 'Jichu sheshi: fazhan yu jianpin de jichu zonghe baogao' ['Infrastructure: A Comprehensive Report on the Basis of Development and Poverty Reduction'], Research Report, *China International Center for Poverty Alleviation*, No. 3, 2011.

20 Zheng Yongnian, '"Yidai yilu" shi kechixu de gonggong chanpin' ['The "Belt and Road" Is a Sustainable Public Goods'], *Renmin ribao* [*People's Daily*], 16 April 2017.

21 Lei Cong, 'Zhongguo-zhongnan bandao jingji zoulang jianshe yu fazhan' ['Construction and Development of the China-Indochina Economic Corridor'], in Li Xihui and Deng Guangqi, eds., *Zhongguo minzu diqu jingji fazhan baogao (2017)* [*Economic Development Report of China's Ethnic Minority Areas (2017)*], Beijing, China: Social Sciences Academic Press, 2017, pp. 155–214.

22 Chen Wenling, '"Yidai yilu" jiang ruhe chongsu quanqiu xinjingji' ['How Will the "Belt and Road" Reshape the New Global Economy?'], *Diyi caijing* [*China Business News*], 15 May 2017, https://www.yicai.com/news/5285143.html.

23 Ding Dou, *Dongya diqu de ciquyu jingji hezuo* [*Sub-regional Economic Cooperation in East Asia*], Beijing, China: Peking University Press, 2001, p. 68.

24 See Mark Granovetter, 'The Strength of Weak Ties', *American Journal of Sociology*, Vol. 78, No, 6, 1973, pp. 1360–1380.

25 Cao Dejun and Chen Jinli, 'Guoji zhengzhi de guanxi wangluo lilun: yixiang xin de fenxi yicheng' ['The Network Theory of Relations in International Politics: A New Analytical Framework'], *Ouzhou yanjiu* [*European Studies*], No. 4, 2011, pp. 69–82.

26 Li Tieli and Jiang Huaiyu, 'Ciquyu jingji hezuo jizhi yanjiu: yige bianjie xiaoying de fenxi kuangjia' ['Research on Sub-regional Economic Cooperation Mechanisms: An Analytical Framework of Border Effects'], *Dongbeiya luntan* [*Northeast Asia Forum*], No. 3, 2005, pp. 90–94.

27 Zou Chunmeng, '*N–X' hezuo jizhi yu zaoqi shouhuo xiangmu: yi Meng Zhong Yin Mian jingji zoulang jianshe wei li* [*The 'N–X' Cooperation Mechanism and Early Harvest Project: Taking the Construction of the Economic Corridor between Bangladesh, China, India and Myanmar as an Example*], Beijing, China: Social Sciences Academic Press, 2016, pp. 125–126.

90 Reglobalisation

28 Zhong Feiteng, '"Yidai yilu," xinxing quanqiuhua yu daguo guanxi' ['The "Belt and Road," New Type of Globalisation and Great Power Relations'], *Waijiao pinglun* [*Foreign Affairs Review*], No. 3, 2017, pp. 1–26.

29 Wang Jinbo, '*Yidai yilu' jingji zoulang yu quyu jingji yitihua: xingcheng jili yu gongneng yanjin* [*The 'Belt and Road' Economic Corridors and Regional Economic Integration: Formation Mechanism and Function Evolution*], Beijing: Social Sciences Academic Press, 2016, p. 43.

30 Wang Liqiang and Wang Lei, eds., '*Yidai yilu' yu yazhou guojia de gongtong de fazhan* [*The 'Belt and Road' and the Joint Development of Asian Countries*], Beijing, China: Social Sciences Academic Press, 2017, pp. 35–37.

31 Feng Yongqi and Huang Hanting, '"Yidai yilu" yanxian guojia dui Zhongguo chanpin shichang de yilaidu ji Zhongguo de duice' ['The Dependence of the Countries along the "Belt and Road" on China's Product Market and China's Policies'], *Dangdai yatai* [*Contemporary Asia-Pacific Studies*], No. 3, 2017, p. 140.

32 Lu Dadao, 'Guanyu 'dian-zhou' kongjian jiegou xitong de xingcheng jizhi fenxi' ['An Analysis of the Formation Mechanism of the "Point to Axis" Spatial Structural System'], *Dili kexue* [*Geographic Science*], No. 1, 2002, pp. 1–6.

33 Wang Lei, Huang Xiaoyan, and Cao Xiao, 'Quyu yitihua shijiao xia kuajing jingji zoulang xingcheng jizhi yu guihua shijian: yi Nancong jingji dai fazhan guihua weili' ['Formation Mechanism and Planning Practice of Cross-Border Economic Corridors from the Perspective of Regional Integration: Taking the Development Planning of Nanchong Economic Belt as an Example'], *Xiandai chengshi yanjiu* [*Modern City Research*], No. 9, 2012, pp. 71-79.

34 Liu Zhi, 'Da Meigonghe ciquyu jingji zoulang jianshe he Zhongguo de canyu' ['The Greater Mekong River Sub-regional Economic Corridor Construction and China's Participation'], *Dangdai yatai* [*Contemporary Asia-Pacific Studies*], No. 3, 2009, pp. 57–65.

35 Abduini, 'Xin Ya'ou daluqiao jingji zoulang jianshe yu fazhan' ['The Construction and Development of the Economic Corridor of the New Eurasian Continental Bridge'], in Li Xihui and Deng Guangqi, eds., *Zhongguo minzu diqu jingji fazhan baogao (2017)* [*The Economic Development Report of China's Ethnic Minority Areas (2017)*], Beijing, China: Social Sciences Academic Press, 2017, pp. 88–107.

36 Office of the Leading Group on Implementing the Belt and Road Initiative, 'Gongjian "yidai yilu:" linian, shijian yu Zhongguo de gongxian' ['Jointly-Building the "Belt and Road:" Concepts, Practices and China's Contributions'], Beijing, China: Foreign Languages Press, 2017, p. 5.

37 China Business Yearbook Editing Committee, *Zhongguo shangwu nianjian 2010* [*China Business Yearbook 2010*], Beijing, China: China Business Publishing House, 2010, p. 393.

38 Chen Zhi and Li Bin, 'Xi Jinping chuxi Zhong E Meng sanguo yuanshou huiwu' [Xi Jinping Attended the Meeting of the Heads of China, Russia and Mongolia'], Xinhuanet .com, 12 September 2014, http://www.xinhuanet.com/world/2014-09/11/c_111244 8718.htm.

39 Office of the Leading Group on Implementing the Belt and Road Initiative, 'Gongjian "yidai yilu:" linian, shijian yu Zhongguo de gongxian' ['Jointly-Building the "Belt and Road:" Concepts, Practices and China's Contributions'], p. 12.

40 Li Ming, 'Zhongguo duiwai touzi e 2012 nian chuang xingao' ['China's Foreign Investment Hit a New High in 2012'], Xinhuanet.com, 7 February 2013, http://sg.xinhu anet.com/2013-02/07/c_124334383.htm.

41 Li Wei, 'Guoji zhixu zhuanxing yu xianshi zhidu zhuyi lilun de shengcheng' ['Transition of International Order and the Formation of the Theory of Realistic Institutionalism'], *Waijiao pinglun* [*Foreign Affairs Review*], No. 1, 2016, pp. 31–59.

42 Yang Yuan, 'Daguo wu zhanzheng shidai baquanguo yu jueqiguo quanli jingzheng de zhuyao jizhi' ['The Main Mechanism of Power Competition between Hegemonic

The Belt and Road Initiative and global governance 91

Powers and Rising Powers in the Age of Great Powers without War'], *Dangdai yatai* [*Contemporary Asia-Pacific Studies*], No. 6, 2011, pp. 6–32.

43 Yang Yuan, 'Jueqiguo ruhe yu baquanguo zhengduo xiaoguo' ['How Rising Powers Compete for Small Powers with Hegemons? A Case Study Based on Ancient East Asian History'], *Shijie jingji yu zhengzhi* [*World Economy and Politics*], No. 12, 2012, pp. 26–52.

44 Li Wei, *Zhidu zhizhan: zhanlue jingzheng shidai de Zhong Mei guanxi* [*War of Institutions: China-US Relations in the Age of Strategic Competition*], Beijing, China: Social Sciences Academic Press, 2017, pp. 176–211.

45 Yan Xuetong, 'Zhongguo ruhe nenggou dabai Meiguo' ['How China Can Beat the United States'], *Guofang shibao* [*Defense Times*], 12 December 2011.

46 Weng Haihua, 'Zhongguo ban "Maxie'er jihua de yijian sandiao"' ['Killing Three Birds with One Stone: the Chinese Version of the "Marshall Plan"'], Sina.com.cn, 6 November 2014, http://finance.sina.com.cn/zl/bank/20141106/132720749143.shtml.

47 Zhong Feiteng, '"Yidai yilu," xinxing quanqiuhua yu daguo guanxi' ['The "Belt and Road," New Type of Globalisation and Great Power Relations'], *Waijiao pinglun* [*Foreign Affairs Review*], No.3, 2017, pp. 1–26.

48 Christopher Layne, 'The Global Power Shift from West to East', *The National Interest*, No. 119, May/June 2012, pp. 21–31; Yan Xuetong, 'Quanli zhongxin zhuanyi yu guoji tixi zhuanbian' ['The Transfer of Power Centers and the Transformation of the International System'], *Dangdai yatai* [*Contemporary Asia-Pacific Studies*], No. 6, 2012, pp. 4–21; Wang Dong, 'Two Asias? China's Rise, Dual Structure, and the Alliance System in East Asia', in Rober S. Ross and Oystein Tunsjo, eds., *Strategic Adjustment and the Rise of China: Power and Politics in East Asia*, Ithaca, NY: Cornell University Press, 2017, pp. 100–134.

49 Zhu Feng, 'Aobama zhengfu 'zhuan shen yazhou' zhanlue yu Zhong Mei guanxi' ['The Obama Administration's 'Pivot to Asia' Strategy and China-US Relations'], *Xiandai guoji guanxi* [*Modern International Relations*], No. 4, 2012, p. 7; Liu Feng, 'Dongya diqu zhixu zhuanxing: anquan yu jingji guanlian de shijiao' ['Order Transition in East Asia: A Perspective of the Security-Economy Nexus'], *Shijie jingji yu zhengzhi* [*World Economy and Politics*], No. 5, 2016, pp. 32–55.

50 Li Wei, 'Dongya diqu zhuyi de zhongjie? Zhidu guosheng yu jingji zhenghe de kunjing' ['The End of Economic Regionalism in East Asia? Excess of Institutions and the Dilemma of Economic Integration'], *Dangdai yatai* [*Contemporary Asia-Pacific Studies*], No. 4, 2011, pp. 6–32.

51 Zhao Yang, 'Zhong Mei zhidu jingzheng fenxi: yi "yidai yilu" weili' ['An Analysis of China-US Institutional Competition: Take the "Belt and Road" Initiative for Example'], *Dangdai yatai* [*Contemporary Asia-Pacific Studies*], No. 2, 2016, pp. 28–57.

52 Sun Yi, 'Guoji zhidu yali yu Zhongguo zimaoqu zhanlue' ['Pressure of International Institutions and China's Free Trade Zone Strategy'], *Guoji zhengzhi kexue* [*The Chinese Journal of International Politics*], No. 3, 2016, pp. 125–161.

53 Qi Huaigao, '"Yidai yilu" dui Zhongguo zhoubian waijiao yu yazhou fazhan de yingxiang' ['The Influence of the "Belt and Road" Initiative on China's Periphery Diplomacy and Asian Development'] *Zhongguo zhoubian waijiao xuekan* [*Chinese Journal of Periphery Diplomacy*], No. 2, 2015, pp. 70–85.

54 Meng Xiaoxu, 'Riben gaozhiliang jichu sheshi hezuo huoban guanxi de goujian yu qianjing' [The Construction and Prospect of Japan's Partnership for Quality Infrastructure], *Guoji wenti yanjiu* [*China International Studies*], No. 3, 2017, pp. 76–88.

55 'Xi Jinping zai jinzhuan guojia gongshang luntan shang de jianghua' ['Xi Jinping's Speech at the Opening Ceremony of the BRICS Business Forum'], Xinhuanet.com, 3 September 2017, http://www.xinhuanet.com//politics/2017-09/03/c_1121596338.htm.

56 Yang Cheng, 'Xin dalu zhuyi: kua ouya yitihua de zhanlue tujing' ['New Continentalism: Strategic Prospects for Trans-Eurasian Integration'], *Wenhua zongheng* [*Beijing Cultural Review*], No. 3, 2015, pp. 20–26.

5 The Asian Infrastructure and Investment Bank pushes forward reglobalisation

> So full of forked paths before, now where are the ways? There shall come a day with gusty winds to help cleave through the waves, for me to make full sail and an open boundless sea navigate.
>
> Li Bai, a famed poet of Tang Dynasty, A Trying Journey I of III

> If you walk alone, you will walk fast; if you walk with others, you will walk far. We welcome everyone to take China's development train. Whether you take the express train or take a free ride, you are all welcome.
>
> Speech by President Xi Jinping during his visit to Mongolia in August 2014

China's great power status has been gradually established based on continuous economic growth and increasing comprehensive national power. In the future, China's policies of and vision for international order need to be demonstrated through various practical actions, and the supply of public goods is one of the best options for this. As China's foreign policy moves from 'keeping a low profile and biding time' (*taoguang yanghui*) to 'striving to accomplish something' (*fenfa youwei*), China's enthusiasm for participating in global governance has become increasingly prominent. The Report of the 18th National Congress of the Chinese Communist Party (CPC) clearly states that 'we should consolidate exchanges and cooperation with other countries in the world and promote the reform of the global governance mechanism', and 'China adheres to the balance of rights and obligations and actively participates in global economic governance'.[1] In his report to the 19th National Congress of the CPC, General Secretary of the CPC Central Committee Xi Jinping clearly pointed out that 'changes in the current global governance system and international order are accelerating', that 'China upholds the global governance concept of wide consultation, joint contributions and shared benefits', and that 'China will continue to play a responsible role as a major power, actively participate in the reform and construction of the global governance system, and continuously contribute China's wisdom and strength'.[2] Overall, the regional and global public goods that China has contributed since

The AIIB, a regional multilateral financial institution established under Chinese leadership, functions mainly to provide capital services for infrastructure development in Asian countries to facilitate investments in various fields, including transportation, energy, telecommunications, agriculture, and urban development.

the new leadership took over in 2012 can be divided into two categories: innovative and traditional public goods that focus on supply. Among them is the Asian Infrastructure Investment Bank (AIIB), which is the most influential international financial organisation created under China's leadership. It is of great significance to the promotion of reglobalisation. As early as October 2013, President Xi Jinping visited Southeast Asia and proposed the idea of building the AIIB. Thereafter, in October 2014, 21 countries, including China, Singapore, and India, signed the Memorandum of Understanding for the Establishment of the AIIB in Beijing. The first signatories came mainly from Central, South, and Southeast Asia. By March 2015, the United Kingdom, South Korea, Russia, Germany, France, and other major economies submitted applications for membership. Except for the United States and Japan, the top ten economies in the world have all applied for membership. By April 2015, all 57 founding members of the AIIB have been confirmed. On 25 December 2015, the AIIB was established. It was the first important international financial organisation initiated by the Chinese government. Although it is only a regional forum, it will continue to move the world with international leverage.

5.1 The motivation for China to build the AIIB

The AIIB, a regional multilateral financial institution established under Chinese leadership, functions mainly to provide capital services for infrastructure development in Asian countries to facilitate investments in various fields, including transportation, energy, telecommunications, agriculture, and urban development. It is an important measure for China to push forward the Belt and Road Initiative (BRI) and the community of a shared future for humankind. The reasons for China to take the lead in establishing the AIIB can be summed up as follows.

First, China sees the provision of international public goods as shouldering the responsibility of a great power. Since the new Chinese leadership took power in 2012, China has led a series of new financial institutions and mechanisms, such as the Brazil, Russia, India, China, and South Africa (BRICS) New Development Bank, the Shanghai Cooperation Organisation Bank, the Silk Road Fund, and the AIIB, which highlight the potential of China's institutional innovation and the spirit of inclusiveness, openness, and cooperation.[3] Li Mingjiang, an associate professor at the Rajaratnam Institute of International Studies at Nanyang University of Technology in Singapore, argued that, despite the weak global economic growth at present, the provision of international infrastructure by China has truly realised the connectivity between countries and regions, laying a solid foundation for the development of countries along the routes in the decades to come.[4] On 23 March 2017, the AIIB announced the formal approval of 13 new members, which was the first expansion of its 57 founding members since its formal opening in January 2016. In June 2017, the Board of Governors of the AIIB approved the three new members – Argentina, Madagascar, and Tonga – and the total number of members increased to 80.[5] On 13 July 2019, the Board of Governors of the AIIB decided to approve the newcomers of Benin, Djibouti and Rwanda, bringing

94 *Reglobalisation*

the AIIB's total membership to 100.[6] The AIIB has surpassed the European Bank for Reconstruction and Development (EBRD) and the Asian Development Bank (ADB) in terms of membership, becoming the second largest multilateral development institution in the world after the World Bank. China has demonstrated its willingness and ability to participate in shaping the international financial order by taking the lead in setting up the AIIB. For the first time in history, China has changed from being a passive participant in globalisation to a proactive leader in reglobalisation, which is of great significance to the change in both China and in the world economic order as a whole. With the sustained growth of China's comprehensive national power, the total amount of regional and global public goods provided by China has increased continuously. As a result, China's role has also changed from that of an initial bystander or beneficiary to that of an advocate, reformer, and supplier. For example, Zhou Xiaochuan, Governor of the People's Bank of China, put forward the idea of creating a super-sovereign currency on the eve of the G20 London Summit in early 2009, which is the ideal goal of the reform of the international monetary system. Building on the Association of Southeast Asian Nations (ASEAN) Plus Three mechanism, China launched monetary diplomacy at the bilateral level, and established currency swap, local currency settlement, currency transaction, and currency settlement partnerships with nearly 50 countries, building up a huge network of monetary partners.[7]

Second, China seeks to build new financial governance models and to reform the international financial order. With the outbreak of the 2008 global financial crisis, the inherent instability and inequity in the international financial system dominated by developed countries has been exposed, and the establishment of the AIIB is the embodiment of China's contributions to the existing international financial system.[8] In recent years, China has achieved initial results in promoting the reform of international economic governance. In addition to the establishment of the AIIB, the BRICS New Development Bank, and the Silk Road Fund, the existing financial governance mechanism has also been reformed and innovated upon. In 2010, China's share in the IMF rose from 3.994% to 6.390% and voting power rose from 3.803% to 6.068%. China's voting power in the International Bank for Reconstruction and Development (IBRD), the key decision-making body of the World Bank, rose to 5.25%. With China's appeals, the international community has continuously strengthened international financial cooperation and coordination, improved the early warning system against international financial risks, and enhanced the capacity to prevent those risks. Adhering to the principles of win-win, inclusiveness, and openness, especially after the joining of emerging economies, the AIIB represents the future development direction of the international financial system and embodies the value of institutional innovation.[9] China has also taken the lead in strengthening regional financial security networks. Promoted by China, East Asian countries have worked together to provide regional public goods to cope with financial shocks.[10] For example, in May 2000, the Chiang Mai Initiative (CMI), with bilateral currency swap networks as its pillar, was adopted at the '1 + 3' Finance Ministers' Conference held in Chiang Mai, Thailand, which provided the region with a crisis relief mechanism. The Asian Bond Markets Initiative (ABMI) aims to promote the development of regional bond markets, and China has been a main supporter and promoter behind it. Since then, China has also built a regional foreign exchange reserve pool of $240 billion for the transformation of the CMI from bilateral swap agreements to multilateral agreements. These regional public goods provide strong support for the development of the Asian financial safety net. In 2014, China, together with Brazil, Russia, India, and South Africa, established the New Development Bank (NDB) and the BRICS Contingent Reserve Arrangement (CRA). The BRICS NDB has a start-up fund of $50 billion and a total authorised amount of $100 billion. The BRICS CRA has a pool of $100 billion to help BRICS countries resist financial risks together.[11] The establishment of the BRICS NDB, the BRICS Emergency Reserve Arrangement, and the AIIB all mark a new stage in China's initiative in the field of international financial governance.

Third, China aims to eliminate regional imbalances in development and promote financial fairness and equity. The inclusive and pluralistic characteristics of the AIIB determine that it can accommodate a higher level and a wider range of regional economic integration and regional infrastructure integration processes. However, compared with the diversity of regional cooperation in Asia, the current infrastructure connectivity in Asia largely depends on the support of concessional loans and aid funds from the ADB, China and Japan.[12] It is very difficult to achieve connectivity and infrastructure integration in Asia through a single financing channel and a limited amount of capital. According to the ADB, the total investment in infrastructure in Asian countries is expected to be around $8.22 trillion from 2010 to 2020. There are about $320 billion worth of gaps in 1,202 inter-regional transport, energy, and communication infrastructure projects (see Table 5.1).[13] This huge funding gap will be difficult to support exclusively through the financing of the public sectors of governments and a limited number of regional development banks if the ADB and World Bank are not strong enough to finance infrastructure network buildup. China is the engine of today's global economy. The establishment of the AIIB will play an important role in the supply of infrastructure financing, making up for the shortcomings of funds provided by traditional international financial institutions, such as the ADB and the World Bank, to help countries with financial difficulties in the region to improve their infrastructure conditions. By taking the AIIB and the Silk Road Fund as platforms, while prioritising the goal of solving the infrastructure bottlenecks in the region, we can promote the rational flow of global funds, reverse imbalances in the development of regions in urgent need of funds, and help lead a new pattern of reglobalisation of balanced development.[14] There is, in the current state of globalisation, an unbalanced distribution of benefits and imbalanced flows of capital. Many developing countries lack funds for infrastructure development and industrial upgrading projects. For a long time, the production process of developed countries grew increasingly capital intensive. Most capital flows preferentially go to areas with high returns on investment, whereas the growth rate of investments in developing countries remains slow.[15]

96   *Reglobalisation*

Table 5.1 Capital gap for infrastructure buildup in Asia from 2010 to 2020

Country/ Region	Percentage of Total Investment in Asia	Investment Demand	Investment Percentage		Average Annual Investment
			New Investment	Investment in Maintenance and Upgrading	
Central Asia	4.554	373657	54	46	33969
Afghanistan	0.318	26142	57	43	2377
Armenia	0.051	4179	41	59	380
Azerbaijan	0.344	28317	64	36	2574
Georgia	0.060	4901	24	76	446
Kazakhstan	0.846	69538	61	39	6322
Kyrgyzstan	0.107	8789	38	62	799
Pakistan	2.172	178558	53	47	16233
Tajikistan	0.139	11468	47	53	1043
Uzbekistan	0.508	41764	48	52	3797
East and Southeast Asia	66.553	5472327	71	29	497484
Cambodia	0.163	13364	51	49	1215
China	53.118	4367642	72	28	397058
Indonesia	5.476	450304	70	30	40937
Laos	0.138	11375	56	44	1034
Malaysia	2.287	188084	79	21	17099
Mongolia state	0.122	10069	37	63	915
Myanmar	0.264	21698	56	44	1973
The Philippines	1.546	127122	53	47	11557
Thailand	2.103	172907	72	28	15719
Vietnam	1.355	109761	53	47	9978
South Asia	28.829	2370497	63	37	215500
Bangladesh	1.762	144903	54	46	13173
Bhutan	0.011	886	30	70	81
India	26.421	2172469	64	36	197497
Nepal	0.174	14330	50	50	1303
Sri Lanka	0.461	37908	52	48	3446

Source: Bhatacharyay, Kawai, and Nag eds., *Asian Development Bank Institute: Infrastructure for Asian Connectivity*, pp. 33–37.

5.2 The cooperation between the AIIB and traditional financial institutions

Since the new leadership assumed office in 2012, China has been more proactively involved in promoting the reform of international economic governance. In addition to the establishment of the AIIB, the BRICS NDB, and the Silk Road Fund, China helped reform and innovate the existing financial governance mechanisms. With the efforts of China and many other stakeholders, the international community has made progress in strengthening international financial cooperation and

The highlights of China's role in establishing and leading the AIIB can be summarised as follows. First, the AIIB adheres to the principles of win-win, inclusiveness, and openness. For China and many Asian countries, a win-win situation can be achieved through the platform of the AIIB. On the one hand, outdated infrastructure has been a major obstacle in the economic development of many Asian countries. The relative weakness of infrastructure buildup in Asia, especially the lack of connectivity, has led to low levels of regional economic cooperation and low overall labour productivity in society. Economic backwardness has resulted in these countries not having enough financial resources to invest in public service systems such as roads, railways, ports, telecommunications, and power grids to support economic growth. Although it can provide some loans to Asian countries, when compared with the huge capital gaps, the ADB's funds are only a drop in the ocean. The AIIB, which focusses on infrastructure development, will undoubtedly help solve the financial bottlenecks faced by these countries and help them industrialise and modernise more effectively. On the other hand, the AIIB also helps enhance China's national interests. One big incentive for the establishment of the AIIB in China is avoiding the fall into the 'middle-income trap', while striving to find new growth drivers after the economy enters the so-called 'new normal'. The AIIB is characterised by inclusiveness and openness. China does not want to make the AIIB a self-centred, closed, and exclusive institution. In contrast, during the preparatory process, China maintained close communication and cooperation with many Asian countries, Western developed countries, and other international organisations, inviting Western developed countries, including the United States and Japan, to join. Although the United States and Japan have not joined yet, the possibility of arranging special plans for their entry in the future cannot be ruled out. On important issues such as the formulation of the charter and the establishment of the institutions of the AIIB, China adheres to the multilateral concepts of openness, consultation, and cooperation; actively consults with other countries; and strives to learn from the management and operation experience of the World Bank and the ADB, rather than impose its will on other countries. In terms of membership size, the AIIB has become the second largest multilateral development institution in the world after the World Bank, surpassing the EBRD and the ADB. The newly approved 13 members for this expansion include five regional and eight non-regional members (see Table 5.2). The regional members are Afghanistan, Armenia, Fiji, Hong Kong, and East Timor. The nonregional members are Belgium, Canada, Ethiopia, Hungary, Ireland, Peru, Sudan, and Venezuela. Jin Liqun, President of the AIIB, said that the interest of the countries in joining the AIIB reconfirmed the remarkable and rapid development of the bank as an international institution since its establishment.[16]

Second, some of the AIIB's functions are similar to those of the World Bank and the ADB, although the positioning is different. Adhering to the principles of win-win, inclusiveness, and openness, especially the absorption of emerging economies, the AIIB represents the future direction of the international financial

98 *Reglobalisation*

Table 5.2 The expansion of the Asian Infrastructure Investment Bank

24 October 2014	21 founding members signed the Memorandum of Understanding for the Establishment of the AIIB and jointly decided to establish the bank. These countries include Bangladesh, Brunei, Cambodia, China, India, Kazakhstan, Kuwait, Laos, Malaysia, Mongolia, Myanmar, Nepal, Oman, Pakistan, the Philippines, Qatar, Singapore, Sri Lanka, Thailand, Uzbekistan, and Vietnam. A month later, Indonesia became the 22nd founding member. At the end of 2014, after Maldives became the 23rd founding member, New Zealand, Tajikistan, Saudi Arabia, Jordan, and other countries joined in succession.
12 March 2015	the UK decided to join as well. Subsequently, France, Germany, and Italy also joined the group. This was followed by the accession of small European countries such as Luxembourg and Switzerland. At the end of March 2015, South Korea, Russia, Australia, and Denmark applied to join the AIIB. The prospective founding members of the AIIB increased to 43.
15 April 2015	the total number of prospective founding members of the AIIB reached 57, expanding its geographical scope from Asia to Europe, Latin America, Africa, and Oceania.
29 June 2015	50 countries that had passed domestic approval procedures formally signed the AIIB Agreement.
25 December 2015	17 founding members (50.1% of the total shares) including China, the UK, South Korea, and Germany ratified the agreement and submitted their instruments of ratification to meet the conditions for the agreement to enter into force as stipulated in its text. The AIIB was formally established. In January 2016, it was officially opened with 57 founding members.
23 March 2017	the AIIB announced the formal approval of 13 new members' applications. This was the first expansion after its establishment, with the total membership reaching 70. The AIIB expanded its membership twice in May and July 2017, approving the applications of 23 members in all. On 19 December 2017, the AIIB approved four economies to join the Bank, including the Cook Islands, Vanuatu, Belarus, and Ecuador, which marked the fourth membership expansion since its founding, bringing the AIIB's total approved membership to 84. This also marked its expansion from within Asia to across the world. In May and June 2018, the AIIB approved the applications of three states, including Papua New Guinea, Kenya, and Lebanon. On 19 December 2018, the AIIB announced that its Board of Governors had approved the membership applications of six more countries, bringing the total membership up to 93. The new group of approved members comprised Algeria, Ghana, Libya, Morocco, Serbia, and Togo.
22 April 2019	the AIIB announced that its Board of Governors had approved membership applications of four more countries, namely Côte d'Ivoire, Guinea, Tunisia, and Uruguay, bringing its total approved membership to 97.
13 July 2019	the Board of Governors of the AIIB decided to approve newcomers, namely Benin, Djibouti, and Rwanda, to join the AIIB, bringing its total approved membership to 100.

Note: Data compiled by the authors.

Table 5.3 Comparison of the rules of the Asian Infrastructure Investment Bank and the World Bank

	Asian Infrastructure Investment Bank	World Bank
Number of Members	There are 57 founding members. Approved 13 new members in 2017; open to members of the IBRD and the ADB	189 countries (including IBRD and International Development Association [IDA] member countries); open to IMF members
Accession Conditions	(1) The Council votes on whether to approve it; (2) An applicant who does not enjoy sovereignty may apply for membership to the AIIB with the consent or representation of its members.	(1) Approval by the Council; (2) To become a member of the World Bank, one must first join the IMF.
Top 5 Shareholders	(1) China (30.34%) (2) India (8.52%) (3) Russia (6.6%) (4) Germany (4.57%) (5) Korea (3.81%)	(1) The United States (17.45%) (2) Japan (7.52%) (3) China (4.42%) (4) Germany (4.39%) (5) France and Britain (4.11%)
Top 5 Voting Members	(1) China (26.06%) (2) India (7.51%) (3) Russia (5.93%) (4) Germany (4.15%) (5) Korea (3.5%)	(1) The United States (16.51%) (2) Japan (7.14%) (3) China (4.61%) (4) Germany (4.18%) (5) France and Britain (3.91%)
Loan Conditions	The basic standpoint of nonpoliticisation.	Loan standards include economic conditions and political requirements.

Source: Compiled by the authors with data drawn from the official websites of the AIIB and the World Bank

system and embodies the value of institutional innovation (see Table 5.3).[17] The World Bank, the ADB, and the AIIB are all multilateral financial institutions providing financing services for development; however, unlike the models of the World Bank and the ADB, which are primarily characterised by intergovernmental cooperation, the AIIB will be open to private investment. It will mobilise private capital and pay attention to market rules, commercial value, and people's livelihoods, while taking investment returns and social welfare into account. The initial capital of the AIIB was $100 billion, which is less than the $165 billion of the ADB, but it does not rule out the possibility of future progress. Asian countries have a 75% stake in the AIIB, which is much larger than their share in the ADB (60%). As a result, they have a greater voice. The ADB is dominated by the United States and Japan. Since the establishment of the ADB in 1966, all its presidents have come from Japan. The main function of the ADB is to help Asia-Pacific countries fight poverty and achieve an 'Asia and Pacific free of poverty'[18]. The

100 *Reglobalisation*

focus of the AIIB is, however, different. The main goal of the AIIB is to utilise a series of support methods to provide financing support for infrastructure projects in Asian countries, including loans, equity investments, and guarantees. In addition to the traditional projects (including major infrastructure projects such as railways, highways, airports, pipelines, ports, bridges, and water resources), they may also be extended to energy savings and emissions reduction and agricultural projects, and so on.[19] The AIIB also covers new frontiers of education and health care, which is a considerable expansion of the most suitable infrastructure investment area for the ADB. There is a view that the acronym ADB actually stands for 'Asian Dams and Bridges'. This leaves broad space for the AIIB to invest in infrastructure connectivity.[20] China is presently seeking investment venues with higher returns for domestic capital that lack value-added channels, meaning that, in the foreseeable future, Chinese capital will 'go abroad'. According to a World Bank estimate, by 2030, China's investment activities will rank first in the world, accounting for 30% of the total global investment.[21]

Third, the AIIB aims to cooperate actively with other international organisations. In preparing for the establishment of the AIIB, China actively communicated and exchanged closely with the World Bank, the IMF, and the ADB, drawing on their experiences and lessons in governance structure, rules, institutional operation, and project management in order to avoid the defects and shortcomings of the old international institutions as far as possible. Adhering to the core concept of being 'lean, clean, and green', the AIIB will refer to the governance principles of international multilateral financial institutions, attach importance to environmental protection and climate change, and act in accordance with the rules of multilateral institutions and international practices to establish a good governance framework. The staff of the AIIB are recruited globally, and this follows the principle of streamlined and efficient institutions and zero tolerance for corruption. At the same time, it also draws lessons from the operation of other international institutions. Compared with the World Bank, the ADB, and other international lending organisations, the AIIB has made innovations in at least the following three ways. First, it is more open. The projects of the AIIB will be open to all bidders. Bidding on contracts at the ADB is open only to its members. Second, the AIIB will give developing countries a greater voice. Members of the Asia-Pacific region retain at least 75% of the voting rights, which gives small- and medium-size Asian countries more of a voice than they do in other global organisations. Third, the AIIB will adopt a more streamlined structure to ensure its efficient operations. Compared with the World Bank and the ADB, the AIIB is simpler in terms of personnel arrangements. It does not have a permanent board of directors and is supervised by an unpaid, nonresident board of directors. This not only helps save costs, but it also helps reduce friction in decision-making processes.

5.3 The historical implications of the AIIB model

The establishment of the AIIB is a strategic measure for China's neighbouring diplomacy and a major strategic test for China to remedy the problems of the

The Asian Infrastructure and Investment Bank   101

existing global governance system. China's proposal to build the AIIB is its second successful attempt to make complementary changes to the current international financial system. Before and after the launch of the AIIB, China took the lead in proposing the establishment of the BRICS NDB and in preparing for the establishment of the Shanghai Cooperation Organisation Bank and similar financial institutions and funds such as the Silk Road Fund. On 29 June 2015, the AIIB Agreement was signed in Beijing. President Xi Jinping, meeting with the heads of delegations attending the signing ceremony, said that the signing of the agreement marked a historic step in the preparation of the AIIB and demonstrated the solemn commitment of all parties, embodying the practical actions of all parties in solidarity, cooperation, openness, inclusiveness, and common development.[22] From the perspective of reglobalisation, the establishment of the AIIB is of great significance.

First, the advent of the AIIB has the potential to promote the reform of global economic governance institutions. The AIIB was not created to compete for regional dominance. So why does China not directly use an existing multilateral development mechanism to promote regional infrastructure buildup? For example, there is the World Bank or the ADB, which has more experience, and even the EBRD, which also invests heavily in Central Asia. One reason is that existing international financial development institutions are still subject to draconian lending conditions. Another reason is that if China utilises the existing multilateral development assistance mechanisms directly, it will inevitably lead to a change in the voting shares in these mechanisms. For example, since its inception in 1966, the ADB has been playing the role of the World Bank in development assistance at the regional level and adopting standards similar to those of the World Bank. The ADB is not only an important recipient of UN development projects in Asia, but also an executive agency of the Food and Agricultural Organization and the WHO in Asia. The ADB distributes voting weights based on capital contributions. At present, it has $165 billion in equity capital. Among the members, the United States and Japan are the largest shareholders, accounting for 15.68% and 15.57% respectively, and they have 12.84% and 12.75% voting rights respectively, occupying leading positions. China is the third largest contributor to the ADB, accounting for 6.47% of the total investment and 5.48% of the voting rights. If China injects large-scale capital into the ADB to promote regional infrastructure development, Japan and the United States need to inject large-scale capital into it as well if they do not want a change in their existing voting weights. Obstacles include high government deficits and complex approval procedures in both countries. Another reason is that developing countries, such as China, still find it difficult to gain the right to speak in proportion to their economic strength. After the 2008 global financial crisis, the Group of Seven (G7) in the West was unable to deal with the crisis alone, so emerging economies were brought in, and the Group of 20 (G20) were pushed to the foreground. As early as in December 2010, the G20 had proposed a reform of IMF governance and share allocation, which increased the share and voting rights of emerging economies such as China, Brazil, India, and Russia. Unfortunately, however, the plan has been stalled in the

102 *Reglobalisation*

US Congress, making it difficult for developing countries to obtain voting and speaking rights commensurate with their economic strength. Therefore, the difference and deviation between the economic strength and the dominant financial structure caused by the lagging reform of the existing international governance institutions is the most direct reason for the establishment of the AIIB. The emergence of the AIIB not only represents the most direct impact of emerging countries on the existing international financial order, but also provides an impetus to reform the existing global financial governance structure.[23]

Second, the AIIB will help regional countries improve infrastructure connectivity in order to lay the groundwork for leapfrog development. It is well known that the material and social infrastructure of emerging economies is relatively backward. Most of the 17 United Nations Sustainable Development Goals (SDGs) involve infrastructure improvement, ranging from clean energy, water, and sanitation facilities to health, education, and sustainable cities. Increasing investment in infrastructure and narrowing gaps in related areas are priorities for many international organisations. However, the links between infrastructure and sustainable employment generation, and between employment and stability are rarely touched upon by the SDGs. Worries around unemployment and lack of economic security are a source of political pressure, which is one of the shaping forces of the global political economy. With the rapid growth of the workforce, some countries along the Belt and Road may face the biggest short-term employment challenges in the history of the world. From 2015 to 2030, the labour force of 39 countries along the Belt and Road will increase by 382 million. This figure is indeed amazing. Absorbing 382 million new workers requires that more new jobs be created within 15 years than the current total workforce of 28 EU countries combined. The AIIB and Silk Road Fund are expected to provide additional opportunities and space for public-private investment partnerships (PPP). As a new institution, the AIIB has the opportunity to innovate and fully mobilise private capital to obtain additional funds and guide related funds to appropriate projects. PPP, in turn, will bring expertise, attract more responsible long-term investment, and create more jobs. Major companies around the world have also seen the potential for sales, profitability, and job creation of Belt and Road projects. Indeed, many multinational corporations in the United States are highly optimistic about the BRI and some have already obtained a large number of orders. It is estimated that every US dollar investment made by the AIIB will lead to new investment of $3–$4 dollars in other sectors, and the investment of $1 billion will create 18,000 jobs in Asia.[24] There is a Chinese saying, 'if you want to get rich, build roads first'. Saying goodbye to the isolationist behaviour building walls and moving to building roads outward is the right way to promote growth and employment.

Third, the AIIB will help contribute toward innovation at international institutions. China has begun to promote the establishment of the BRICS NDB, the AIIB, the Silk Road Fund, and new governance initiatives with a pragmatic attitude. In the next 10 years, China will focus on institutionalising and multilateralising these achievements to form a preliminary network of international rules and mechanisms.[25] From the supply side, global public goods can release the influence

The Asian Infrastructure and Investment Bank   103

of supplier countries through the use and integration of resources, in which institutions are the key to leveraging resources.[26] Evelyn Goh, a scholar at Australian National University, believed that, in order to understand the logic of China's supply of public goods, it is necessary to explain how it transforms its growing power resources into the actual policy impact on the target country. There are two ways in which China can exert positive global influence. On the one hand, China can use its economic strength and attractiveness skillfully to implement coercive, inducing, or persuasive actions; on the other hand, it depends on the distribution effect and leadership enhancement brought about by international institutions.[27] In the next ten years, China should take the development of the Belt and Road connectivity and interoperability as an entry point to promote the diversification of international financial mechanisms, solve the problems of inefficient and unfair institutions, reintegrate regional resources, and stimulate competition between regional systems.[28] At the same time, it should urge countries to reflect on and improve the existing international financial system. The institutional public goods promoted by China inevitably have some overlap and competition with those by the ADB, the World Bank, and other institutions. To make full use of its own advantages, developing special features is key. The establishment of the AIIB is a strategic test for China to reform and shape the international financial order. Most Asian countries are at the early stages of industrialisation and urbanisation and require large amounts of capital, technology, and experience in infrastructure development. On 23 March 2017, the AIIB announced the formal approval of 13 new members, which was the first expansion from its 57 founding members since its formal opening in January 2016, taking its total membership to 70. The AIIB has surpassed the EBRD and the ADB in terms of membership and has become the second largest multilateral development institution in the world after the World Bank.[29] The development potential released by the AIIB will become key to initiating inclusive and shared economic benefits of reglobalisation.

Notes

1 Tan Jingjing and Pan Jie, 'Zoujin shijie wutai zhongxin: dangde shibada yilai waijiao gongzuo chengjiu zongshu' ['Approaching the Center of the World Stage: A Summary of the Achievements in Diplomatic Work since the Eighteenth Congress of the CPC'], Xinhua News Agency, 27 August 2017, http://news.xinhuanet.com/politics/2017-08/27/c-1121549869.htm.

2 Xi Jinping, 'Yuecheng quanmian jiancheng xiaokang shehui, duoqu xinshidai Zhongguo tese shehui zhuyi weida shengli: zai Zhongguo gongchandang di shijiuci quanguo daibiao dahui shang de baogao' ['Secure a Decisive Victory in Building a Moderately Prosperous Society in All Respects and Strive for the Great Success of Socialism with Chinese Characteristics for a New Era—Delivered at the 19th National Congress of the Communist Party of China'], 18 October 2017, *Renmin ribao* [*People's Daily*], 18 October 2017, p. 1.

3 Tu Yonghong and Wang Jiaqing, 'Yatouhang: Zhongguo xiang quanqiu tigong gonggong wupin de lichengbei' ['Asian Infrastructure and Investment Bank: A Milestone for China to Provide Public Goods to the World'], *Lilun shiye* [*Theoretical Vision*], No. 4, 2015, pp. 62–65; Cao Dejun, 'Zhongguo waijiao zhuanxing yu quanqiu gonggong

104 *Reglobalisation*

wupin gongji' ['China's Diplomatic Transition and Global Public Goods Supply'], *Zhongguo fazhan guancha [China Development Observation]*, No. 5, 2017, pp. 33–35.

4 Li Xuedi, et al., 'Zongshu: "yidai yilu" cu gongying, lizu changyuan hui shijie: haiwai zhuanjia xuezhe ping lianghui' ['Summary: The "Belt and Road" Initiative Promotes Win-Win Situations, Based on Long-Term Benefits to the World—Comments of Foreign Experts and Scholars on the Two Sessions'], Xinhua News Agency, 6 March 2017, https://www.yidaiyilu.gov.cn/xwzx/hwxw/9136.htm.

5 Chen Shangwen, 'Yatouhang zaikuo pengyouquan' ['The AIIB Expands Its Friendship Circle Again'], People.com.cn, 16 June 2011, http://world.people.com.cn/n1/2017/0616/c1002-29345038.html.

6 Liu Mingyue, 'Yatouhang chengyuan zengzhi baiming, 2019 nian zuixin yatouhang chengyuanguo mingdan yilan' ['Membership of the AIIB Reaching 100: An Overview of the Most Updated List of AIIB Members'], ChinaIRN.com, 15 July 2019, http://www.chinairn.com/hyzx/20190715/114620197.shtml.

7 Li Wei, 'Huoban, zhidu yu huobi: renminbi jueqi de guoji zhengzhi jichu' ['Partners, Institutions, and International Currency: The International Political Basis for the Rise of the RMB'], *Zhongguo shehui kexue [Chinese Social Sciences]*, No. 5, 2016, pp. 79–100.

8 Xiong Aizong et al., 'Dongya gouzhu jinrong haixiao 'fangbodi': xiezai Yazhou jinrong weiji baofa 20 zhounian' ['Building a 'Breakwater' against a Financial Tsunami in East Asia: On the 20th Anniversary of the Outbreak of the Asian Financial Crisis'], *Renmin ribao [People's Daily]*, 27 July 2017.

9 Xu Chao, 'Xin kaifa yinhang yu quanqiu jinrong zhili tixi gaige' ['The New Development Bank and the Reform of the Global Financial Governance System'], *Guowai lilun dongtai [Foreign Theoretical Trends]*, No. 11, 2016, pp. 105–114.

10 Yang Quan, 'Quanqiu jinrong dongdang Beijing xia dongya diqu shuangbian huobi huhuan de fazhan: dongya jinrong hezuo zouxiang ji renminbi juese tiaozheng' ['The Development of Bilateral Currency Swaps in East Asia under the Background of Global Financial Instability: The Direction of East Asian Financial Cooperation and the Adjustment of the Role of Renminbi'], *Guoji jinrong yanjiu [Studies of International Finance]*, No. 6, 2010, p. 33.

11 Wang Hongying, 'Zhongguo zai guoji jinrong tixi zhong de jueqi: jinzhan yu juxianxing' ['The Rise of China in the International Financial System: Progress and Limitations'], in Institute of International and Strategic Studies at Peking University, ed., *Zhongguo guoji zhanlue pinglun [China International Strategy Review (2016)]*, Beijing, China: World Affairs Publishing House, 2016, pp. 41–53.

12 Zhu Caihua, Guo Hongyu, Feng Xingyan, et al., 'Dongya jichu sheshi hulian hutong rongzi: wenti yu duice' ['Financing for East Asian Infrastructure Connectivity: Problems and Solutions'] *Guoji jingji hezuo [International Economic Cooperation]*, No. 10, 2013, pp. 24-29.

13 Biswa Nath Bhatacharyay, Masahiro Kawai, and Rajat M. Nag, eds., *Infrastructure for Asian Connectivity*, Cheltenham, UK: Edward Elgar Publishing, 2012.

14 Wang Jinbo, 'Yatouhang yu quanqiu jingji zhili xiti de wanshan' ['The AIIB and the Perfection of the Global Economic Governance System'], *Guowai lilun dongtai [Foreign Theoretical Trends]*, No. 12, 2015, pp. 22-32.

15 Zong Liang and Huang Xuefei, 'Xinxing quanqiuhua de qianjing, lujing yu Zhongguo juese' ['Prospects, Paths, and the Role of China in New Globalisation'], *Jinrong luntan [Finance Forum]*, No. 6, 2017, pp. 7–13.

16 Wang Lin, 'Yatouhang pizhun 13 ge xinchengyuan, chengyuan guimo chao Yakaihang' ['The AIIB Has Approved 13 New Members, Whose Membership Is Larger than that of the Asian Development Bank'], *Xinjing bao [Beijing News]*, 24 March 2017.

17 Xu Chao, 'Xin kaifa yinhang yu quanqiu jinrong zhili tixi gaige' ['The New Development Bank and the Reform of Global Financial Governance System'], *Guowai lilun dongtai [Foreign Theoretical Trends]*, No. 11, 2016, pp. 105–114.

The Asian Infrastructure and Investment Bank   105

18 Asian Development Bank, *Strategy 2020: The Long-term Strategic Framework of the Asian Development Bank*, Mandaluyong City, Phil: Asian Development Bank, 2008, https://www.adb.org/sites/default/files/institutional-document/32121/strategy2020-print.pdf, p. 1.

19 Chen Shaofeng, 'Yatouhang: Zhong Mei yatai quanshi gengti de fenshui ling' ['The AIIB: A Watershed of Power Shift between China and the United States in the Asia-Pacific'], *Meiguo yanjiu [American Studies]*, No. 3, 2015, pp. 14–33.

20 Robert M. Orr, 'The Asian Development Bank and the Asian Infrastructure Investment Bank: Conditional Collaboration?' PacNet #39, 4 May 2016, https://www.csis.org/analysis/pacnet-39-asian-development-bank-and-asian-infrastructure-bank-conditional.

21 The World Bank, *Capital for the Future: Saving and Investment in an Interdependent World*, Washington, DC: The World Bank, 2013, p. 5.

22 'Xi Jinping huijian chuxi 'Yazhou jichu sheshi touzi yinhang xieding' qianshu yishi geguo daibiaotuan tuanzhang' ['Xi Jinping Received Heads of the Delegations Attending the Signing Ceremony of the 'Asian Infrastructure Investment Bank Agreement'], Xinhuanet.com, 29 June 2015, http://news.xinhuanet.com/2015-06/29/c_1115756477.htm.

23 Wang Yong, 'Quanqiu jingji zhili zouxiang 'hou Meiguo shidai'?' ['Global Economic Governance Heading towards the Post-American Era?'], FTChinese.com, 31 March 2015, http://www.ftchinese.com/story/001061284.

24 Makmun Syadullah, 'Prospects of Asian Infrastructure Investment Bank', *Journal of Social and Development Sciences*, Vol. 5, No. 3, September 2014, pp. 155–156.

25 Tu Yonghong, 'Zhongguo zai "yidai yilu" jianshe zhong tigong de quanqiu gonggong wupin' ['Global Public Goods Provided by China in the Construction of "Belt and Road"'], *Guangming ribao [Guangming Daily]*, 22 June 2015, p. 5.

26 Thomas Risse-Kappen, 'Quanqiuhua yu quanli: shehui jiangou zhuyi de shijiao' ['Globalisation and Power: A Social Constructivist Perspective'], *Shijie jingji yu zhengzhi [World Economy and Politics]*, No. 10, 2013, pp. 24–37.

27 Evelyn Goh, *Rising China's Influence in Developing Asia*, Oxford, UK: Oxford University Press, 2016, pp. 1–5.

28 Li Wei, 'Xianshi zhidu zhuyi de shengcheng' ['The Formation of the Realist Institutionalism'], *Waijiao pinglun [Foreign Affairs Review]*, No. 1, 2016, pp. 31–59; Chen Qi and Guan Chuanjing, 'Guoji zhidu sheji de lingdaoquan fenxi' ['An Analysis of the Leadership of International Institutional Design'], *Shijie jingji yu zhengzhi [World Economy and Politics]*, No. 8, 2015, pp. 4–28.

29 Sun Yi, 'Gongxian fazhan jiyu: wanshan quanqiu zhili' ['Contributing Development Opportunities and Improving Global Governance'], *Renmin ribao (haiwai ban) [People's Daily (Overseas Edition)]*, 24 March 2017, p. 1.

6 Digital Economy 2.0 and Alibaba's reglobalisation story

> It's an age that destroys you but has nothing to do with you; it's an age of cross-border robbery and you can't fight back; it's an age when you wake up too slowly to wake up at all; it's not that your opponent is better than you, it's that you don't even know who your opponent is.
>
> Speech by Jack Ma at the Second World
> Internet Conference on 18 December 2015

> He who is good at playing is good at plotting for momentum, and he who is not good at playing is good at making schemes.
>
> Sun Tzu, *The Art of War*

China's entry point in leading the process of reglobalisation is closely related to institutional innovation. Since the twenty-first century, with the rapid development of global internet technology and e-commerce, major changes have taken place in international trade enterprises, trade patterns, business models, and organisational methods. This historical change is reflected in the rise of internet trade.[1] The 40th China Internet Development Report, published by the China Internet Network Information Center in August 2017, shows that, as of June 2017, there were 751 million internet users in China, accounting for one-fifth of the total number of internet users worldwide. The internet penetration rate was 54.3%, which exceeded the global average by 4.6 percentage points.[2] China has the largest number of internet users in the world. The advantages of having more than 700 million internet users will have a huge impact on the world's consumption and business models. At present, China's e-business model is facilitating the coverage and innovation of global business rules. For example, in 2016, China's online payments doubled from the previous year, exceeding 37.1 trillion yuan, 50 times those of the United States, and more than Japan's GDP of that year. Behind this huge number, Tencent and Alibaba stood out as the two giants of China's internet world. They continue to expand their mobile payment business to other parts of the world. In 2012, Yu'ebao, China's first internet fund, designed especially for Alipay, came into being. It led to what would become a part of a revolution in electronic payment systems across the world. In 2016, Tencent made full

Digital Economy 2.0 and Alibaba's reglobalisation story   107

use of the advantages of the more than 1.15 billion users of WeChat, a Chinese version of Twitter, to launch a comprehensive campaign on the mobile payment business. With 'WeChat Pay' as the main force, by the end of September 2016, Tencent garnered 830 million mobile payment users, while Alipay had 400 million users, and scan code payment became the mainstream choice in the market.[3] Mary Meeker, known as the 'Queen of the Internet', noted in her report *Internet Trends 2017* that China had become the world's internet leader in many ways. China's mobile payment transactions grew from almost zero in 2012 to $5 trillion in 2016. With Alipay and WeChat Pay as the main driving force, a revolution of 'electronic globalisation' or reglobalisation began to unfold in China.[4]

6.1 Alibaba promotes reglobalisation

On Singles' Day, 11 November 2016, the transactions of Alibaba's largest online retail platform in Asia, Tmall.com, surged to 120.7 billion yuan, setting a new world record. On that day, a new world record in logistics was also set by Alibaba's Cainiao Network, which received 657 million logistics orders. The total number of payments in Alipay was 1.05 billion, which indicated an increase of 48% year on year. The number of payments made peaked at 120,000 per second, depicting an increase of 1.4 times, also breaking the record of the previous year of 2015. From the turnover of 50 million yuan since its launch in 2009 to 91.2 billion yuan in 2015, and then to more than 100 billion yuan on Singles' Day in 2016, the rapid growth and revolutionary transformation of Alibaba's ecosystem was behind it all. It has been 16 years since Ma Yun, nicknamed Jack Ma, started his business in a humble apartment in Hangzhou, the capital city of Zhejiang Province, China. For 16 years, many people questioned this idealist, because his aim remains the subversion of the existing forms of the economy and trade in China, which has not yet been modernised fully, and to let the internet connect everything.

China's huge 'demographic dividend' has provided unique advantages for the overall rise in Chinese internet enterprises. China has the world's largest population and largest number of internet users. Its internet development level has approached that of the United States, making it an internet superpower and creator of several new business models. In the past few years, China witnessed the great development of its domestic industries through the mobile platform and became the largest market in several fields. The Better Than Cash Alliance under the UN released a report in April 2017, which suggests that under the impetus of Alipay and WeChat Pay, the scale of China's social network payment market reached $ 2.9 trillion in 2016, an increase of 20 times over the past 4 years.[5] China's mobile payment transactions are currently far ahead of those of the rest of the world (see Figure 6.1). In 2017, Ipsos, a global market research company, surveyed 18,000 consumers across 23 countries and regions around the world and found that 77% of Chinese consumers often used mobile payment tools, a number that ranks first in the world. India also has a high mobile payment penetration rate of 76%. Paytm, a subsidiary of China's Alibaba Group, is reported to be India's leading payment service provider. Surprisingly, the penetration rate of mobile

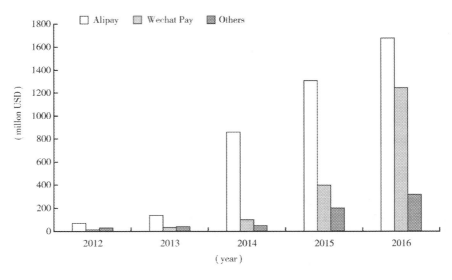

Figure 6.1 The transaction volume of China's mobile payments.

payment in some developed countries is rather low, that is, 48% in the United States and Germany, and Japan, at 27%, ranking the lowest among all the countries and regions surveyed. As industry analysts suggest, this is because developed countries in Europe and the United States have already entered a mature credit card society, and the convenience of credit card consumption, ironically, may have prevented developed economies from transitioning to mobile payment.[6] Take Alibaba and Tencent as an example, and we can see the microcharacteristics of the new round of globalisation, that is, reglobalisation.

First, as a model of financial innovation, Alibaba-led global internet finance has the characteristics of openness, equality, cooperation and sharing and is an important commercial force to promote reglobalisation. Internet finance can connect traditional capital flow, information flow, and commodity flow of business transactions and create more opportunities for enterprises. Internet finance also solves the problems of complex business models and asymmetric information between both sides of financing in traditional financial modes so that enterprises can adopt different modes of financing at different stages of their development to meet the capital demand. With the continuous development of internet finance, cross-border settlement and foreign exchange become easier, which in itself provides more convenient conditions for global trade and is conducive to promoting upgraded trade by means of financial innovation. The 'Internet+' mode with big data, cloud computing, and mobile internet as its core will create a more equitable and universal pattern of reglobalisation. In recent years, Jack Ma has made frequent speeches on the international stage, telling the story of Alibaba's globalisation. In April 2017, as one of the most important carriers of Alibaba's

Digital Economy 2.0 and Alibaba's reglobalisation story   109

globalisation, AliExpress announced that it had more than 100 million overseas buyers across 220 countries around the world, covering 18 languages, with wireless sales accounting for 59.3% of total sales. In the world's major consumer countries, Alibaba's Cainiao Network began to implement a series of logistical upgrading programmes. The number of overseas buyers of AliExpress has currently exceeded 100 million, with 45.4% of the users in countries participating in the Belt and Road Initiative (BRI). The Cainiao Network has built a wide network of cooperation with the postal service, special express, and warehousing logistics of the countries along the Belt and Road. The Cainiao Network has established 17 overseas warehouses within the Belt and Road countries, which are distributed in Russia, India, and Southeast Asia. Along the Belt and Road, AliCloud has built data centres in places such as Hong Kong, Singapore, the Middle East, and Europe and has set up 14 geographical nodes around the world, providing cloud computing and big data services to the countries and regions along the routes with China's own research and development technology.[7] On Singles' Day, that is, 11 November 2015, buyers from 214 countries and regions placed millions of orders on AliExpress of which 155 came from Greenland, the northernmost part of the Earth; 415,479 from Chile; 608 from Fiji, the easternmost and westernmost part of the Earth; 356 from Seychelles, the island country of the Indian Ocean; 30 from Lesotho, a country with the highest average elevation in the world; 15 from the Vatican, the smallest country; and 18 from war-torn Syria; AliExpress sent out 21.24 million packages to the world in 24 hours.[8]

Second, cross-border e-businesses help China and the various countries along the Belt and Road to build the 'Digital Silk Road'. The promotion of cross-border e-businesses will help to narrow the digital divide between different countries, regions, and populations and release data dividends to fully assist the implementation of the BRI. Against the backdrop of stalled global trade negotiations, Alibaba actively calls for the establishment of the 'Electronic World Trade Platform' (eWTP) to promote global inclusive trade and digital economic growth and incubate new rules of global trade in the internet era (see Table 6.2). Since the initiative was put forward in 2016, it has received positive responses and high recognition from international organisations, government agencies, business circles, and think tanks, including the UN. In September 2016, eWTP, as a core policy recommendation of the Business Twenty (B20), was supported and adopted by the leaders of the Group of Twenty (G20) and written into the G20 Leaders' Communique at the Hangzhou Summit. At the same time, the establishment of the eWTP pilot areas around the world is also picking up steam. In March 2017, the first eWTP pilot area was established in Malaysia. China and Malaysia vowed to jointly build the Digital Free Trade Area (eHub). As infrastructure for the development of the digital economy, the Digital Free Trade Area will become a digital hub of logistics, payment, customs clearance, and data integration, as well as a window for small and medium-size enterprises in Malaysia and Southeast Asia to reach the rest of the world.[9] The innovation of this network operation mode reflects the concept of inclusive and mutually beneficial development. It is not only a platform for creating new rules of governance, but also one for pursuing inclusive trade.[10]

110 *Reglobalisation*

According to the big data of the cross-border e-commerce of Alibaba, the Ali Research Institute has compiled the E-Commerce Connectivity Index (ECI) of the Belt and Road countries, which measures the degree of closeness of the cross-border e-commerce trade between China and the Belt and Road countries. With a higher ECI export index, a country would purchase more goods made in China. With a higher ECI import index, Chinese consumers would purchase more goods from that country (see Table 6.1).

Finally, we should build a platform for sharing. Relying on the new infrastructure of the cloud network, the internet has created a new business environment. Information flow is no longer restricted in the supply chain of the industrial economic system. The distance between suppliers and consumers is greatly shortened and transaction costs are greatly reduced, which directly supports the formation of large-scale business collaboration. The most important feature of the emerging Digital Economy 2.0 is the high degree of digitisation. The flow and sharing of data push business processes across enterprise boundaries and weave new ecological and value networks. Digital Economy 2.0 has the characteristics of everyone participating, building, and sharing, and of realising inclusive technology, finance, and trade. In the field of global trade, Digital Economy 2.0 has brought a new situation of inclusive trade to the whole world. Inclusive trade means that all kinds of trade entities can participate in and benefit from global trade, and the trade order will be fairer and just. Alibaba has created a platform for a sharing economy, has rewritten the business landscape, and has made the process of reglobalisation more convenient and inclusive. On 11 November 2016, Alibaba's online shopping platform generated huge sales of $17.8 billion in the Singles' Day Global Shopping Festival, an increase of 32% year on year. As a young and informal festival, Singles' Day has already far surpassed Black Friday in terms of trade volume. Alibaba is mining big data collected through its retail, streaming, and payment platforms. In 2018, Alibaba launched its first pilot programme for shoppers on Single's Day in Southeast Asia. Jack Ma likened his 'World Electronic Trade Platform' programme to

Table 6.1 ECI indexes of countries along the Belt and Road

Rank	Country	ECI Export Index	ECI Import Index	ECI Total Index
1	Russia	29.0	0.9	29.9
2	Israel	10.9	2.8	13.7
3	Thailand	4.6	6.9	11.5
4	Ukraine	10.3	0	10.3
5	Poland	8.4	0.7	9.1
6	Czech Republic	6.8	1.1	7.9
7	Moldova	7.8	0	7.8
8	Turkey	7.4	0.2	7.7
9	Belarus	7.0	0	7.1
10	Singapore	4.0	2.3	6.4

Source: Ali Research Institute.

Digital Economy 2.0 and Alibaba's reglobalisation story 111

Table 6.2 The sharing connotation of eWTP

According to the Business 20 (B20) consensus, eWTP is a private sector-led, market-driven, open, transparent, multistakeholder public-private partnership platform. It aims to explore the trends, problems, and policy recommendations of global digital economy and electronic trade, share business and best practices, incubate and innovate new rules and standards of trade, and promote the development of global digital economy infrastructure. We will work together to promote inclusive and sustainable development of the global economy and society. Therefore, the eWTP ecosystem will include three levels of content:	
Rule level	Stakeholders discuss and incubate new rules and standards in the digital age, such as digital customs, tax policy, data flow, credit system, and consumer protection that are directly related to e-commerce.
Business level	relevant parties carry out business exchanges and cooperation in the field of digital economy and e-commerce and establish new infrastructure in the internet era, such as e-commerce platforms, financial payment, logistics warehousing, integrated foreign trade services, marketing, education, and training, etc.
Technical level	Technical level – jointly establish eWTP technology architecture based on internet, big data, cloud computing, internet of Things, artificial intelligence, and so on.
These three levels are closely related and are interdependent. Discussions at the rule level mainly come from practices at the business and technical levels, and their results and consensus will promote business cooperation and innovation and development of new technologies in the digital economy.	

Source: Ali Research Institute, 'Shijie dianzi maoyi pingtai changyi (eWTP) 2017 niandu baogao' ['Annual Report of the Electronic World Trade Platform Initiative (eWTP) 2017'], pp. 1–3.

a 'dispute-free WTO', which he believed would help 80% of companies and developing countries that do not have the opportunity to participate in global trade sell goods overseas. In Jack Ma's view, Alibaba is becoming a 'consumer-to-business' company, rewriting retail rules so that retailers can know what shoppers want to buy through big data.[11]

6.2 Chinese e-businesses leading global internet consumption

Although China is still a developing country and lags behind many developed countries in terms of industrialisation and modernisation, this backwardness is not necessarily a disadvantage. In the internet era, if China can seize the opportunity to surpass others, it will show a unique advantage inherent in backwardness. At present, China is the largest online retail market in the world. The scale and volume of online shopping users rank first in the world and dominate the development of mobile e-commerce. According to a report by Ipsos, in 2016, for the first time, China became one of the most popular online shopping destinations in the world.[12] Chinese enterprises represented by Alibaba have been at the forefront of the world in mobile payment, cross-border electronic trade, and massive data processing. The data released by the Ministry of Commerce (MOFCOM) show that China's cross-border e-commerce import and export volume reached

112 *Reglobalisation*

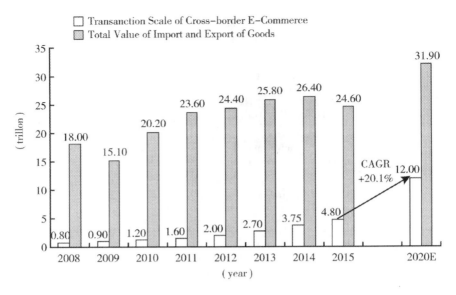

Figure 6.2 The rapid development trend of cross-border e-commerce in china.

RMB6.3 trillion in 2016 and that the scale of cross-border e-commerce trade in China is expected to reach RMB12 trillion by 2020, accounting for 37.6% of China's total import and export volume (see Figure 6.2). In the coming years, China's e-commerce and cross-border trade will usher in another major development opportunity under the impetus of the BRI. Cross-border e-commerce has set up a free, open, universal, and inclusive global trading platform on which billions of consumers can buy from all over the world and small and medium-size enterprises can sell to the world, truly realising global connectivity and global linkage. From the global wave of e-commerce led by China, we can see three development trends.

First, as a new cross-border consumption mode, cross-border business-to-consumer (B2C) e-commerce will become a new engine of cross-border trade growth in consumer goods thanks to its strong growth momentum. According to a report released by the UN Conference on Trade and Development (UNCTAD) in May 2017, China had already become the largest cross-border B2C e-commerce market in the world, with a market size of $617 billion. The future development of cross-border B2C e-commerce will not only increase its scale and expand the scope of products and services, but also present three major trends: value-added platform services, integration, intensification of services, and online and offline platform integration. This will also change the multilink chain pattern of traditional cross-border business-to-business-to-consumer (B2B2C) trade in consumer goods and form a collection of services. The trading platform touches digital consumers and drives the seamless delivery of products and services for

Digital Economy 2.0 and Alibaba's reglobalisation story   113

the offline business ecosystem. Its trading process is flatter. Across all regions in the world, the differences in economic development level and industrial structure allow regional markets to present different characteristics and development trajectories. With leading market size and strong growth, the Asia-Pacific region has become the most important regional market in the world. In 2014, cross-border B2C e-commerce transactions in the Asia-Pacific region accounted for 30% of the global total, which is expected to rise to 48% in 2020. The consumer goods industry in the whole region is more developed and countries are experiencing staggering development, which has become the source of market growth. Among these countries, those in East Asia, along with China, Japan, and South Korea as the main players, have developed sophisticated infrastructure and a high penetration rate of mobile internet, which is the core of the whole Asia-Pacific market. It is estimated that by 2020, cross-border B2C e-commerce transactions in East Asia will account for 86% of the total Asia-Pacific region and 39% of the global total. Owing to the rapid progress of regional economic integration and the huge potential of economic development, Southeast Asia has become another hotspot for e-commerce in the Asia-Pacific region. The continuous development of cross-border B2C e-commerce will have a far-reaching impact on cross-border consumption and the global economy. Cross-border consumption patterns will be more diversified, new digital service providers will emerge in large numbers, and the process of globalisation will continue to accelerate.[13]

Second, China has become the world's leading country in both physical and e-commerce trade, highlighting its huge potential in shaping the global political and economic patterns. In 2015, China's cross-border e-commerce transactions amounted to RMB4.8 trillion, accounting for 19.5% of China's total imports and exports. It is estimated that, by 2020, China's cross-border e-commerce market will reach RMB1.2 trillion, and its share in the total imports and exports will reach 37.6%.[14] China is the only country in the world in which both physical and e-commerce trade are at the forefront of the world, which shows the potential energy of shaping the future pattern of reglobalisation. In 2015, despite the slowdown of global trade growth, the growth rate of cross-border e-commerce in China was still significantly higher than that of the import and export of goods, and the penetration rate of e-commerce in China's import and export trade continues to increase.[15] According to the data released by the China E-Commerce Research Center, cross-border e-businesses play a significant role in promoting the international competitiveness of Chinese products and promoting the development of foreign trade under the Belt and Road framework.[16] Taking Alibaba's trading scale as an example, in 2016, the trading volume of the Singles' Day Global Shopping Festival exceeded RMB120.7 billion, covering 235 countries and regions. Logistics orders shattered the world record again, with a total of 600 million. In the process of moving from rapid growth to revolutionary transformation, Alibaba strives to build the infrastructure of future businesses, including the trading market, payment, logistics, cloud computing, and big data. It not only connects businesses with the internet, but also gathers global demand and connects businesses and consumers from all over the world. In Jack Ma's words,

114 *Reglobalisation*

'creating an economy that has never been born in history, spanning borders, time and space'.[17] He hopes that by 2036, the total sales of the Alibaba platform will exceed the GDP of the world's fifth largest economy, only after the United States, China, Japan and the European Union. Its development goal is to have 2 billion users, which is equivalent to quarter of the Earth's population according to current figures. After more than ten years of cultivation, Alibaba's ecosystem has begun to gather global demand, connect global businesses and consumers, and change the efficiency of upstream manufacturing, logistics, and financial allocation, forming new production relations and new lifestyles through the internet.[18]

Finally, in terms of information security, Alibaba also has world-class technology and management experience. The safety guarantee of Singles' Day is to ensure the safe and smooth operation of the whole ecosystem covering platforms, businesses, suppliers, and logistics. This huge security system includes early detection of cyber-attacks, identifying abnormal activity at any time, and automatic tracing of high-risk cases. On Singles' Day, 11 November 2016, Alibaba's cloud shield protection system withstood 2,000 DDos attacks, 500 million web attacks, and 600 million password cracking attempts.[19]

6.3 Digital economy and the 'four new inventions'

'There were the four great inventions: the compass, paper-making, gunpowder, and printing in ancient times. There are now four new inventions: high-speed rail, Alipay, sharing bicycles, and online shopping'. In 2017, this was a popular saying about the Chinese internet in 2017. Although slightly exaggerated, it does describe China's future innovation potential. The so-called four new inventions listed here is a summary made by the media of China's leading new consumer products or consumption patterns.[20] Two of the four new inventions listed above are directly related to Alibaba, namely Alipay and online shopping. They represent the innovation capacity of the internet world and manifest the shaping ability of reglobalisation.

First, digital infrastructure has become a new infrastructure for reglobalisation. Generally speaking, the core of Digital Economy 1.0 was information technology (IT), at which time the internet was just beginning to develop. At this stage, IT had been used widely in traditional industries. This represented the installation period of IT, but it had yet to coalesce into a mature internet business model that could be scaled to the wider society. In recent years, the digital economy, based on digital technology and the internet platform as an important carrier, has begun to take shape. We call this the Digital Economy 2.0. The core of Digital Economy 2.0 is data technology (DT), which means that everything is connected online. With unprecedented growth, data has become the core component driving both business innovation and development. The Digital Economy 2.0 architecture is based on the new infrastructure of cloud computing. The internet platform, a brand new economic organisation, has grown and brought about revolutionary changes in business, organisational, and employment models.[21] Digital infrastructure refers to at least one part of the infrastructure that contains IT, which

Digital Economy 2.0 and Alibaba's reglobalisation story   115

generally includes hybrid or dedicated infrastructure. Hybrid digital infrastructure refers to a combination of traditional physical infrastructure and digital components. For example, water pipes that are equipped with sensors and digital parking and traffic systems. Dedicated digital infrastructure refers to infrastructure with a digital essence, such as broadband, wireless networks, and so on. Together, these two types of infrastructure provide necessary conditions for the development of the digital economy in various fields. In recent years, the breakthroughs and integration of IT, such as mobile internet, big data, cloud computing, the internet of Things (IoT), and artificial intelligence (AI), have promoted the rapid development of the digital economy. The development of mobile internet has fundamentally cast off restrictions and constraints of wired internet, expanded the scope of the application of the internet, and promoted the extensive innovation of mobile applications. The development of mobile internet, low-cost sensors, and cloud computing have promoted the development of the IoT. It is estimated that 50 billion interconnected devices will be online by 2020. In the foreseeable future, the number of terminals accessing the IoT will increase by 10 times and even 100 times, and the data capacity of the IoT will increase exponentially, doubling itself once every 2 years. The development of AI technology has significantly improved the ability of big data autonomous analytics. Without intelligent technology, the collection, processing, and analysis of big data cannot be possible, new meanings cannot be discovered, and new value cannot be produced. AI technology can summarise the implicit rules and support intelligent decision-making by understanding video, audio, and human natural language and analysing a large number of trivial, unstructured data in the IoT. Therefore, the effective use of big data and AI technology will promote the development of the IoT and realise the leap from quantitative to qualitative changes in the IoT.[22]

Second, the sharing economy makes the development of reglobalisation more inclusive and balanced. In 2016, the sharing economy opened a new page in China's business history. When China's traditional 'three carriages' of investment, consumption, and export to stimulate economic growth slowed down, the 'Internet+' sharing economy brought new impetus to China. In the shared transportation market, China has been at the forefront of the world. At present, Chinese consumers have produced more than 10 billion shared trips a year, accounting for 67% of the global market share. The 'originated in China' business model represented by Ofo and Mobike has begun to go global, growing from technological innovation to mode creation, which has triggered the replication and imitation of bicycle sharing companies such as Spin in the United States. Shared bicycles have become popular in China since 2016. In less than 2 years, the number of bicycles issued and used in China has exceeded the sum of all other shared bicycles in the world. China is experimenting with a revolutionary sharing economy. Individuals and data comprising innumerable bicycles are a huge IoT, like a moving spider web that can obtain big data from different scenes. Among them, smart locks, big data analysis, battery systems, and bicycle manufacturing all involve high technology. For example, the Global Navigation Satellite System (GLONASS), built in by Mobike, supports GPS, Beidou, and GLONASS and constitutes the largest

116 *Reglobalisation*

mobile IoT system in the world. Founded on the campus of Peking University, Ofo is the world's first and largest bicycle sharing platform; it has provided more than 400 million trips to more than 30 million users in 46 cities across the world and has connected more than 2.5 million shared bicycles.[23] By August 2017, Ofo had covered seven countries in the world: China, Singapore, the United States, the United Kingdom, Kazakhstan, Thailand, and Malaysia. During the same period of time, Mobike's presence was expanded to Singapore, Britain, Japan, and Italy. The sharing economy is not a closed economy for self-entertainment. The new economic revolution has expanded from China to the whole world. In the global planning of Mobike, the business plan of sharing bicycles in 2017 was projected to extend to 20 countries and regions, and the tide of sharing bicycles in China was felt the world over. The sharing economy outside bicycles is also prevalent around the world. In January 2016, General Motors invested $500 million in Lyft, the second largest ride-sharing company in the US, to launch Maven, a car-sharing service that allows customers to access vehicles and drive their own cars using smartphone software or other smart devices. Four months later, in May 2016, Toyota Motor Company and Uber announced that they were going to jointly develop a car-pooling business. Shortly thereafter, the Volkswagen Group also launched a new independent brand, Moia, which can provide bus- and taxi-like software services, and vehicles can be called on through the mobile app, and users can share vehicles.

Finally, China's leading smart technology will open up new space for promoting a new model of reglobalisation. AI endows the machine with certain audio-visual perception and thinking ability, which not only promotes the improvement of productivity, but also has a positive effect on the operation of the economy and society. AI was first commercialised in 2016. After the AlphaGo Robot defeated a South Korean professional Go player, winning the series 4–1, AI attracted attention worldwide. Now IBM, Microsoft, Facebook, Baidu, and other leading internet companies have also opened AI platforms. The accelerated commercialisation of AI has made the government aware of the important role of AI in economic development and industrial upgrading. *Made in China 2025*, released by the Chinese government in 2015, takes intelligent manufacturing as the focus of development and embeds AI technology in the manufacturing industry. In 2016, many industrial policies put forward the establishment of AI industrial systems as soon as possible to promote the development of AI technology and industrial application.[24] According to data from the Wuzhen Think Tank, global AI enterprises are mainly concentrated in the United States, United Kingdom, and China. In 2016, the number of AI enterprises in the United States (2,905 enterprises), China (709 enterprises), and the United Kingdom (366 enterprises) together accounted for 65.73% of the global total (see Figure 6.3).[25] The rapid development of AI enterprises in China is playing an increasingly important role in the international arena.

In China, the internet giants represented by Baidu, Alibaba, and Tencent (BAT) mainly benefit from their own massive data advantages to promote 'AI+' in all fields of application and strive to occupy the starter advantage in basic technology and key fields of application. For example, Baidu set up a research institute

Digital Economy 2.0 and Alibaba's reglobalisation story 117

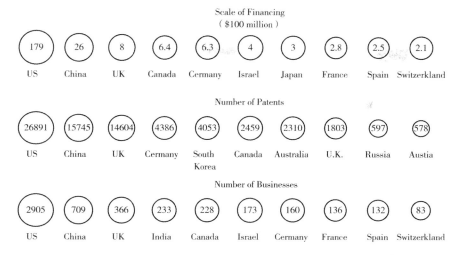

Figure 6.3 Development pattern of world artificial intelligence technology in 2016.

focussing on AI, launched 'Secretary Xiaodu' on the application level, developed vision technology for autonomous vehicles, and developed 'Baidu Brain' at the basic level. Alibaba pays great attention to cloud computing in AI. Currently, its AI products are mainly used in the electronics business. At the service level and the business end, Alibaba has launched an intelligent robot customer service platform, and opened DT PAI, China's first AI computing platform. Tencent launched a writing robot called Dreamwriter, opened the visual recognition platform Tencent Youtu, and established an AI laboratory in 2016. Both China and the United States consider AI as the dominant strategy in the future and have formulated strategic development plans to promote the process from a national level in order to take the initiative toward reglobalisation in the future. As the largest developing country, China has made attempts to plan and deploy strategic guidance and project implementation. Both China and the United States have established a relatively complete research and development base at the national level to promote the development of AI.

China is currently the world's largest online retail market, ranking first in terms of the number of online shopping users and transaction volume. In 2016, the trading volume of Tmall Singles' Day exceeded 100 billion yuan, with consumers in 235 countries and regions in the world, creating a record in the history of global retail. According to a report by the International Trade Center, a subsidiary body of UNCTAD and the WTO, China was the largest retail e-commerce market in the world in 2016. With more and more consumers turning online, offline channels began to play a more complementary role in online sales. China is taking the lead in areas such as online and mobile payment, the sharing economy, and AI.[26]

118 *Reglobalisation*

Notes

1 Kevin Martin, 'Zhongguo shuzihua xiaofei heyi lingxian shijie?' ['Why China's Digital Consumption Leads the World?'], FTChinese.com, http://www.ftchinese.com/story /001070473?page=2.
2 China Internet Network Information Center, *Di 40 ci Zhongguo hulian wangluo fazhan zhuangkuang tongji baogao* [*The 40th China Internet Development Statistics Report*], 2017, http: //free.eol.cn/edu-net/edudown/CNNIC40.pdf, p. 13.
3 Wu Yakun, 'Rimei: Zhongguo qunian shouji zhifu'e wei Meiguo 50 bei, guimo chao Riben GDP' ['Japanese Media: Last Year China Made 50 Times More Mobile Payments than the United States, Exceeding Japan's GDP in Scale'], guancha.cn, 27 March 2017, https://www.guancha.cn/economy/2017_03_27_400713.shtml.
4 Mary Meeker, 'Internet Trends 2017: Code Conference', 31 May 2017, http://dq756f9p zlyr3.cloudfron.net/file/Internet+Trends+2017+Report.pdf.
5 Zennon Kapron and Michelle Meertens, 'Social Networks, e-Commerce Platforms, and the Growth of Digital Payment Ecosystems in China: What It Means for Other Countries', Research Report, April 2017, Better than Cash Alliance.
6 Ipsos, '2017 Mobile Payment Usage in China', 17 August 2017, https://www.ipsos.co m/sites/default/files/ct/publication/documents/2017-08/Mobile_payments_in_China-2017.pdf; 'Woguo yidong zhifu pujilv 77% quanqiu diyi, Meiguo jin 48%, Riben 27%' ['China's Mobile Payment Penetration Rate of 77% Ranks First in the World, with That of the US at 48% and Japan at 27%'], China.com.cn, 5 September 2017, http://tech.chi na.com.cn/internet/20170906/320637.shtml.
7 Ali Research Institute and DT Finance, 'eWTP zhuli "yidai yilu" jianshe: Alibaba jin-gjiti de shijian' ['eWTP Promotes the "Belt and Road" Construction: The Practices of the Alibaba Economy'], Research Report, 21 April 2017, http://i.aliresearch.com/img /20170421/20170421181400.pdf.
8 Ali Research Institute and DT Finance, 'eWTP zhuli "yidai yilu" jianshe: Alibaba jin-gjiti de shijian' ['eWTP Promotes the "Belt and Road" Construction: The Practices of the Alibaba Economy'].
9 Ali Research Institute, 'Dudong G20 sida zhuti: dongxi shuju shidai jingji fazhan Dongxiang' ['Understanding the Four Topics of G20: Comprehending the Trends of Economic Development in the Digital Age'], Research Report, August 2016, http://i.a liresearch.com/file/20160831/20160831103441.pdf.
10 Ali Research Institute, 'Shijie dianzi maoyi pingtai xieyi (eWTP) 2017 niandu baogao' ['Annual Report of the Electronic World Trade Platform Initiative (eWTP) 2017'], Research Report, March 2017, http://i.aliresearch.com/img/20170323/20170323182812.pdf.
11 Liu Junlin, 'Alibaba ni xiang quanqiu shuchu "guanggun jie"' ['Alibaba plans to export 'the Singles' Day' to the world'], 8 November 2016, china.com.cn, http://www.china. com.cn/news/world/2016-11/08/content_39658569.htm.
12 Wang Hualei, Wang Liying, and Ji Qingqing, '2016 nian shijie xinxihua fazhan xianzhuang ji 2017 nian zhanwang' ['Current Situation of World Informatization Development in 2016 and Prospects for 2017'], in Yin Libo, ed., *Shijie xinxihua fazhan baogao (2016-2017)* [*World Informatization Development Report 2016-2017*], Beijing, China: Social Sciences Academic Press, 2017, p. 17.
13 Accenture Strategy and Ali Research Institute, 'Quantiu kuajing B2C dianshang shichang zhanwang: shuzihua xiaofei chongsu shangye quanqiuhua' ['Global Cross-Border B2C E-Commerce Market Prospects: Digital Consumption Reshaping Commercial Globalisation'], Research Report, 2015, http://i.aliresearch.com/file/ 20150611/20150611113848 pdf, p. 12.
14 Ali Research Institute and Ali Cross-Border E-Commerce Research Center, '2016 Zhongguo kuajing dianshang fazhan baogao: maoyi de weilai: kuajing dianshang lian-jie shijie' ['China Cross-Border E-Commerce Development Report 2016—The Future of Trade: Cross-Border E-Commerce Connecting the World'], September 2016, http://i .aliresearch.com/img/20160901/20160901101059 pdf, pp. 4–5.

Digital Economy 2.0 and Alibaba's reglobalisation story   119

15 Ibid.
16 China E-Commerce Research Center, '2016 nian (shang) Zhongguo dianzi shangwu shichang shuju jiance baogao' ['China's Electronic Commerce Market Data Monitoring Report for the First Half of 2016'], September 2016, http://www.100ec.cn/zt/upload-data/B2B/EC.pdf.
17 Sina Technologies, '2016 Tianmao shuangshiyi dangtian jiaoyi'e chao 1207 yi, wuxian chengjiao zhanbi jin 82%' ['Tmall 2016 Singles' Day Sales in 2016 Surpassed 120.7 Billion Yuan, with Nearly 82% Coming from Wireless Transactions'], Sina.com.cn, 12 November 2016, http://tech.sina.com.cn/i/2016-11-12/doc-ifxxsmic6065504.shtml.
18 China E-Commerce Research Center, '2016 nian (shang) Zhongguo dianzi shangwu shichang shuju jiance baogao' ['China's Electronic Commerce Market Data Monitoring Report for the First Half of 2016'], September 2016, http://www.100ec.cn/zt/upload-data/B2B/EC.pdf.
19 Ali Research Institute, 'Weilai shangye xinchangtai: 2016 nian "shuang 11" shendu dongcha' ['The New Normal of Future Business: Deep Insight on the 2016 Singles' Day'], Research Report, November 2016.
20 It should be pointed out that, although the four new inventions seem to be products provided by enterprises rather than public goods in a strict sense, they share a common feature with consumption, that is, 'sharing' requires a dialectical understanding of the relationship between public goods and private goods. In fact, the boundaries between public goods and private goods are not absolute. Sometimes private goods may be converted into public goods at other times. For example, innovative technology within the term limit of intellectual property rights is a private product; but after the period of protection, it becomes a public good and can be used by anyone. Often the prototype of major public goods is the result of some enterprise innovation. For example, the internet. See Liu Yuanju, '"Xin sida faming" jianzheng Zhongguo yixie qiye chuangxing de jieguo, liru hulianwang' ['The "Four New Inventions" Witness China's Economic Transformation'], *Xinjing bao* [*Beijing News*], 1 September 2017.
21 Ali Research Institute, 'Shuzi jingji 2.0 baogao: gaobie gongsi, yongbao pingtai' ['Digital Economy Report 2.0: A Farewell to Companies, an Embrace of Platforms'], January 2017, http: //i.aliresearch.com/file/20170109/20170109174300.pdf.
22 Tencent Research Institute, 'Zhongguo "hulianwang +" shuzi jingji zhishu (2017)' ['China's "Internet+" Digital Economic Index (2017)'], 20 April 2017, http://www.ten-centresearch.com/4868.
23 Wang Yi, 'Ofo xiaohuangche qixing chuang shijie' ['Ofo Yellow Bikes Riding into the World'], *Renmin ribao* [*People's Daily*], March 29, 2017, p. 14.
24 Jiantuo Huake Investment Co., Ltd., *Zhongguo zhihui hulian touzi fazhan baogao (2017)* [*China's Intelligent Interconnection Investment Development Report 2017*], Beijing, China: Social Sciences Academic Press, 2017, p. 35.
25 Wuzhen Think Tank, Netease Science and Technology, Netease Intelligence, *Wuzhen zhishu: quanqiu rengong zhineng fazhan baogao (2016) (kuangjia pian)* [*Wuzhen Index: Global Artificial Intelligence Development Report (2016) (Framework)*], October 2016, p. 7, http://h5.iwuzhen.org/pdf/AI-Overview.pdf.
26 Yin Libo, ed., *Shijie xinxihua fazhan baogao (2016-2017)* [*World Informatization Development Report 2016-2017*], Beijing: Social Sciences Academic Press, 2017.

7 The mechanism of reversal pressure and the experience of special economic zones in China

> We should be bolder in reform and opening up, dare to experiment and not be like women with small feet. If you are sure of it, try boldly and make bold progress. The important experience of Shenzhen is daring to break through. Without a bit of the 'dashing' and 'daring' spirit, we can't muster the strength and energy to make a good road, a new road or a new career.
>
> Deng Xiaoping's 'South Tour Talks' in
> January 1992

> We should form a mechanism of reversal pressure by deepening the opening up, add new impetus to the revitalisation of our national industries and stimulate new vitality.
>
> Premier Li Keqiang's remarks at State
> Council executive meeting in
> November 2015

China has been an important driving force for the reform of the international order and for the reconstruction of the process of globalisation. However, there is still a long way to go to attain comprehensive leadership. The stories of the Shanghai Shipping Capability Trading Platform, Alibaba, and the Belt and Road Initiative (BRI) tell us that profound changes are taking place in the relationship between China and the world. It is time to bid farewell to traditional linear thinking and to realise that an increasingly powerful China will shape and influence the characteristics and process of globalisation. Reglobalisation presents a two-way interactive feature, emphasising domestic and international linkages – linkages between emerging countries and the world and marginal and central linkages. It transcends the narrow thinking of Western-centrism and advocates a more inclusive and shared global order. The reversal pressure mechanism is important in the process of globalisation. At the beginning of the reform and opening up era, the Chinese government set up special economic zones (SEZ) such as Shenzhen, where special policies were implemented. In the mid-1980s, 14 coastal open cities were established successively, and some cities under the jurisdiction of coastal open cities were designated as coastal economic open zones. With the deepening of reform and opening up, economic and

The mechanism of reversal pressure and the experiences   121

technological development zones and high-tech development zones were established throughout the country. The enterprises that can enter the development zones enjoy certain preferential policies. In the early 1990s, more than 10 new national-level zones appeared one after another, and in recent years, free-trade zones have been established. These are the internal reforms of China in adapting to the process of globalisation. China's successful experiences have now gained popularity world over, and this, in turn, shapes a new process of globalisation and leads to reglobalisation.

7.1 Promoting reform through opening up: innovative experiments in China's free-trade zones

As early as in the Third Plenary Session of the Eleventh National Congress of the Chinese Communist Party (CPC) in 1978, reform and opening up were proposed as an integrated strategy. While reform is an internal self-adjustment mechanism, opening up is an external adjustment mechanism. Both formed a dual engine for China's pursuit of 'four modernisations', which support and complement each other. Practice shows that whenever domestic reform lacks momentum, or even falls into controversy, the expansion of opening up will often play the role of the 'rescuer' of reform, and the role of the 'reversal pressure'. Classic examples include the establishment of SEZs in 1980 and China's accession to the WTO in 2001. In the history of reform, the success of these two instances of opening up exerting a reversal pressure on reform has laid the foundation for the free-trade area model to blossom everywhere in recent years. In the course of China's reform and opening up, the types of industrial parks include economic and technological development zones, high-tech industrial development zones, border economic cooperation zones, export processing zones, duty-free zones, duty-free ports, comprehensive duty-free zones, duty-free logistics parks, logistics parks, cross-border industrial zones, and free-trade pilot zones, etc. They each enjoy different kinds of policy support and have different functions.

Overall, behind China's economic phenomenon, there are various development and high-tech zones that have become the bases of innovation experiments. The layout of various 'new areas' (*xin qu*) in China has an obvious driving effect on local development and have become a regional growth engine with radiating effects. For example, Shanghai's Pudong New Area has different degrees of driving effects on the economic growth of the Yangtze River Delta, the southeast coastal areas, and the regions along the river. Chongqing's Liangjiang New Area has important driving effects for the economic growth and development of Chongqing as a whole. As of 2017, if we count the Xiong'an New Area in Hebei Province, the total number of new areas at the national level is 19. China's SEZs with various orientations, ranging from the local to the national level and then to the international level, provide an important platform for institutional innovation for China to participate in and lead a new round of globalisation, that is, reglobalisation (see Table 7.1). Special zones differ in their functions:

Table 7.1 China's new zones, special economic zones, development zones, and free-trade zones

	New Zones	Special Economic Zones	Development Zones	Free-Trade Pilot Zones
Number	19	7	219	11
Typical Examples	Xiong'an New Area, Pudong New Area, and Tianjin Binhai New Area	Shenzhen, Zhuhai, Xiamen, Shantou, Hainan, Kashgar, and Horgos	Each province has different levels of development zones	Shanghai Free Trade Zone, etc.
Characteristics	Highlighting regional development and resource integration and giving full play to the radiating role of the economic centre.	Relying on special policy support, giving full play to local comparative advantages, and establishing an independent economy.	There are unified preferential policies and industrial planning for industrial agglomerations and production parks.	Innovation in foreign trade systems, tariffs, approval, and management policies.

Note: Table compiled by the authors.

The mechanism of reversal pressure and the experiences 123

- SEZs – To promote reform properly, China follows a gradual reform strategy of partial piloting before popularising the experience. In the early period of reform and opening up, several SEZs, such as the Shenzhen Special Economic Zone and the Zhuhai Special Economic Zone (in both cases, two big cities, Shen Zhen and Zhu Hai, grew out of the SEZs), were established, and special policies were implemented in each. The nature of the comprehensive reform pilot area is similar to that of the special administrative area, but the content of the experiments is clearer. For example, some are aimed at the coordinated development of urban and rural areas, and others at dealing with problems of resources and environment.
- Economic and technological development zones – They focus on both industrial and regional development. Especially in the 1980s and 1990s, many policies were designed to promote the complementarity of different industries, highlighting the advantages of industrial agglomeration. Enterprises that can enter the zones enjoyed certain preferential policies such as preferential treatment for industrial land and tax relief.
- High-tech industrial development zones – They focus more on industrial development. In the early stage of development, the high-tech industry needs the guidance and assistance of the government. For that purpose, the Ministry of Science and Technology formulated a detailed catalogue of industrial guidance for the development of high-tech zones.
- Free-trade zones – They have flexible tariff approval and management policies that are applicable to production, trade, and investment activities in the zone. Sometimes, such zones are not mutually exclusive, and the same place can have several zones at the same time.

China needs to combine domestic and international development and explore the new direction of global development based on domestic policy innovations in order to explore the new rules of reglobalisation. The creation of various types of development zones for field experiments and policy innovation is a unique wisdom of reform (see Table 7.2). In March 2013, Li Keqiang, Premier of China's State Council, discussed the idea of establishing a free-trade zone in Shanghai at a symposium. He said, 'We should expand domestic demand with openness, form a mechanism of reversal pressure with openness, and promote a new round of reform with openness'.[1] This was the first time that Li Keqiang had put forward the strategic thinking behind the establishment of the Shanghai Free Trade Zone. *The General Plan of China's Shanghai Pilot Free Trade Zone*, released by the State Council, puts forward the guiding principles of the free-trade zone as follows: 'Closely revolving around the national strategy, further emancipating the mind, adhering to the principle of trying first, promoting reform and development through opening up', which reiterates the idea that 'opening up promotes reform'. The key point of this strategy is to promote internal system adjustment with the help of external reversal pressure brought about by the opening up. Specifically, through the experiment of the Shanghai Free Trade Zone, China can establish

124 *Reglobalisation*

Table 7.2 The '1+3+7' pattern of China's pilot free-trade zone

Batch (Time)	Name	Strategic Positioning
First Batch (29 September 2013)	China (Shanghai) Pilot Free-Trade Zone	It aims to deepen and improve the investment management system with negative list management as the core, the trade supervision system with trade facilitation as the key point, the financial innovation system with the goal of convertibility of capital account and opening up of financial service industry, and the ex post facto supervision system with the transformation of government functions as the core in order to form an institutional innovation system linked with the general rules of international investment and trade; to give full play to the radiating role of key function-bearing areas such as finance and trade, advanced manufacturing, scientific and technological innovation; and to build a free-trade zone with the highest degree of openness, convenience for investment and trade, free currency exchange, efficient and convenient supervision, and standardised legal environment.
Second Batch (21 April 2015)	Tianjin Pilot Free-Trade Zone	With institutional innovation as the core task and replicability and promotion as basic requirements, it strives to become a high-level open platform for Beijing-Tianjin-Hebei coordinated development; a pilot area of national reform, opening up, and institutional innovation; and a high-level free-trade pilot area facing the world.
	Fujian Pilot Free-Trade Zone	Focussing on the strategic requirements of building a foothold on both sides of the Taiwan Strait; serving the whole country and facing the world; giving full play to the advantages of reform first, creating an international, market-oriented, and rule-of-law-based business environment; building the free-trade pilot area into a reform and innovation pilot field; giving full play to the advantages of Taiwan; taking the lead in promoting the process of investment and trade liberalisation with Taiwan; and building the free-trade pilot area into a deepening cross-strait economy. The Demonstration Zone of Economic Cooperation gives full play to the frontier advantage of opening up, builds the core area of the Twenty-First Century Maritime Silk Road, and creates a new highland of opening up and cooperation for countries and regions along the Twenty-First Century Maritime Silk Road.
	Guangdong Pilot Free-Trade Zone	Relying on Hong Kong and Macao, serving the mainland and facing the world, it aims to build the free-trade pilot area into a demonstration zone of deep cooperation among Guangdong, Hong Kong, and Macao, an important hub of the Twenty-First Century Maritime Silk Road and a pioneer of the new round of reform and opening up in China.
The Third Batch (31 March 2017)	Liaoning Pilot Free-Trade Zone	With system innovation as the core and replicability and popularisation as basic requirements, it aims to speed up the reform of the market-oriented system and mechanism, actively promote structural adjustment, and strive to build a pilot free-trade zone as a new engine to enhance the overall competitiveness of the old industrial bases in Northeast China and the level of opening up to the outside world.
	Zhejiang Pilot Free-Trade Zone	With institutional innovation as the core and replicability and promotion as basic requirements, the pilot free-trade zone will be built into an important demonstration area of open sea ports in eastern China, a pilot area of international commodity trade liberalisation, and a resource allocation base with international influence.

(Continued)

The mechanism of reversal pressure and the experiences 125

Table 7.2 (Continued)

Batch (Time)	Name	Strategic Positioning
	Henan Pilot Free-Trade Zone	With system innovation as the core and replicability and popularising as basic requirements, it aims to speed up the development of a modern three-dimensional transportation system and a modern logistics system connecting the north and south, the east and the west, and making the pilot free-trade zone into a modern, comprehensive transport hub serving the BRI, a full-scale reform and opening experimental field, and an inland open economic demonstration zone.
	Hubei Pilot Free-Trade Zone	With system innovation as the core and replicability and popularising as basic requirements, based in the central region, radiating to the entire country and to the world beyond, it strives to become a demonstration area for the orderly undertaking of an industrial transfer, a cluster area for strategic emerging industries and high-tech industries, a pilot field for comprehensive reform and opening up, and a new highland for inland opening up.
	Chongqing Pilot Free-Trade Zone	With institutional innovation as the core and replicability and popularising as basic requirements, it aims to fully implement the requirements of the CPC Central Committee and the State Council on giving play to the important role of Chongqing as a strategic fulcrum and junction, increasing the opening of the cities in the western regions, and building the pilot free-trade zone as an important hub for the connectivity of the BRI and the Yangtze River economic belt and an important fulcrum for the Strategy of Western Development.
	Sichuan Pilot Free-Trade Zone	With system innovation as the core and replicability and popularising as basic requirements, it aims to serve the entire country and face the world based on the inland system, connect the east and the west, and build the pilot free-trade zone into a leading area of development and opening up in a western port city, a pilot area of inland opening strategy, an international open channel hub, a new inland open economic highland, and a demonstration zone of coordinated opening of inland and coastal border rivers.
	Shaanxi Pilot Free-Trade Zone	With system innovation as the core and replicability and popularising as basic requirements, the requirements of the CPC Central Committee and the State Council should be fully implemented to give full play to the role of the BRI in the development of the western regions and the opening up of the cities in the western regions as important fulcrums of economic cooperation and people-to-people exchange.

Note: Table compiled by the authors based on data drawn from 'Zhongguo (Shanghai) ziyou maoyi shiyanqu zongti fang'an de tongzhi' ['The Notice of the General Plan of China (Shanghai) Pilot Free Trade Zone'] and 'Jinyibu shenhua Zhongguo (Shanghai) ziyou maoyi shiyanqu gaige kaifang fang'an' ['Further Deepening the Reform and Opening up Plan of China (Shanghai) Pilot Free Trade Zone'].

a good image of the government's willingness to reform and boost the national confidence in reform and can also try to promote the transformation of the financial and trade management system. Through this, China can also explore the feasible path of industrial upgrading, find the appropriate mode of integration of the East Asian economy and ultimately provide a reference for comprehensive

126 *Reglobalisation*

reform. On 2 December 2013, the People's Bank of China issued *Opinions on Financial Support for the Construction of China (Shanghai) Pilot Free Trade Zone*. The Shanghai Free Trade Zone was allowed to carry out pilot reforms in the areas of promoting cross-border use of the RMB, the convertibility of the RMB capital account, and the marketisation of interest rates and foreign exchange management, which marked the deepening of the financial reforms in the Shanghai Free Trade Zone. On 31 March 2017, the State Council issued *The Reform and Opening Up Plan for the Comprehensive Deepening of China's (Shanghai) Pilot Free Trade Zone*, signifying that the Shanghai Free Trade Zone had entered the 2.0 era. The plan clearly points out that the Shanghai Free Trade Zone should strengthen the system integration of the reform, build a comprehensive reform pilot area that combines openness and innovation, and speed up the convergence with international rules while also establishing a risk and stress testing area for an open economic system. It should transform the functions of the government and create a leading area to enhance governance abilities. It should also innovate cooperative development modes to build a bridgehead to serve the Belt and Road development and push market players to 'go global'. It must serve the overall situation of reform and opening up in the whole country and form more institutional innovations that can be replicated and promoted.[2] From the perspective of system innovation, China can draw up a roadmap to further the opening up of the market, integrate into economic globalisation and adjust the national economic development model by building the Shanghai Free Trade Zone, and explore a new model for promoting the linkage between domestic development and globalisation. The Shanghai Free Trade Zone is the frontier of China's connection with the new round of globalisation rules that can promote the incubation of reform and development modes with Chinese experience and characteristics and accumulate local experience to lead the reglobalisation process.[3]

7.2 'Development is the absolute principle': the global implications of China's experience

China's development achievements in the past 40 years of reform and opening up have brought about an unprecedented sea change for China and a great reversal of the historical coordinates for the world. China's rise is one of the most consequential historic events in our time. In many ways, Western theories have fallen short of fully explaining China's stunning rise. Faced with such dramatic changes in history, there is a need to theorise China's extraordinary experiences. At the beginning of the reform and opening up era, China's paramount leader Deng Xiaoping declared loudly, 'Development is the absolute principle! Practice is the sole criterion for testing truth'. China's top leaders believe that the basic issue for all humankind is to develop. Asian, African, and Latin American countries are at an important stage in which they are in urgent need of development experience and paths. These countries are eager to find a development path that is in line with their own national conditions. At

The mechanism of reversal pressure and the experiences 127

the beginning of its preamble, the 'United Nations Sustainable Development Agenda 21' solemnly points out,

> Humanity stands at a defining moment in history. We are confronted with a perpetuation of disparities between and within nations, a worsening of poverty, hunger, ill health and illiteracy, and the continuing deterioration of the ecosystems on which we depend for our well-being. However, integration of environment and development concerns and greater attention to them will lead to the fulfilment of basic needs, improved living standards for all, better protected and managed ecosystems and a safer, more prosperous future. No nation can achieve this on its own; but together we can – in a global partnership for sustainable development.[4]

As the first country in the world to achieve the goal of halving poverty, China has made outstanding contributions to world development. The global implications of China's development experience can be highlighted in two areas.

First, China should play a unique role as a bridge to facilitate the common development of developing countries. In the international arena, it has three identities, namely those of a major, developing, and non-Western country. These identities can serve as a bridge between the Global North and the Global South. On the one hand, in the multilateral frameworks of the United Nations Security Council, the United Nations General Assembly, and the G20, China helps urge developed countries to fulfil their North-South assistance obligations, playing the role of a 'promoter' of global public welfare. On the other hand, in South-South cooperation, China helps developing countries reduce poverty and pursue sustainable development. For example, at the Forum on China-Africa Cooperation, the Forum of China and the Community of Latin American and Caribbean States, and the China-ASEAN (10+1) Leaders' Meeting, China supports and encourages underdeveloped countries to participate in the process of China's economic development. In April 2015, President Xi Jinping made a solemn commitment at the commemorative activities of the 60th anniversary of the Asian and African Conference, also known as the Bandung Conference to give zero tariff treatment to 97% of the tax items of the least developed countries that have established diplomatic relations with China and to increase assistance without any political conditions attached; to share the development dividend of the BRI, the Asian Infrastructure Investment Bank (AIIB), and Silk Road Fund; and to provide 100,000 training spots to developing countries in Asia and Africa in the next 5 years. Sharing China's development experience through the construction of industrial parks is also an important means for China to play the role of the 'transmission belt'. By the end of 2016, Chinese enterprises had built 77 cooperative development zones in 36 countries with a total investment of $24.19 billion, 1,522 enterprises, a total output of $70.28 billion, and paid $2.67 billion in taxes and fees to host countries, which created 21.2 million jobs locally, and played an active role in promoting industrial upgrading in host countries and the development of bilateral economic

128 *Reglobalisation*

Table 7.3 Selected overseas industrial parks established by China

Name	Content
China-Belarus Industrial Park	The China-Belarus Industrial Park, initiated by the heads of state of China and Belarus, is a landmark project for the cooperation between the two countries to build the Silk Road Economic Belt, which is located at an important node extending from the Silk Road Economic Belt to Europe. The industrial park is the largest investment project in Belarus and the largest economic and technological cooperation project between China and Belarus, with an investment of about $5.6 billion, covering an area of 91.5 square kilometres. It focusses on the development of electronic information, biomedicine, fine chemicals, high-end |manufacturing, and other industries. The start-up area of the first phase of the industrial park was put into operation in June 2017.
Thai-Chinese Rayong Industrial Zone	Located in Rayong Prefecture on the east coast of Thailand, the park is one of China's first overseas economic and trade cooperation zones and China's first overseas industrial park to be developed in Thailand. The enterprises and projects of the park were welcomed locally. At present, more than 80 enterprises from China have invested in the park. The total investment of Chinese enterprises in the park exceeds $2.5 billion. This has created more than 20,000 jobs for the local people. More than 90% of the local staff work in the park, with an average monthly wage of RMB3,000.
Malaysia-China Kuantan Industrial Park	Together with the China-Malaysia Qinzhou Industrial Park, the Kuantan Industrial Park has become the first sister zone in the world to build industrial parks with each other, creating a new model of 'two countries and two parks'. Qinzhou Industrial Park has invested more than RMB3 billion in infrastructure. Currently at the Kuantan Industrial Park, more than 50 projects have decided to focus on the development of industries with traditional comparative advantages, such as iron and steel, aluminium deep processing, palm oil processing, etc., to accelerate the development of new industries, such as information and communication, electrical and electronic, and environmental protection industries, and to actively develop financial and insurance industries.
The Central European Trade and Logistics Cooperation Zone in Hungary	According to the planning of China's MOFCOM, the park is the first state-level overseas economic and trade cooperation zone and the first state-level logistics-based overseas economic and trade cooperation zone constructed in the European region in accordance with the model of 'one region and multiple parks'. With a total investment of USD 264 million US, the park has basically completed the planning, layout, and construction of 'one district, three parks'. The park has initially formed a distribution network system covering major cities in Europe and China, with an annual import and export volume of USD 245 million.

(Continued)

The mechanism of reversal pressure and the experiences   129

Table 7.3 (Continued)

Name	Content
China-Oman Al Duqm Industrial Park	On 19 April 2017, the founding ceremony of the park was held. It is the largest Industrial Park set up with the investment of foreign investors in Oman. The total investment of the proposed project in the park is RMB67 billion, including nine areas that include petrochemical industry, building materials, e-commerce, and so on. In April 2017, 10 Chinese enterprises from Ningxia, Hebei and other regions signed a residence agreement with a total investment of USD 3.2 billion. The signing contents include the bromine extraction project of desalination combined with production of seawater and the project of power station, etc.
Uzbekistan Pengsheng Industrial Park	The Industrial Park is located in Syr Darya State, Republic of Uzbekistan, with a total investment of about USD 90 million. It has become one of the successful examples of China's investment in private enterprises in Uzbekistan. By the end of 2015, the total number of employees in the park was over 1500, of which more than 1300 were employed locally, contributing to local economic growth and improvement of people's livelihoods. The Industrial Park intends to develop additional construction materials, leather products, electrical machinery, textiles, and other industries.
China-Kazakhstan Horgos International Border Cooperation Center	The cooperation centre covers cross-border economic and trade zones and regional cooperation projects established at the port of Horgos between China and Kazakhstan. It is the first international border cooperation centre established between China and other countries. From the official launch of the centre in April 2012 to the end of 2016, the number of people entering and leaving the centre exceeded 10 million, with a total investment of more than RMB20 billion. Nearly 30 projects have been stationed at the centre. Among these, 18 have begun construction, RMB6.27 billion of investment has been made, and more than 4000 businesses have settled in.
Cambodia Sihanoukville Port Special Economic Zone	The park is one of China's first overseas economic and trade cooperation zones approved by the Ministry of Commerce (MOFCOM) and the Ministry of Finance. It is a model for cooperation in China-Cambodia relations. After completion, it can accommodate 300 enterprises, with 100,000 industrial workers working in the park and 200,000 people living in a liveable new city. At present, land access, electricity, water, communications, sewage, and flat land have been basically realised in the 5 square kilometres area of Sihanoukville Port Special Economic Zone. More than 100 enterprises from China, Europe, the United States, Japan, South Korea, and other countries and regions have been stationed.
Zambia-China Economic and Trade Cooperation Zone	The zone is the first overseas economic and trade cooperation zone established by China in Africa and the first multifunctional economic zone announced by the Zambian government. The China Nonferrous Mining Group is responsible for the development, construction, operation, and management of the zone. Economic and trade cooperation zones are divided into two: the first planned area is 11.58 square kilometres, and the planned area of Lusaka Park is 5.7 square kilometres. Currently, nearly $1.4 billion has been attracted and over $1.2 billion has actually been invested.

Source: Data compiled by the authors.

130 *Reglobalisation*

and trade relations. The construction of the cooperation zones along the Belt and Road has achieved remarkable results (see Table 7.3).

Second, China pays attention to overall planning and adheres to the concept of sustainable development. In the early 1980s, the Chinese government put forward the strategic goal of three steps to achieve modernisation: first, from 1981 to 1990, the gross national product (GNP) would double to solve the problem of people's food and clothing; second, from 1991 to the end of the twentieth century, the GNP would double again, and the people's living standards will reach an affluent (*xiao kang*) level; and third, by the mid-twenty-first century, the GNP would quadruple, and the people will be relatively rich, reaching the level of moderately developed countries. In 1997, the Chinese government concretised the third strategic goal of the abovementioned three steps and put forward a new three-step development strategy for China for the first half of the twenty-first century: to double the GNP in the first decade of the twenty-first century when compared with 2000, and to make people's affluent lives more prosperous. China will become a relatively complete socialist market economy. After ten years of efforts, on the 100th birthday of the founding of the Communist Party of China, the national economy will be more developed, and various systems will attain a state of perfection; by the middle of the twenty-first century, on the 100th anniversary of the People's Republic of China (PRC), modernisation would be achieved and a prosperous, strong, democratic, and civilised socialist country would be built. Since entering the twenty-first century, China has put forward the strategic plan of building a well-off society in an all-round way (*quanmian jianshe xiaokang shehui*). Since 2012, the new leadership has clearly set fulfilling people's yearning for a better life as its governing goal, and further put forward the 'Two Hundred-Year' goal (*liangge bainian*). By 2020, on the 100th anniversary of the founding of the CPC, China will achieve the goal of the first Hundred-Years; that is, upon comprehensively solving the problem of food and clothing, the Chinese people should live a comparatively affluent life and should have already accomplished the goal of building a well-off society. By the middle of the twenty-first century, on the 100th birthday of the PRC, it will achieve the goal of its second hundred years, with per capita GDP reaching the level of that of moderately developed countries and thus realising the goal of building a 'prosperous, strong, democratic, civilised, and harmonious modern socialist country'.[5] In order to achieve the above goals, the Chinese government emphasises sustainable development and prioritises the development of an 'ecological civilisation' (*shengtai wenming*) with a vow to build a China that is not only economically well-off, but also environmentally friendly.

7.3 China promotes the new development of global governance

The provision of global public goods for development is a key goal of global governance. The United Nations 2030 Agenda for Sustainable Development contains 17 sustainable development goals (SDGs) and 169 related goals, one of which

The mechanism of reversal pressure and the experiences 131

is to advocate that the world strive to eradicate all forms of poverty and hunger, achieve equality and harmony by 2030, and ensure that no one is left behind. This is an extraordinarily comprehensive plan for human development and global governance, as well as a new goal for the domestic, regional, and global supply of public goods in various countries. China's participation in the supply of global public goods for development has a long history, especially when it comes to foreign aid, climate and ecological protection, and global health, which are three key areas in which China contributes to global governance.[6]

First, China adheres to aid on an equal footing. With the characteristics of global public goods, foreign aid is conducive to achieving the SDGs and can help to promote the balanced development of underdeveloped countries.[7] Over the past 60 years, China has assisted four-fifths of the less-developed countries in the world and has made important contributions toward promoting North-South equality. The South-South aid model initiated by China emphasises the principles of mutual aid and solidarity, common development, and noninterference in internal affairs, which can be viewed as a kind of horizontal aid with mutual respect and on an equal footing.[8] The idea of aid on an equal footing is best embodied in the 'Eight Principles of Foreign Economic and Technical Assistance' put forward by China in 1964.[9] China not only pays attention to respecting the equal status of recipient countries, but also encourages them to develop independently from its own experiences with development and poverty alleviation. In April 2016, the Institute of South-South Cooperation and Development at Peking University was officially established. Mid-career and senior officials and leaders of nongovernment organisations (NGOs) from 27 developing countries in Africa, South and Central Asia, the Middle East, and Latin America came together to learn from China's development experiences.[10] Many developing countries believed that the paths that China had just walked over the past 30 years was what they were about to face. China has become a model for learning and serves as a reference for other developing countries.[11]

Second, important progress has been made in promoting global climate governance. It is all the more commendable that China, as a developing country burdened with the task of industrialisation and economic modernisation, is willing to commit to combating climate change, even at the expense of its economic growth rate, thus making valuable contributions to global environmental governance. According to a report released in September 2016 by the Chinese Ministry of Foreign Affairs on China's plan to implement the UN 2030 Agenda for Sustainable Development, after years of effort, China's per unit GDP carbon dioxide emissions in 2014 decreased by 33.8% when compared with 2005 and the forest stock increased by 2.681 billion cubic metres when compared with 2005, all of which have contributed toward zero growth of desertification ahead of time.[12] It is not easy for a rapidly industrialising country with a population of 1.4 billion. Faced with rising expectations of the international community, China, while optimising its development structure, is actively making contributions to global climate governance.[13] For example, it was one of the first countries to sign the Paris Accord, and promoted its ratification jointly with the United States during the

132 *Reglobalisation*

G20 Hangzhou Summit,[14] setting off a Chinese-style 'green wave'. China is also actively using the platform of the BRI, G20, and the BRICS (Brazil, Russia, India, China and South Africa) to provide public goods in global climate governance. In November 2015, President Xi Jinping announced at the opening ceremony of the Paris Conference on Climate Change that China will launch 10 low-carbon demonstration zones, 100 climate mitigation and adaptation projects, and 1,000 cooperation projects on climate change training in developing countries through the so-called '10-100-1000 Plan'. It has also been announced that China will establish a $3.1 billion China South-South Climate Change Cooperation Fund.[15] At the G20 Summit in Hangzhou in 2016, China took the lead in creating the G20 Energy Ministers Meeting Beijing Communique, the Enhancing Energy Access in the Asia and the Pacific: Key Challenges and G20 Voluntary Collaboration Action Plan, the G20 Voluntary Action Plan on Renewable Energy, and the G20 Energy Efficiency Leadership Program, which raised the level of climate governance to new heights and won high appraise and wide recognition from the international community.[16]

Since the new leadership took office in 2012, China's supply of environmental public goods has taken on new features. First, Beijing set up clear domestic objectives and has strictly enforced environmental law and regulations. A series of laws and regulations were passed between 2012 and 2017, such as the Action Plan for Air Pollution Prevention and Control, the Action Plan for Water Pollution Prevention and Control, and the Action Plan for Soil Pollution Prevention and Control. At the same time, the new Environmental Protection Law, billed as 'the most stringent Environmental Protection Law in the history of China', has been implemented since 2015, with unprecedented enforcement and supervision.[17] Guided by the ideal of green development, the energy consumption and water consumption per GDP unit of China's economy in 2016 were 17.9% and 25.4%, respectively, lower than those in 2012. The effect of reduced emissions of major pollutants is remarkable.[18] Second, China has played a leading role in launching green initiatives on the multilateral stage. At the Paris Climate Conference, President Xi Jinping announced China's new support programme for developing countries, namely the '10-100-1000 Plan'.[19] At the same time, China took the lead in signing the Paris Accord and submitted an aggressive plan for 'nationally determined contributions' (NDCs). Third, China focussed on the development and innovation of new energy and building a sustainable society. Of the installed capacity of 76 gigawatts (GW) of new energy in the world in 2011, China contributed 31 gigawatts, ranking first in the world for four consecutive years.[20] At the same time, it is also the largest investor in new energy in the world. During the period of the 12th Five-Year Plan (2011–2015), China's proportion of the installed capacity of nonfossil energy increased from 27% in 2010 to 35% in 2015, exceeding the planned target. In 2016, China's growth of installed capacity of coal power slowed down significantly, while the newly installed capacity of nuclear, wind, and solar power grew substantially.[21]

Finally, the shortcomings in global health governance need to be remedied. For a long time, there has been a widening gap between the Global North and the

The mechanism of reversal pressure and the experiences 133

Global South in the distribution of global public health resources.[22] According to the World Health Organization (WHO), the child mortality rate in low-income countries was about 8% in 2012, 13 times higher than that in high-income countries. Reproductive health service coverage in these low-income countries is only 46%, less than half of that in almost all high-income countries. In addition, 70% of the newly infected human immunodeficiency virus (HIV) patients live in sub-Saharan Africa.[23]

At the same time, the problem of the fragmentation and decentralisation of the global health governance system has become increasingly prominent.[24] For China, with a dense population of 1.4 billion and a massive population flow, the risk of infectious disease epidemics is huge and the prevention and control of an epidemic, should it break out, will be extremely challenging. However, in this unfavourable environment, China has made positive contributions to domestic and international health governance. For example, after years of efforts, China has established one of the largest medicare systems in the world and plans to exceed all the targets of the United Nations Agenda for 2030. The Chinese government has promised to reduce the maternal mortality rate to 12/100,000 by 2030, which will be significantly less than the target of 70/100,000 set by the UN Agenda for 2030. As for the prevention and control of pathogens, the National Action Plan on Antimicrobial Resistance (2016–2020), issued by the Chinese government in 2016, is considered by the WHO as a turning point in human efforts to cope with antibiotic resistance. As a WHO official put it, 'without China playing a leading role, the global war on antibiotic resistance will be difficult to win'.[25] In recent years, China's health diplomacy has been making remarkable progress. It has set high standards for both domestic and global public health undertakings. While giving full play to the advantages of traditional health governance, it also highlights two new changes.

On the one hand, China is engaging in regional health cooperation across the Belt and Road. To promote the prevention and control of infectious diseases, health system reform, health capacity-building, and talent cooperation in countries along the routes, China has promoted the publication of the Prague Declaration on Health Cooperation and Development between China and Central and Eastern European Countries, the Suzhou Joint Communique of the Second Forum of Health Ministers between China and Central and Eastern European Countries, the Nanning Declaration on China-ASEAN Health Cooperation and Development, and other multilateral communiques. China has also implemented 41 projects, such as the China-Africa Public Health Cooperation Plan and the China-ASEAN Health Personnel Training Plan. Through multilateral and bilateral cooperation, China and the countries along the Belt and Road routes have actively expanded exchanges and cooperation in the field of traditional Chinese medicine. At the time of writing, 43 overseas centres of traditional Chinese medicine (TCM), such as the China-Czech TCM Center, have been established, and TCM cooperation agreements have been signed with 35 countries.[26] On the other hand, China is actively expanding soft health assistance,[27] which has the advantages of going deep into the grassroots level and being close to the people. It is

134   *Reglobalisation*

more conducive to accumulating the 'soft power' of a country. In global health governance, emerging economies, such as China and India, lead the South-South cooperation model in international aid, which emphasises the role of 'soft aid' for health and pays attention to individual health support. Within the framework of the China-Africa Cooperation Forum, China has helped Africa build 89 hospitals and 30 malaria control centres since 2007, and has provided antimalarial drugs valued at RMB190 million, as well as a large number of other medical equipment and medicines.[28] China has been sending medical teams to Africa since 1963 and takes a serious and responsible attitude in curing diseases and rescuing people, serving the general public, bringing great changes to the lives of patients in poor areas, and winning wide praise from the African people.[29]

The outbreak of the COVID-19 pandemic in January 2020 has caused tremendous loss of life and disruption of economies across the world, putting humankind on the edge of an unprecedented global depression, heretofore unseen in decades. In response to the call to combat the common threat, China joined hands with the international community to fight COVID-19, an enemy that holds no regard for border, race, or ideology. On 26 March 2020, President Xi Jinping attended a G20 leaders' virtual summit to advance a coordinated response to the deadly coronavirus disease and its huge human, social, and economic implications. In addition, he had made phone calls with many heads of state and international organisations to coordinate bilateral and multilateral measures to fight the COVID-19 pandemic. During his phone call with UN Secretary-General Antonio Guterres, President Xi Jinping noted that the pandemic had 'demonstrated that mankind is a community with a shared future that share weal and woe', adding that 'in the era of economic globalisation, COVID-19 will not be the world's last major emergency, and various traditional and non-traditional security issues will constantly bring about new tests'.[30] In demonstration of solidarity with the world, the Chinese government announced that it was going to provide emergency assistance including testing kits, masks, and other medical supplies for 83 countries as well as international and regional organisations, including the WHO and the African Union. The National Health Commission and the Red Cross Society of China have sent expert teams to Italy, Spain, Iran, Iraq, Serbia, Pakistan, Cambodia, Laos, Venezuela, and other countries that have been severely affected by the pandemic.[31] From 1 March to 4 April 2020, China exported major epidemic prevention and control materials worth RMB10.2 billion, including about 3.86 billion masks worth RMB7.72 billion, 37.52 million protective suits worth RMB910 million, 2.41 million infrared thermometers worth RMB330 million, 16,000 ventilators worth RMB310 million, 2.84 million COVID-19 testing kits, and 8.41 million pairs of goggles.[32] The Chinese Centre for Disease Control and Prevention shared the complete genome sequences of three viruses with the world. Research teams rapidly published papers in leading international academic journals, which established a scientific basis for identifying the source and route of infection and for developing prevention and control strategies.

The mechanism of reversal pressure and the experiences   135

Chinese enterprises worked around-the-clock to supply the international market with drugs in bulk, daily necessities, and epidemic prevention supplies. For instance, Huawei donated epidemic prevention supplies and medical equipment to Japan, Italy, the United States, Bangladesh, Zambia, and Iraq. Both the Jack Ma and Alibaba Foundations have donated medical supplies including masks and testing kits to Japan, South Korea, Iran, Italy, Spain, the United States, Afghanistan, Bangladesh, Cambodia, Laos, Maldives, Mongolia, Myanmar, Nepal, Pakistan, Sri Lanka, 54 African countries including Ethiopia, and 24 Latin American countries including Argentina.[33]

China also supported the UN and the WHO in fulfilling their mandates in improving global public health governance, cooperated with other countries to build a community of common health for humankind, and provided a roadmap for global health governance. China quickly released the Protocol on Prevention and Control of COVID-19 (as of writing, the pamphlet had been updated to the sixth edition) to share its experience with the world and to enhance exchange and collaboration with other countries in drug research, virus strain isolation, vaccine development, and epidemic prevention. China proposed reliance on the WHO to enhance information sharing on epidemic prevention and control and to promote comprehensive, systematic, and effective prevention and control guidelines. China suggested that all countries should jointly explore and establish a regional public health emergency liaison mechanism, accelerate the response to public health emergencies, and hold high-level meetings on global public health security. Through virtual meetings such as webinars, China Association for Science and Technology (CAST) had organised international academic exchanges with 208 international organisations and foreign institutions to help diffuse knowledge and to develop shared an understanding and response to the unprecedented spread of COVID-19.[34]

Notes

1 Lu Nan, '"Gaige cujin kaifang" yihuo "kaifang daobi gaige"' ['"Reform Promotes Openness" or "Opening Puts Reversal Pressure on Reform"'], *Wenhua zongheng* [*Beijing Cultural Review*], No. 6, 2013, pp. 74–76.

2 Xinhua News Agency, 'Guowuyuan yinfa 'Quanmian shenhua Zhongguo (Shanghai) ziyou maoyi shiyanqu gaige kaifang fang'an' ['The State Council Issued the Reform and Opening-up Plan for China (Shanghai) Pilot Free Trade Zone'], Xinhuanet.com, 31 March 2017, http://www.xinhuanet.com/politics/2017-03/31/c_1120732782.htm.

3 Zheng Yongnian and Wang Luyao, 'Quanqiu jingji xinguize xia de zimaoqu shiyan' ['Free Trade Zone Experiments under the New Rules of the Global Economy'], *Wenhua zongheng* [*Beijing Cultural Review*], No. 6, 2013, pp. 60–67.

4 United Nations, 'United Nations Sustainable Development Agenda 21', United Nations Conference on Environment & Development, Rio de Janerio, Brazil, 3–14 June 1992, https://sustainabledevelopment.un.org/content/documents/Agenda21.pdf.

5 The Commentator of Xinhua News Agency, 'Wei shixian "liangge bainian" fendou mubiao er nuli' ['Striving for Realization of the Goal of 'Two Hundred-Year'], Xinhuanet.com, 31 July 2017, http://www.xinhuanet.com/politics/2017-07/31/c_112 1409397.htm.

6 The Ministry of Foreign Affairs of China and the United Nations System in China, *Report on China's Implementation of the Millennium Development Goals (2000-2015)*,

136 Reglobalisation

July 2015, https://www.cn.undp.org/content/china/en/home/library/mdg/mdgs-report-2015-.html.

7 Jiang Mozhu, 'Pengyou yu liyi: guoji gonggong chanpin shijiao xia de Zhongguo duiwai yuanzhu' ['Friends and Interests: China's Foreign Aid from the Perspective of International Public Goods'], *Dongbeiya luntan* [*Northeast Asia Forum*], No. 5, 2016, pp. 40–49.

8 Pang Xun, 'Xinxing yuanzhuguo de 'xing' yu 'xin': chuizhishi yu shuiping fanshi de shizheng bijiao yanjiu' ['The Rise and Breakthroughs of Emerging Donor Countries: An Empirical Comparative Study on the Vertical and Horizontal Paradigms'], *Shijie jingji yu zhengzhi* [*World Economy and Politics*], No. 5, 2013, pp. 31–54.

9 The Eight Principles of Foreign Economic and Technical Assistance were put forward by Chinese Premier Zhou Enlai during his visit to Ghana in 1964. The specific contents are as follows: the two sides of assistance are equal and mutually beneficial; the sovereignty of the recipient country is strictly observed without any conditions or privileges; economic assistance is provided in the form of interest-free or low-interest loans; helping the recipient country become self-reliant and achieve independent development is a priority; projects assisted in the construction industry are aimed at moderate investment with quick returns; China provides the best quality equipment and materials it can produce and negotiates prices based on international market prices; any technical assistance provided comes with assurances that the recipient country's personnel fully grasp this technology; experts dispatched enjoy the same material treatment as their own experts in recipient countries. See Zhou Enlai, 'Zhongguo zhengfu duiwai jingji jishu yuanzhu de baxiang yuanzhu' [Eight Principles of the Chinese Government's Foreign Economic and Technical Assistance], January 1964, in the Ministry of Foreign Affairs of the PRC and the Documentation Research Office of CPC CC eds., *Zhou Enlai waijiao wenxuan* [*Selected Diplomatic Works of Zhou Enlai*], Beijing, China: Central Documentation Publishing House, 1990, pp. 388–389.

10 Ji Peijuan et. al, 'Zai Zhongguo, women zengqiang le fazhan xinxin' ['In China, We Have Increased Our Confidence in Development'], People.cn, 17 April 2017, http://world.people.com.cn/n1/2017/0417/c1002-29214338.html.

11 China International Economic Exchange Center and the United Nations Development Program, 'Chonggou quanqiuzhili: youxiaoxing, baorongxing ji Zhongguo de quanqiu juese' ['*Reconfiguring Global Governance: Effectiveness, Inclusiveness and China's Global Role*'], *Report of the 2013 High-level Policy Forum on Global Governance*, August 2013, p. 28.

12 Ministry of Foreign Affairs of the PRC, *Zhongguo luoshi 2030 nian kechixu fazhan yicheng: guobie fang'an* [*China's National Plan on Implementing the 2030 Agenda for Sustainable Development*], September 2016, https://www.fmprc.gov.cn/web/ziliao_674904/zt_674979/dnzt_674981/qtzt/2030kcxfzyc_686343/P020161012715836816237.pdf, pp. 3–4.

13 Ministry of Foreign Affairs, *China's Position Paper on Implementing the 2030 Agenda for Sustainable Development*, 22 April 2016, https://www.fmprc.gov.cn/web/ziliao_674904/zt_674979/dnzt_674981/qtzt/2030kcxfzyc_686343/t1357699.shtml.

14 On the afternoon of 3 September 2016, President Xi Jinping, US President Barack Obama, and UN Secretary-General Ban Ki-moon jointly attended the ceremony for the deposit of instruments by China and the United States to join the Paris Accord on Climate Change in Hangzhou. However, on 1 June 2017, US President Donald Trump unilaterally announced US withdrawal from the Paris Accord.

15 Xinhua News Agency, 'Xin Jinping zai qihou bianhua Bali dahui kaimushi shang de jianghua' ['Xi Jinping's Speech at the Opening Ceremony of the Paris Conference on Climate Change'], Xinhuanet.com, 1 December 2015, http://news.xinhuanet.com/world/2015-12/01/c-1117309642.htm.

The mechanism of reversal pressure and the experiences 137

16 Chen Weiwei, 'G20 chengyuanguo jiang licu kezaisheng nengyuan fazhan' ['G20 Member States will Promote Renewable Energy Development'], Xinhua News Agency, 1 July 2016, http://www.xinhuanet.com/energy/2016-07/01/c_1119144665.htm.

17 Xu Yang and Sun Renbin, 'Zhongguo shishi "shishang zuiyan" huanbaofa, kaiqi yifa zhiwu xinjiyuan' [China Implements the Most Stringent Environmental Protection Law, Unleashing the New Epoch of Regulating Pollution According to Law], Xinhuanet .com, 1 January 2015, http://www.xinhuanet.com/politics/2015-01/01/c_1113849 726.htm.

18 Hou Xuejing and Gao Jing, 'Tuijin meili Zhongguo jianshe: dang de shibada yilai shengtai wenming jianshe chengjiu zongshu' ['Promoting the Development of a Beautiful China: Summary of the Achievements in the Construction of Ecological Civilization since the Eighteenth National Congress of the CPC'], Xinhua News Agency, 12 August 2017, http://news.xinhuanet.com/politics/2017-08/12/c-1121473465.htm.

19 Gan Junxian, 'Zhongguo yu quanqiu qihou anquan zhili xin jinzhan yu xin qianjing (2013-2015)' ['New Progress and Prospects of Climate Security Governance in China and the World (2013-2015)'], Yu Xiaofeng, et al., eds., *Zhongguo feichuantong anquan yanjiu baogao (2015-2016) [Report on China's Non-traditional Security Research (2015-2016)]*, Beijing, China: Social Sciences Academic Press, 2016, pp. 174–188.

20 Raj Prabhu, 'Mercom Forecasts 76 GW in Global Solar Installations in 2016, a 48% Year on Year Increase over 2015', 26 November 2016, https://mercomindia.com/m ercom-forecasts-76-gw-global-solar-installations-2016-48-yoy-increase-2015/.

21 Huang Xiaoyong, et al., 'Shijie nengyuan fazhan xianzhuang, weilai qushi ji Zhongguo de nengyuan fazhan zhanlue' [The Current Situation and Future Trend of Global Energy and China's Energy Development Strategy], in Cui Minxuan and Huang Xiaoyong, eds., *Shijie nengyuan fazhan xianzhuang, weilai qushi ji Zhongguo de nengyuan fazhan zhanlue [The Current Situation and Future Trend of Global Energy and China's Energy Development Strategy]*, Beijing: Social Sciences Academic Press, 2017, pp. 1–91.

22 Alan Ingram, 'The New Geopolitics of Disease: Between Global Health and Global Security', *Geopolitics*, Vol. 10, No. 3, 2005, pp. 522–545.

23 World Health Organization, 'WHO/UNICEF Highlight Need to Further Reduce Gaps in Access to Improved Drinking Water and Sanitation', 8 May 2014, https://www.who .int/mediacentre/news/notes/2014/jmp-report/en/.

24 Colin McInnes, 'WHO's Next? Changing Authority in Global Health Governance after Ebola', *International Affairs*, Vol. 91, No. 6, 2015, pp. 1299–1316.

25 Bernhard Schwartländer, 'China Can Help Stop Misuse of Antibiotics', World Health Organization, 22 September 2016, https://www.who.int/china/news/detail/22-09-2016 -china-can-help-stop-misuse-of-antibiotics.

26 Office of the Leading Group for Promoting the Belt and Road Initiative, *The Belt and Road Initiative: Progress, Contributions and Prospects*, pp. 29–30.

27 Soft aid refers to nonmaterial and non-financial support, focussing on technical, human, and capacity-building support. See Song Yantao and Wei Xuan, 'Zhongguo duiwai yuanzhu zhong de "ruan yuanzhu" tanjiu' ['Exploration of "Soft Aid" in China's Foreign Aid'], *Shandong keji daxue xuebao [Journal of Shandong University of Science and Technology (Social Science Edition)]*, No. 6, 2012, pp. 86–91.

28 Li Anshan, 'Zhong Fei yiliao hezuo 50 nian: chengjiu, tiaozhan yu weilai' ['50 Years of China-Africa Medical Cooperation: Achievements, Challenges and the Future'], in the Center for Global Health Research at Peking University, ed., *Quanqiu weisheng shidai Zhong Fei weisheng hezuo yu guojia xingxiang [The Image of China-Africa Health Cooperation and Countries in the Age of Global Health]*, Beijing, China: World Affairs Publishing House, 2012, pp. 9–26.

29 Peilong Liu, et al., 'China's Distinctive Engagement in Global Health', *The Lancet*, Vol. 384, No. 9945, August/September 2014, pp. 793–804.

138 *Reglobalisation*

30 Xinhua News Agency, 'Xi Talks with UN Chief, calling for Urgent International Action against COVID-19', People.cn, 13 March 2020, http://en.people.cn/n3/2020/0313/c9 0000-9667730.html.

31 Tenghan, 'Zhongguo yi xuanbu xiang 83 ge guojia tigong yuanzhu, zhichi guoji she-hui kangyi' ['China Has Announced to Offer Help to 83 Countries and International Organizations, Supporting the International Community to Fight the Pandemic'], China.com, 26 March 2020, https://news.china.com/socialgd/10000169/20200326/3 7979563.html.

32 The Joint Prevention and Control Mechanism of the State Council, 'Guowuyuan lian-fang liankong jizhi 4 yue 5 ri xinwen fabuhui' ['The April 5 Press Conference of the State Council Joint Prevention and Control Mechanism'], www.gov.cn, 5 April 2020, http://www.gov.cn/xinwen/gwylflkjz82/index.htm.

33 Jack Ma Foundation, '3 yue gongyi yuebao' ['Monthly Public Welfare Report (March)'], 3 April 2020. https://www.mayun.xin/index.html#/topic-detail/19334.

34 Liu Li, 'Zhongguo kexie huyu shijie gongjian zhongda chuanran jibing yufang tixi' ['CAST Appealed to the World to Build a Major Infectious Diseases Prevention System'] Gmw.cn, 6 April 2020, https://tech.gmw.cn/2020-04/07/content_33720408 .htm.

8 Embracing the era of reglobalisation

Although Dao is near, it can't be reached without you getting there; though things are small, they can't be done without your action.

Xunzi: Self-Cultivation

We should stick to an open development concept and make economic globalisation more open, inclusive, and balanced so that its benefits are shared by all.

President Xi Jinping's Remarks at the Boao
Forum for Asia Annual Conference, April
2018

As an emerging country, China has long enjoyed the dividends of the late-starter advantage and has benefited a lot from globalisation, such as the introduction of modern technology, drawing lessons from international management experience, learning from market economic systems, formulating free-trade rules, promoting freedom of navigation, and stabilising the international security situation. China's rise has benefited from the development dividend of global public goods.[1] However, it is impossible for the international community to allow China to be a free-rider forever, especially when the global order is chaotic and China's own strength is significantly enhanced; China will be expected to play a leading role. At the critical juncture of globalisation and global governance, China needs to seize the opportunity and make full use of it. For China, opportunities and challenges coexist in the process of reglobalisation.

8.1 China's advantage in leading reglobalisation

The international community seems confident of China's rise in 2030. Experts have pointed out that even in the case of slow growth, China's gross domestic product (GDP) growth rate can still reach 6.2%, 5.3%, and 4.3% annually in the three periods of 2015–2020, 2021–2025, and 2026–2030.[2] According to this estimate, in the Fourteenth Five-Year Plan period (2021–2025), China will cross the 'middle-income trap' and enter the ranks of high-income countries. Justin Yifu Lin, a top Chinese economist who has served as the Chief Economist of the World

140 *Reglobalisation*

Bank, also predicted that China's economy will be the largest in the world by 2030. After 2030, the gap between China and other developed countries will narrow significantly. China will enter the ranks of developed countries, and the centre of the world economy will shift to China.[3] A more optimistic forecast predicts that by 2030, China's total economic output will reach $66.4 trillion, equivalent to twice the total economic output of the United States at that time. China will also rank first in terms of research and development (R&D) investment, technology exports, talent, science and technology, and cultural strength in 2030. Similarly, the US National Intelligence Council has calculated a global power index based on GDP, population, military expenditure, and scientific and technological prowess to assess the growth and decline of great powers. The results of this index system show that China will be on the path to becoming the world's most powerful country in the next 20 to 30 years and will surpass the United States by 2030. The National Intelligence Council later adjusted the power index, adding three new indicators: health, education, and governance. The system is more comprehensive, and the forecast results show that China will become the world's most powerful country by 2040.[4] These predictions and indicators show that after decades of development, China has achieved what it took other countries a few centuries to accomplish.[5] The success of China's development reveals its great potential, of which three points are most prominent.

First, in the construction of large-scale infrastructure, China gives full play to its technological and cost advantages. Undoubtedly, the construction of roads, bridges, canals, and ports will lay the foundation for future Asian economic development and prosperity. China has significant advantages in terms of infrastructure development. On the one hand, it has the world's cutting-edge technology in large-scale infrastructure construction, with rich experience in large-scale construction projects.[6] For example, China is the world's largest producer of renewable energy. Its hydropower technology is very mature, and the allocation capacity of domestic hydropower facilities has ranked first in the world for a long time.[7] For example, China has the longest high-speed railway network in the world. By the end of 2016, China's high-speed railway operation mileage had exceeded 20,000 kilometres, accounting for about 65% of the world's total.[8] On the other hand, China's technology and labour costs are relatively low, and the comparative advantage of exporting large-scale infrastructure construction projects is obvious.[9] In terms of scale and quality, China's leading 'super projects' can be roughly listed as follows.

- China has established the largest floating solar power plant in the world. It generates 40 megawatts of electricity as opposed to the previous world record of only 6.3 megawatts, which fully demonstrates China's technological prowess in wind, hydro, and solar power.
- China has completed its super telescope projects. Since 2016, it has been building the world's largest telescope, the Five-Hundred-Metre Aperture Spherical Telescope (FAST). The project is located in a naturally formed depression in Guizhou Province in southwestern China. It is much larger than

the previous and the world's first Arecibo telescope (with an aperture of 305 metres) and can effectively receive the deepest radio waves in the universe. Radio waves will play a very important role in space exploration.

- China is planning to build a super collider. The European Organization for Nuclear Research (CERN) has built the world's largest and most energetic Large Hadron Collider, developed by more than 10,000 scientists and engineers from 10 countries. China is planning to build a collider with a perimeter of 50–100 kilometres, which will generate seven times as much energy as that of CERN.
- China is working on the South-North Water Transfer Project and the Three Gorges Dam Project. The total water transportation mileage of the South-North Water Transfer Project is 4,350 kilometres, and 44.8 billion cubic metres of water resources are transferred every year. It ranks first in the world in terms of water transportation capacity and mileage. The Three Gorges Dam Project is the largest hydroelectric power project in the world. It took 12 years to complete. The cumulative power generation exceeded 1 trillion kWh, setting many world records in the field of hydroelectricity.
- China's Cross-Sea Bridge Project is a major advancement. The Hong Kong-Zhuhai-Macao Bridge is 55 kilometres long. It integrates bridges, islands, and tunnels. It is the longest cross-sea bridge in the world with the longest steel structure bridge body and the longest submarine tunnel.
- China is engaged in the development of space technology such as quantum satellites and Mars probes. Its first probe landed on the moon in 2013 and then launched the world's first quantum science experimental satellite, Mozi, in August 2016, to achieve space-to-ground quantum key distribution, enabling secure network communication between multiple nodes; this was hailed as a milestone in science.[10]

Second, China's development experience can provide new ideas for developing countries. China has multiple identities. It is not only a rising power but also a developing country. It is currently experiencing the stage of industrialisation and postindustrialisation almost at the same time. The coexistence of this ladder-like development has provided China with sufficient experience to cope with the development gap.[11] For example, China is committed to sharing its experiences and knowledge in agriculture and poverty relief and alleviation with many developing countries. In Tanzania, Chinese-assisted hybrid rice technology yields 9–12 tonnes per hectare, four times higher than the yield of traditional local planting techniques.[12] Owing to the complexity in its national conditions, China has taken a stepwise and gradualist approach to reform and opening up. Since reform and opening up began in 1978, China has adopted this approach by accumulating experiences through pilot projects before carrying out every large-scale reform measure. Prominent examples include the rural household responsibility contract system pilot project, Shenzhen Special Economic Zone reform pilot project, the coastal urban belt for opening up pilot project, and the Shanghai Free Trade Zone pilot project. This gradualist approach helps to accumulate replicable and

142 Reglobalisation

extendable experience in institutional innovation, connect national conditions with international rules effectively, and reduce the risk that comes with reform. China has presently established free-trade zone pilot projects from the south to the north and from the east to the west.[13] The unprecedented scale of China's processes of modernisation, industrialisation, and urbanisation will solve a series of major development problems. These experiences and practices are important points of reference for developing countries working to generate growth and bring about prosperity.[14]

In August 2017, the Center for International Knowledge on Development (CIKD) was established as an important platform for China to share expertise and produce knowledge on development with the international community. Actively carrying out research on development and promoting international academic exchanges, the CIKD has compiled and studied representative cases in China's development process and has systematically summarised the experience of modernisation concerning national governance capacity, pilot SEZs, poverty alleviation, etc. (see Table 8.1).[15] Prior to that, in April 2016, the Institute of South-South Cooperation and Development was officially launched at Peking University, one of China's most prestigious universities. In addition to sharing development experience, the institute aims to enhance developing countries' capacity to implement sustainable development goals (SDGs) by providing academic degrees and graduate education programmes. China took measures to help form an international research community on global governance. To promote the development of high-quality research institutions and to increase the supply of regional and global public goods, China is exploring the establishment of an extended network of high-quality public knowledge centres, research institutions, and think tanks across the globe. When scholars gather, new governance schemes and technological innovations may emerge, and knowledge diffusion will take place.[16]

Third, China has great potential in emerging fields of technology such as the internet, artificial intelligence (AI), big data analysis, and so on. According to some estimates, China will build the world's largest broadband network and information infrastructure system by 2030 with the world's largest information society and the largest population covered by IT.[17] China leads in both digital economy and internet consumption because of its huge population and vast market. Today, the world's internet enterprises are divided into those in China and those in the United States. Baidu, Alibaba, Tencent, and JD.com (BATJ) are among the top 10 internet companies in the world, accounting for almost half the world's internet consumption. The internet giants represented by BATJ have vigorously promoted the research and development of AI by virtue of their massive data advantages. For example, Baidu set up a research institute focussing on AI to develop 'Baidu Brain', an open AI technological platform; Alibaba launched an intelligent robot customer service platform in the area of AI focussing on cloud computing, which opened the first domestic AI computing platform, DT PAI; and Tencent launched a writing robot, Dreamwriter, and established an AI laboratory in 2016.

Embracing the era of reglobalisation 143

Table 8.1 Projects by the Center for International Knowledge on Development

Projects	Contents
Research on the Development Experience of China's Industrial Parks	Summarises the development experience of China's industrial parks. The World Bank provides the data on Pakistan, the United Nations Industrial Development Organization provides the data on Ethiopia, and the European Bank for Reconstruction and Development provides the data on Belarus.
Silk Road Think Tank Network (SiLKS)	Works with SiLKS members and partners to carry out thematic research on the Belt and Road Initiative (BRI).
Seminar on Experiences and Cases of China's Development for Developing Countries	A total of 447 officials and scholars from 94 countries have been trained for 14 consecutive years. The training includes China's basic national conditions and development experiences, policies, systems, and planning, etc. It also enables trainees to visit various parts of China for research.
Sustainable Development of Children	Works with the United Nations International Children's Emergency Fund (UNICEF) to promote sustainable development for children in China and the Belt and Road countries. Research focusses on three areas: summarising and disseminating China's experience in child nutrition and health; carrying out studies on early childhood development in Asia; and monitoring the progress of sustainable development goals related to children in all countries along the BRI.
China's Implementation of the UN's 2030 Agenda for Sustainable Development	The report was published in 2019, in cooperation with China's Ministry of Foreign Affairs. It reviewed the progress that China has made in implementing the 2030 Agenda, summarised typical cases, and proposed guidelines and goals for the next phase.
Research on Transformation of Global Development Governance and China's Responsibility	To be released in cooperation with the UK Department for International Development and other agencies.
Research on Humanitarian Assistance	To be released in cooperation with the UK Department for International Development and other agencies.
Research on the Belt and Road Initiative and the China-Indochina Peninsula Economic Corridor	To be released in cooperation with the Asian Development Bank and other institutions.

Source: Compiled by the authors with data from the official website of China's Center for International Knowledge on Development, http://www.cikd.org/english/.

144 *Reglobalisation*

8.2 The China plan in the age of reglobalisation

A roadmap can be envisioned for China to engage in leading the reglobalisation process. From the perspective of public goods provision, China has a major role to play. First, by 2020, China will focus on consolidating and upgrading the existing regional public goods and domestic public goods initiatives. These efforts can help boost the Belt and Road Initiative (BRI) and connect it with the United Nations (UN) 2030 Agenda, strengthen domestic air pollution governance and environmental protection, and establish an East Asian cooperation mechanism on disaster prevention and an early warning system. Second, in the ten years from 2020 to 2030, the focus of public goods provision is to accelerate the implementation of the UN Agenda 2030, to further consolidate regional public goods, and to plan investment in global public goods. For example, we can envision building a regional if not global high-speed railway network, an Asia-Pacific Free Trade Zone, a world electronic trade and payment platform, and a global research and development centre for big data. At this stage, we can bring into play the advantages of traditional projects and emerging technologies of China's infrastructure and expand regional cooperation to the global level. Third, in the 20 years from 2030 to 2050, China will successfully accomplish the goals of the 'Two Hundred-Year' plan, ranking first in influence and strength at the global level. At that time, the world may face more fragmentation and diversification of governance problems. China, along with other stakeholders, can play a leading role in preventing large-scale natural disasters, dealing with astronomical disasters, such as asteroid impacts on Earth and solar storms, promoting the establishment of norms for global cyberspace order and AI, establishing lunar and Mars experimental stations in aerospace, and strengthening cross-border joint research and development.

The short-, medium-, and long-term vision in time, combined with the domestic, regional, and global levels of supply in space, constitutes a three-dimensional global public goods supply roadmap (see Table 8.2). In short, the steps of China's supply of public goods should be aligned with its own growth, and at the same time, China should actively leverage its comparative advantage and devote itself to innovating the supply mode of public goods. In addition to continuing to make contributions in the traditional field, China may also open up new areas for the supply of public goods, which is conducive to avoiding fierce competition with hegemonic powers and increasing the space for China to supply new public goods.[18]

First, before 2020, harvesting the achievements of regional governance will be the main task. In the near future, while avoiding direct competition with other great powers, China should gradually strengthen domestic governance, while upgrading regional public goods, so that the platforms of the BRI, the Asian Infrastructure Investment Bank (AIIB), and the BRICS (Brazil, Russia, India, China, and South Africa) Bank will be more institutionalised and networked. Based on regional governance, China can accumulate high-level governance capabilities and experiences and prepare for full participation in promoting global governance. Therefore, China needs to lay a solid foundation and continue to make good use

Embracing the era of reglobalisation 145

Table 8.2 A roadmap for China to take Part in leading reglobalisation

Stages	Before 2020 (accomplish the goal of building a well-off society)	Before 2030 (achieving the goals of the UN 2030 agenda)	Before 2050 (accomplish the 'Two Hundred-Year' goal)
Objectives	Strengthening supply of domestic public goods and optimising provision of regional public goods	Strive toward provision of global public goods in key areas	Rise to world power, enhance global leadership, pay attention to the future of humankind and the Earth
Advantages	Support from the UN 2030 Agenda	China's own experience and regional leadership status	Deepening of the community of a shared future for humankind and recognition of China's global leadership
Focus	Domestic and regional levels	Transregional and global levels	Global level
Examples	The BRI connecting with the UN 2030 Agenda; air pollution governance and environmental protection; building a moderately prosperous society; and cooperation in regional disaster prevention early warning system.	Establishment of a transregional high-speed rail network; establishment of the Asia-Pacific Free Trade Zone; world electronic trade and payment platform; establishment of the Global Big Data R&D Center, etc.	Preventing large-scale natural disasters; preventing the impact of solar storms and asteroid collisions with Earth; developing global norms in emerging domains (i.e. cyberspace order, Artificial Intelligence Ethics Committee); Mars Laboratory Station.

Note: Table compiled by the authors.

of existing platforms, such as international economic and financial organisational structures (i.e. the AIIB, the BRICS Bank, the BRI, the Boao Forum for Asia, and the Dalian Summer Davos Forum) and regional security management patterns (i.e. Shanghai Cooperation Organisation [SCO], Conference on Interaction and Confidence Building Measures in Asia, and the Xiangshan Forum), as well as progressive concepts such as the new Asian security concept, and a community of shared future for humankind.

On the one hand, China is working to connect the BRI with the UN 2030 Agenda. The BRI is the largest global public good that China has ever provided. At the regional level, the BRI is a transregional public product with a focus on Asia and extension to Europe, Africa, and Oceania. However, instead of rushing

146 *Reglobalisation*

to expand the scope of the BRI, China should concentrate on domestic and neighbouring areas to prevent strategic overreach.[19] The Belt and Road Forum for International Cooperation held in May 2017 in Beijing, is an important step toward institutionalising the BRI. Connecting the BRI with the UN 2030 Agenda can maximise the international effectiveness of the BRI. By combining the BRI with the international development agenda in which all countries in the world participate, we can achieve platform grafting and promote a win-win situation. In addition to connecting with professional platforms such as the UN General Assembly, the UN Security Council, the Food and Agriculture Organization of the United Nations and UNESCO, China should actively use relevant platforms, such as the Group of 77 and China's South-South Cooperation platform, the Group of Twenty (G20) platform for South-South and North-South Cooperation, and the BRICS.[20] At the Hangzhou Summit, China called on the G20 member states to take the first step in implementing the 2030 Agenda and to list 'implementing the 2030 sustainable development agenda, eliminating poverty and achieving common development' as one of the four major areas of work for the G20.[21] These are all attempts by China to align existing initiatives with the agenda of the United Nations.

On the other hand, China is also actively committed to working to resolve regional and international crises, playing a constructive role in bridging differences, persuading and facilitating talks, and maintaining regional stability and peace. China will continue to participate in the diplomatic process of resolving regional crises such as the North Korea nuclear issue, the Iranian nuclear issue, the Afghanistan issue, and the Syria issue, among others, and work with other stakeholders to address global challenges such as terrorism, cybersecurity, climate change, epidemics, and refugees.

Second, before 2030, the core task is to improve the global governance system. In the medium-term (before 2030), China can leverage its competitiveness and contribute to the creation of a transregional high-speed railway network, build a new financial governance platform, lead the trends of innovation and economic development, improve the global governance system, and design a new form of global public goods. On the one hand, China should upgrade the Belt and Road and improve global connectivity. By that time, the Belt and Road will have expanded into a global network system that is interconnected with all kinds of things. Through the internet, the soft internet of Things (IoT), and the infrastructure network of high-speed railways, highways, and aviation; pipeline; and port networks, the whole world will move toward becoming a more closely knit community.[22] China has carried out high-speed rail construction in Thailand, Brazil, Russia, and other countries and regions the world over. China's high-speed rail 'going out' diplomacy has been extended to Africa, Asia, Europe, America, Oceania, and other regions.[23] In recent years, China has taken part in nearly 20 overseas railway projects, including the Jakarta-Bandung high-speed rail in Indonesia, the China-Laos railway, the Lahore Metro's Orange Line trains in Pakistan, the Hungary-Serbia railway, the China-Thailand railway, the Singapore-Kuala Lumpur high-speed rail, the Moscow-Kazan high-speed rail,

Embracing the era of reglobalisation 147

and the United Kingdom high-speed rail. The Hungary-Serbia railway project has become a flagship project of the '16+1' cooperation between China and Central and Eastern Europe. In June 2017, the Fuxing (meaning 'rejuvenation'), China's standard electric multiple unit (EMU) model with the lowest global operating energy consumption and indigenous intellectual property rights, was officially opened to the public and has the potential to add to China's competitiveness.[24] The current 1.0 version of high-speed rail has a speed limit of 350–500 kilometres per hour, and may take about 40 hours from Shanghai to London (as opposed to 16 days for the China-European trains and more than a month for shipping); by 2030, it may be upgraded to version 2.0, and theoretically, the vacuum tube maglev high-speed rail can reach 3,500–5,000 kilometres per hour, so it will take only 20 minutes to travel from Beijing to Shanghai, and only 4 or 5 hours from Beijing to New York.[25] With the development of the Trans-Asian Railway (TAR) project, China can participate in the construction of the global high-speed rail network on five continents in 2030, laying the foundation for the establishment of new networked global relations.

On the other hand, China may take the initiative to help establish global data sharing centres and build an information community. The inseparable relationship between big data and the internet determines that big data has openness in its genes, so it is an inevitable trend to establish big data sharing centres. As open data refers to data that anyone can freely access and use for free, it is a new type of public good.[26] In 2009, the United States took the lead in opening the national data platform website, data.gov. After that, developed countries such as the United Kingdom and Canada announced their government data opening plans as well. Opening government data quickly became a global phenomenon. The Action Guideline to Promote the Development of Big Data issued by China's State Council in 2015, proposed the creation of a national open data platform by the end of 2018, and the goal of opening data to the society in the fields of transportation, medical treatment, public health, environmental protection, weather forecasting, and business registration and supervision should be gradually realised by 2020. In keeping with this pace of opening up, by 2030, China will be able to build a regional or global big data sharing centre. By then, China will become one of the knowledge centres of the world, continuously providing big data support for global governance efforts. Global big data centres can be developed cooperatively across borders, as China will have acquired leading digital capabilities by 2030. In 2017, Chinese companies had already been at the forefront of the world in terms of big data. For example, Alibaba's Singles' Day Shopping Festival created a world record sales of RMB120.7 billion in 2016. The logistics of shipping all the orders made during the shopping festival also broke the global record, resulting in 657 million orders having been placed in a single day. In terms of payment, the total number of payments made by Alipay reached 1.05 billion, an increase of 48% over the same period of the previous year. The number of payments peaked at 120,000 per second, which also refreshed the record of peak global traffic.[27] WeChat, with nearly 900 million users, produces more data in a day than all paper books in human history combined. Therefore, China's big data capability can be

148 *Reglobalisation*

transformed into public goods for the benefit of the region and the world when conditions are ripe in the future.

Third, from now on until 2050, China, together with other stakeholders, may focus on leading the world toward a community of a shared future. The world's leading powers are bound to be forward-looking and imaginative. Thinking about the future, we have to learn from the current technological changes and the development trends in human society. In 2016, AlphaGo, an AI robot developed by Google, defeated the world's top Go player, a historic moment in the history of AI. According to forecasts, AI will be popularised in the next 20 to 30 years. In the next 30 years, the speed of progress of science and technology and its impact on human beings will be immeasurable.[28] The speed of technological changes in the next 30 years is likely to exceed that of the past 100 years. This more drastic and subversive change requires a new response. By 2050, China will have completed the goal of great national rejuvenation, becoming a global power that has the will and capacity to lead the world jointly with other stakeholders.

By 2050, the global prosperity of humankind will be elevated to a new height. Both reality and the virtual network will converge more deeply. By that time, human beings may face astronomical natural disasters such as asteroids hitting the Earth, solar storms, and so on. The rise in sea levels may inevitably lead to the reduction of available land and even species extinction. Hopefully, we will rise above the 'clash of civilisations' and build a community of shared future for humankind. In this highly developed and risky world in 2050, China, as a global leading power, will join hands with other stakeholders to tackle global challenges. Regardless of linguistic and cultural differences, the global sense of a community of shared future for humankind will deepen further.[29] In this new interactive model of global relations, the 'Oriental wisdom' advocating inclusive integration and convergence will play an important role.

In the next 30 to 50 years, humans may suffer from various threats from nature and outer space, and more advanced public goods are thus necessary. For example, the destruction of an old satellite in outer space can lead to a chain reaction that threatens most satellites in orbit. According to data compiled by the Union of Concerned Scientists (UCS), more than 1,100 active satellites are in orbit today, about 60% of which are used for communication. In addition to the active satellites, there are about 2,500 inactive satellites that are real threats.[30] In addition, space governance also includes the prevention of asteroid impacts. There are hundreds of millions of pieces of debris scattered in the solar system, ranging in size from pebbles to thousands of kilometres in diameter. Some of these are likely to hit the Earth. It is estimated by scientists that about 1,500 asteroids that are 1 kilometre in diameter have passed or are passing through the Earth's orbit.[31] The collision between near-Earth asteroids and Earth is only a matter of time. Once a large enough asteroid rushes into the Earth's atmosphere without having melted, debris will cause great harm. Scientists have also warned that an asteroid 390 metres wide, known as Apophis, could collide with Earth in 2036, releasing 100,000 times more energy than the Hiroshima atomic bomb.[32] China

Embracing the era of reglobalisation 149

will become a space power in 2050. According to the Chinese government's plan, China will land on Mars in the 2020s and build a Chinese space base.[33] At that time, China's ability to respond to space disasters will also rank high in the world, and China will join forces with other countries to establish a global early warning system for blocking asteroids flying to Earth.[34] The peak of the solar storm will also have a disastrous impact on Earth's communications facilities. On 13 March 1989, a solar storm swept through northern Canada, causing power outages for over 9 hours in 90,000 households in the region.[35] These public hazards need to be dealt with jointly by the whole world, and China is also duty-bound to contribute.

China will also pay attention to the ethics of AI technology and take the lead in forging a consensus on AI governance. In addition to cloud computing and big data, AI and intelligent commodities will also become the major trend in development in the next 30 years. AI endows computers with certain abilities to perform human-like feats of cognition including learning, problem-solving, and perception, which not only promotes productivity, but also generates ethical problems.[36] As early as more than 20 years ago, the supercomputer 'Deep Blue' developed by IBM beat the world chess champion and shocked the world. Today, IBM's computer Q&A system Watson, Google's AlphaGo and unmanned vehicles, Apple's voice assistant Siri, and various other face recognition technologies represent the trends in the future development of AI. In the near future, most commodities will be intelligent and a part of the IoT, which will profoundly change humankind's way of life.[37] It is no exaggeration to say that the rules of the world will change dramatically in the next 20–30 years. China needs to plan ahead of time and enhance its ability to contribute to the global community in the future. According to data from the Wuzhen Think Tank, in 2016, a number of AI companies in the United States, China, and the United Kingdom accounted for 66% of the world's total, and the growth rate of the AI industry in China was astonishing.[38] In July 2017, the State Council issued the Plan for the Development of New Generation Artificial Intelligence. According to this plan, China aims at play a leading role globally in R&D for AI and becoming a major AI innovation centre by 2030.[39] However, ethical concerns of AI are also new issues to be considered. It has been reported that by 2030, computers or robots will have the same storage capacity and processing speed as human brains and will even be able to replace human thinking completely. Will robots with strong decision-making power replace humans? Or will it be used by extremists for the purpose of perpetuating crimes, starting a war, or committing a massacre? By 2050, it is likely that China will become one of the global leaders in science and technology. Therefore, it is necessary for China to take the shared responsibility to initiate the creation of the ethical norms of AI and to assess, supervise, and inspect the risks that emerging technologies may bring about, so as to ensure the overall safety of humankind. The above imaginations may seem remote, but they are not unfamiliar. After all, 30 years ago, people could not have imagined the ethical problems of today's internet world.

150 *Reglobalisation*

Notes

1 Zhang Shiquan, *Guojia jingji liyi yu quanqiu gonggong wupin* [*National Economic Interests and Global Public Goods*], Beijing, China: Intellectual Property Publishing House, 2016, pp. 148–149.
2 Li Xuesong, et al., '*Shisanwu' ji 2030 nian fazhan mubiao yu zhanlue yanjiu* [*Research on Development Goals and Strategies for the 13th Five-Year Plan and 2030*], Beijing, China: Social Sciences Academic Press, 2016, p. 6.
3 'Lin Yifu: 2030 nian Zhongguo jiang chengwei shijie diyida jingjiti' ['Justin Yifu Lin: China Will Become the World's Largest Economy by 2030'], Chinanewsnet.com, March 26, 2017, http://www.chinanews.com/cj/2017/03-26/8183838.shtml.
4 US National Intelligence Council, *Global Trends 2030: Alternative Worlds*, December 2012, https://www.dni.gov/files/documents/GlobalTrends_2030.pdf, p. 16.
5 Wang Tian, 'Felix kaituo Zhongguo tese daguo waijiao xin jumian' ['Striving to Open Up a New Pattern of Situation for Great Power Diplomacy with Chinese Characteristics'], *Renmin ribao* [*People's Daily*], 31 August 2017.
6 KPMG, *Infrastructure in China: Sustaining Quality Growth*, Hong Kong, China: KPMG International, 2014, https://home.kpmg.com/cn/en/home.html.
7 International Hydropower Association 'China Statistics', https://www.hydropower.org/country-profiles/china.
8 Xin Wen, 'Zhongguo gaotie lichen da 2 wan gongli, zhan quanshijie gaotie zongliang 65% zuoyou' ['China's High-Speed Rail Mileage Has Exceeded 20,000 Kilometers, Accounting for 65% of the World's Total'], China.com.cn, 29 December 2016, http://www.china.com.cn/news/2016-12/29/content-4005460.htm.
9 China's high-speed railway has the highest speed at 350 kilometers per hour, and its standard basic unit cost is $17 million–$21 million. The developed countries in Europe have a speed of up to 300 kilometers per hour, with an estimated cost of $25 million–$39 million per kilometer, while the construction cost of high-speed railway in the United States and Japan is even higher, reaching almost $52 million per kilometer. See International Transport Forum, December 2013, http://www.itf-oecd.org/search/statistics-and-data?f=field-publication-type%#A648&f=field-publication-type%3A657.
10 Wu Jingjing, Yang Weihan and Xu Haitao, 'Woguo chenggong fashe shijie shouke liangzi kexue shiyan weixing "Mozi hao"' ['China Successfully Launched the World's First Quantum Science Experiment Satellite "Mozi"'], Xinhuanet.com, 16 August 2016, http://www.xinhuanet.com/world/2016-08/16/c_129231459.htm
11 China International Economic Exchange Center and the United Nations Development Program, *Report of the 2013 High-level Policy Forum on Global Governance—Reconstructing Global Governance: Effectiveness, Inclusion and China's Global Role*, August 2013, p. 28.
12 Qian Wenrong, 'Lianheguo yingzai liangshi anquan quanqiu zhili zhong fahui zhudao zuoyong' [The United Nations Should Play a Leading Role in Global Governance of Food Security], in Zhang Guihong and Guo Fengcheng, eds., *Zhongguo, Lianheguo yu quanqiu zhili* [*China, the United Nations and Global Governance*], Beijing, China: Current Affairs Publishing House, 2014, pp. 158–159.
13 Wang Meng and Lu Zehua, 'Zimaoqu yinling Zhongguo quanfangwei kaifang, gouzhu fushe "yidai yilu" wangluo' ['Free Trade Zones Lead China to Open up in All Directions and Build a Radiated Network of the "Belt and Road"'], *Renmin ribao (haiwaiban)* [*People's Daily (Overseas Edition)*], March 29, 2017.
14 Jia Yanning, 'Zhongguo guoji fazhan zhishi zhongxin qidong, wei shixian quanqiu kechixu fazhan gongxian Zhongguo zhihui' ['China Center for International Knowledge on Development Launched to Contribute China's Wisdom to the Realization of Global Sustainable Development'], CRI Online, 22 August 2017, http://news.cri.cn/20170822/3c4f7f39-8e42-c9fa-8323-7736549c1a68.html.

Embracing the era of reglobalisation 151

15 China Center for International Development on Knowledge, 'Xi Jinping xiang Zhongguo guoji fazhan zhoshi zhongxin qidong yishi ji 'Zhongguo luoshi 2030 nian kechixu fazhan yicheng jincheng baogao' fabuhui zhi hexin' ['Xi Jinping's Congratulatory Letter to the Launch Ceremony of the China Center for International Development on Knowledge and the Press Conference of China's Progress Report on the Implementation of the Sustainable Development Agenda of 2030'], Xinhua News Agency, 23 August 2017, http://zj.people.com.cn/n2/2017/0823/c186327-30643365 .html; Ministry of Foreign Affairs of the PRC, 'Zhongguo luoshi 2030 nian kechixu fazhan yicheng: jinzhan baogao' ['Progress Report on China's Implementation of the Sustainable Development Agenda 2030'], August 2017, pp. 363–365, http://www.fmpr c.gov.cn/web/ziliao-674904/zt-674979/dnzt-674981/qtzt/2030kcxfzyc-686343/P02 0161012715836816237.pdf.

16 Fan Yongming, Qian Yaping, and Rao Yunyan, *Quyu guoji gonggong chanpin yu dongya hezuo [Regional International Public Goods and East Asian Cooperation]*, Shanghai, China: Shanghai People's Publishing House, 2014, p. 13.

17 Hu Angang, '2030 Zhongguo: waixiang gongtong fuyu' (xia)' ['China 2030: Towards Common Prosperity (Part 2)'], *Nongchang jingji guanli [Farm Economic Management]*, No. 4, 2012, pp. 16–23.

18 For the stages of global governance, see Wang Yizhou and Cao Dejun, 'Tianjian dandaoyi: Zhongguo canyu lianheguo zhili de xin lujing, xin yuanjing' ['Shoulder Moral Responsibilities: A New Path and Vision for China's Participation in UN Governance'], in United Nations Association of China, ed., *Lianheguo 70 nian: chengjiu stryu tiaozhan [70 Years of U.N.: Achievements and Challenges]*, Beijing, China: World Affairs Press, 2015, pp. 475–487.

19 Shi Yinhong, 'Chuantong Zhongguo jingyan yu dangjin Zhongguo shijian: zhanlue tiaozheng, zhanlue touzhi he weida fuxing wenti' ['Traditional Chinese Experiences and China's Current Practice: Strategic Adjustment, Strategic Overdraft, and the Great Rejuvenation'], *Waijiao pinglun [Foreign Affairs Review]*, No. 6, 2015, pp. 57–68.

20 Zhang Chun and Gao Wei, 'Lianheguo 2015 nian hou fazhan yicheng he quanqiu shuju huoban guanxi' ['United Nations Post-2015 Development Agenda and Global Data Partnership'], *Shijie jingji yu zhengzhi [World Economy and Politics]*, No. 8, 2015, pp. 88–105.

21 Cao Jiahan, '"Yidai yilu" changyi yu 2030 nian kechixu fazhan yicheng de duijie yiyi, tiaozhan yu fangxiang' ['The Meaning, Challenge and Direction of the Connecting of the "Belt and Road" Initiative and the 2030 Agenda for Sustainable Development'], in Zhang Ning and Li Yongquan, eds., *Sizhou zhilu jingjidai he ouya jingji lianmeng duijie yanjiu [The Silk Road Economic Belt and Eurasian Economic Alliance]*, Beijing, China: Social Sciences Academic Press, 2017, pp. 55–69.

22 Chen Wenling, '"Yidai yilu" jiang ruhe chongsu quanqiu xinjingji' ['How Will the "Belt and Road" Reshape the New Global Economy?'], *Diyi caijing [China Business Network]*, 15 May 2017.

23 For comments on the prospect of high-speed railway diplomacy, see Xu Fei, *Zongheng 'yidai yilu': Zhongguo gaotie quanqiu zhanlue [Across the 'Belt and Road:' China's Global Strategy for High-speed Rail]*, Shanghai, China: Gezhi Press and Shanghai Renmin Publishing House, 2017.

24 Qi Hui, '"Fuxing hao" laile!' ['The "Fuxing" is Coming!'], *Jingji ribao [Economic Daily]*, 26 June 2017, http://paper.ce.cn/jjrb/html/2017-06/26/content_337339.htm.

25 Jinqiao Think Tank, 'Zhongguo gaotie gang zouchu guomen, Zhongguo feiche youyao laile' ['China High-speed Railway Just Arrived Overseas, and China's Flying Cars Are Coming Too'], chnrailway.com, 2 September 2017, https://www.chnrailway.com/html /20170902/1727661.shtml.

26 Gao Qiqi, 'Dashuju gonggong zhili: siwei, goucheng yu caozuohua' ['Public Governance of Big Data: Thinking, Composition and Operationalization'], *Renwen zazhi [Humanities Magazine]*, No. 6, 2016, pp. 103–111.

152   *Reglobalisation*

27 Ali Research Institute and Ali Cross-Border E-Commerce Research Center, '2016 Zhongguo kuajing dianshang fazhan baogao—maoyi de weilai: kuajing dianshang lianjie shijie' ['China Cross-Border E-Commerce Development Report 2016—The Future of Trade: Cross-Border E-Commerce Connecting the World'], pp. 4–5.

28 Jun Bin, 'Guge jiqiren dabai Hanguo weiqi gaoshou, rengong zhineng zaixian taolun gaochao' ['Google's Robot Defeats Korean Go Player, and Artificial Intelligence Reaches a Climax of Discussions'], Fx168.com, 10 March 2016, https://news.fx168.com/politics/us/1603/1817102.shtml.

29 Qin Yaqing, 'Rule, Rules, and Relations: Towards a Synthetic Approach to Governance', *The Chinese Journal of International Relations*, Vol. 4, No. 2, 2011, pp. 117–145.

30 UCS Satellite Database, https://www.ucsusa.org/resources/satellite-database

31 Li Yiming, *Renlei miezhong de 10 zhong keneng* [*Ten Possibilities of Human Extinction*], Beijing, China: New World Press, 2012.

32 Ling Shuo, 'Diqiu huo mianlin qida zainan' ['Earth May Face Seven Major Disasters'], *Xi'an ribao* [*Xi'an Daily*], 9 December 2014.

33 Xu Yanhong, 'Zhongguo toulu 2020 nian denglu Huoxing tance jihua: sanci renwu yici wancheng' ['China Discloses Its Mars Landing Exploration Plan in 2020: Three Missions to Be Completed at Once'], *Cankao xiaoxi* [*Reference News*], 22 April 2016.

34 Qu Ting, Yu Fei and Wang Cong, 'Kaiqi taikong 'xin changzheng': Zhongguo zhunbei le naxie liqi?' ['What Edge Tools Have China Prepared for the Opening of the New Long March in Space?'], Xinhua News Agency, 21 April 2016, http://www.xinhuanet.com/world/2016-04/21/c_128919170.htm.

35 Fan Lilang, '2014 nian shi Taiyang fengbao huodong fengnian amei jiexi qi dui renlei yingxiang' ['2014 is the Peak Year of Solar Storm Activity: An Analysis of Its Impact on Human Beings'], China.com.cn, January 22, 2014, http://www.china.com.cn/news/world/2014-01/22/content_31273442.htm.

36 So-called artificial intelligence is the sum of all kinds of activities, such as material means, methods, and knowledge, that human beings have mastered in the process of utilising and transforming machines, which includes robots, language recognition, image recognition, natural language processing and expert systems.

37 Liu Qiangdong, 'Disici linshou geming jiang lailin, jiang you yici chaoyue hulianwang' ['The Fourth Retail Revolution is About to Surpass the Internet Again'], ifeng.com, 10 July 2017, http://tech.ifeng.com/a/20170710/44650274-0.shtml.

38 Wuzhen Think Tank, Netease Science and Technology, Netease Intelligence, *Wuzhen zhishu: quanqiu rengong zhineng fazhan baogao (2016) (kuangjia pian)* [*Wuzhen Index: Global Artificial Intelligence Development Report (2016) (Framework)*], October 2016, http://h5.iwuzhen.org/pdf/AI-Overview.pdf, p. 7.

39 The State Council, 'Guowuyuan guanyu yinfa xinyidai rengong zhineng fazhan guihua de tongzhi' ['The Notice by the State Council on the Issuance of the Plan for the Development of New Generation of Artificial Intelligence'], 20 July 2017, The Central People's Government of the PRC, http://www.gov.cn/zhengce/content/2017-07/20/content_5211996.htm.

Conclusion

Reglobalisation: When China meets the world again

In discussing the relationship between China's rise and globalisation, liberal order seems to be an indispensable phrase. Often used by Western academia and policy circles in describing the existing international order, the term 'liberal order' is distinctly Western-centric. When Western politicians and pundits talk about the international order, they take a Western-centric perspective as if they own the property rights to the existing international order. In the Western narrative of international order, there is an implicit context when China is mentioned: 'Does China seek to challenge and overthrow the existing order?' From such a perspective, this liberal order operates under a set of norms and rules constructed by the United States and its allies. When the West looks at China, there is an ostensible arrogance: 'You (China) have to behave well to qualify as a legitimate member of the existing international order'. There is an evident absurdity in this mentality. It is almost like quantum physics: 'Is China in or not in the existing international order? It is both in and not in'. After more than 40 years of reform and opening up, China surely has been deeply embedded in the existing order; however, because of ideological prejudices, Western politicians, pundits, and the media often consider China as belonging to a different kind, and subconsciously believe that it does not have the legitimacy to become a member of the existing international order. Therefore, when Western policymakers and scholars use the concept of liberal order to describe the existing international order, there are obvious limitations because China is neither totally assimilated into the Western liberal order, nor is it totally cut away from it but rather is embedding itself in it to unleash the power of reform and integration gradually.

In traditional international relations, the West emphasises a zero-sum game, that is, 'I win, and you lose'. China comes with a different mindset shaped by Confucian cultural-psychological traditions that place a premium on harmony, inclusiveness, and relationality. China emphasises win-win and all-win scenarios and cooperates with others to complement each other's strengths and weaknesses. China's rise is reshaping the process of globalisation and ushering in a new stage of what we call 'reglobalisation'. It is also Chinese wisdom to let nature take its course. 'The highest good is like water', as the classic *Daode Jing* (The Book of Dao and Its Virtues) put it. Strategically, it is called *moushi* (meaning 'to study the situation with the intent to shape it,' and *shunshi erwei*, meaning to act in

154 *Reglobalisation*

accordance with the situation'. In this context, *moushi* means to form a momentum: 'I am not trying to swallow you; rather, I am trying to form a momentum, and then you will think that if you do not participate, you will fall behind'. To some extent, the Belt and Road Initiative (BRI) is a manifestation of such Chinese wisdom. Once the shared vision is set, through wide consultation, joint contributions, and shared benefits, more and more countries will join the initiative. Finally, those who reject the BRI will find that the initiative is not just for the self-interests of China. In contrast, the BRI aims to build a big cooperative platform on which everyone will be better off by playing a positive-sum rather than zero-sum game.

Since the 2008 global financial crisis, the deficiencies in the old version of globalisation have been characterised by the rising inequality between not only developed and underdeveloped countries, but also between the rich and the poor within developed countries, and is highlighted by the rise of antiglobalisation, populism, and protectionism. Globalisation has not ceased. The world has not entered a deglobalisation era, either. Rather, we argue in this book that globalisation has entered a new stage that can be called reglobalisation. Many processes are driving the megatrend of reglobalisation. In a way, one may argue that the BRI, the Regional Comprehensive Economic Partnership (RCEP), and the Comprehensive and Progressive Agreement for Trans-Pacific Partnership (CPTPP) – a multilateral free-trade agreement formerly known as the Trans-Pacific Partnership (TPP) – all contribute to reglobalisation. In particular, this book has highlighted the leading role that China has played in the shaping and reshaping of globalisation, that is, reglobalisation. In conclusion, reglobalisation has two far-reaching implications.

First, to restore the legitimacy of the globalisation narrative. The globalisation narrative has been tainted in the West and has received harsh attacks from populists. Western analysts tend to take a zero-sum perspective in understanding the relationship between China and globalisation (seen as a West-led process), seeing China's increasingly prominent profile in globalisation as posing an existential threat to the West-dominated liberal order. However, since the reform and opening up began more than 40 years ago, China has never attempted to overthrow the existing international order. Rather, it aims to contribute to the reform and improvement of the existing order. When some Western politicians flirt with deglobalisation, fanning up protectionism and xenophobia, China assumed responsibility and joined forces with other emerging countries in promoting a new round of globalisation or reglobalisation.[1] China's thousands of years of history and the rise and fall of dozens of dynasties have made it more keenly aware of the fragility of the 'winner-takes-all' mentality.[2] Since 2016, with Brexit, Trump's withdrawal of the US from the TPP, and the rise in protectionism, the trend of deglobalisation has been on the rise. In stark contrast, China has been actively promoting reglobalisation through major initiatives such as the BRI, the Asian Infrastructure Investment Bank (AIIB), and the RCEP.

Second, when global uncertainty is on the rise, reglobalisation restores certainty. As an emerging power, China is a learner of the rules of globalisation. The international impact unleashed by China's domestic reform can promote the process of globalisation. China's unique 'pilot mode' of development has

Conclusion 155

provided a creative way of thinking for South-South cooperation. Justin Yifu Lin, former Chief Economist of the World Bank, noted that South-South cooperation can enable other developing countries to learn from China's successful experience, especially through planning special economic zones (SEZs) and industrial parks, developing infrastructure, and leveraging on comparative advantages to achieve leapfrog development.[3] Since the reform and opening up in 1978, China accumulated experience through pilot projects before carrying out every major reform measure. The most successful examples of pilot projects including the following: the Rural Household Responsibility Contract System reform, the economic reform pilot project of Shenzhen Special Economic Zone, the coastal urban belt opening up pilot project, and the Shanghai Pilot Free Trade Zone. Such a gradualist pilot mode helps to accumulate replicable and extendable experience in institutional innovation, effectively connect national conditions with international rules, and reduce the risk of reform. China has formed a new pattern of '1+3+7' free-trade zone pilot programmes across the nation.[4] Aiming at institutional innovation, the pilot free-trade zones can accumulate experience of reform for less developed countries. In 2007, China set up 19 economic parks overseas, extending the pilot mode of China abroad.[5] The cooperative model promoted by the pilot project has stabilised partnerships between China and host countries. This kind of a cooperative model has the nature of gift-giving and contributes to the formation of long-term and sustainable friendship between countries.[6] Overall, the more China promotes domestic reform, the more it can contribute to reglobalisation.

China has been an important driving force for the reform of the international order and even for the reshaping of the process of globalisation; however, there is still a long way to go for China to obtain comprehensive leadership. The stories of the Shanghai Shipping Freight Exchange Company (SSFEC), the BRI, the AIIB, and Alibaba all remind us that profound changes are taking place in the relationship between China and the world. An increasingly powerful China will reshape the dynamics and process of globalisation. As a result, reglobalisation has become a two-way street, emphasising linkages between China's domestic reforms and international environment and between emerging countries and the world, transcending the Western-centrism and leading to a global order that is more inclusive and equitable going forward. If the encounter between China and the world in 1840 can be defined as one of passivity and suppression, today's encounter between China and the world is characterised by cooperation and symbiosis, a process of dialogue, mutual growth, and evolution in a genuine sense. As China meets the world again, it is bound to create a new pattern of globalisation, one that has not been seen before. It is a historical process of reglobalisation. Although this process will not be accomplished overnight, changes are expected. Fortunately, today we are standing at this great starting point of history.

Notes

1 Gao Bai, 'Weishenme quanqiuhua hui fasheng nizhuan: ni quanqiuhua xianxiang de yinguo jizhi fenxi ['Why Globalisation Reverses: An Analysis of the Causal

156 *Reglobalisation*

Mechanism of the Phenomenon of De-globalisation'], *Wenhua zongheng* [*Beijing Cultural Review*], No. 6, 2016, pp. 42–50; Zheng Yu, 'Quanqiuhua Jincheng bingwei nizhuan' ['The Process of Globalisation Has Not Been Reversed'], *Wenhua zongheng* [*Beijing Cultural Review*], No. 6, 2016, pp. 22–35.

2 Shi Yinhong, 'Chuantong Zhongguo jingyan yu dangjin Zhongguo shijian: zhanlue tiaozheng, zhanlue touzhi he weida fuxing wenti' ['Traditional Chinese Experiences and China's Current Practice: Strategic Adjustment, Strategic Overdraft, and the Great Rejuvenation'], *Waijiao pinglun* [*Foreign Affairs Review*], No., 2015, pp. 57–68.

3 Justin Yifu Lin and Yan Wang, *Going Beyond Aid: Development Cooperation for Structural Transformation*, Cambridge, UK: Cambridge University Press, 2016.

4 Wang Meng and Lu Zehua, 'Zimaoqu yinling Zhongguo quanfangwei kaifang, gouzhu fushe "yidai yilu" wangluo' ['Free Trade Zones Lead China to Open Up in All Directions and Build a Radiated Network of the "Belt and Road"'], *Remin ribao (haiwaiban)* [People's Daily (Overseas Edition)], 29 March 2017. .

5 Deborah Brautigam and Xiaoyang Tang, 'Going Global in Groups: China's Special Economic Zones Overseas', *World Development*, Vol. 63, 2014, pp. 78–91. Deborah Brautigam and Tang Xiaoyan, 'African Shenzhen: China's Special Economic Zones in Africa', *The Journal of Modern African Studies*, Vol. 49, No. 1, 2011, pp. 27–54.

6 Li Ruichang, 'Jieding 'Zhongguo tedian de duikou zhiyuan': yizhong zhengzhixing kuizeng jieshi' ['Defining 'Point to Point Aid with Chinese Characteristics': An Interpretation of Political Gifts'], *Jingji shehui tizhi bijiao* [*Comparison of Economic and Social Systems*], No. 4, 2015, pp. 194–203.

Index

Afghanistan issue 146
Alibaba 6, 106–113, 115–120, 135, 142, 147, 155
AliExpress 109
Alipay 106–107, 114, 147
Al-Qaeda 30
America First 2, 27, 31
Americanisation 29
anti-globalisation/ antiglobalisation 2, 4, 12, 26, 29, 45n2, 154
artificial intelligence (AI) 115–117, 142, 144, 148–149
Asian Development Bank (ADB) 94–95, 97, 99–101, 103
Asian Infrastructure Investment Bank (AIIB) 6, 14, 17, 20, 23, 53, 58, 82–84, 87, 93–105, 127, 144–145, 154–155
Asia-Pacific Economic Cooperation (APEC) 14, 17, 38, 61n27
Asia-Pacific Free Trade Zone 144–145

B2C e-commerce 112–113
Baidu 116–117, 142
Baidu, Alibaba, Tencent, and JD.com (BATJ) 142
Beijing Consensus 11
The Belt and Road Forum for International Cooperation 20, 23n16, 25n34, 53, 146
Belt and Road Initiative (BRI) 6, 8, 14, 17, 19–20, 48, 50, 53, 57–59, 63–65, 67–73, 76–79, 82–84, 87–88, 93, 102, 109, 112, 120, 125, 127, 132, 143–146, 154–155
Better Than Cash Alliance 107
big data 108–113, 115, 142, 144, 147, 149
Boao Forum for Asia 2, 47, 56, 139, 145
BRICS (Brazil, Russia, India, China and South Africa) 14, 33, 36–37, 45n26, 84, 93, 95,132, 144,146
BRICS Bank/ the New Development Bank (BRICS NDB) 2, 17, 93–96,101–102, 145

BRICS Industrial and Commercial Forum 84, 146

Cainiao Network 107, 109
capital flow 32, 44n18, 95, 108
Center for International Knowledge on Development (CIKD) 142
Centre-periphery economic structure 33, 87–88
Chiang Mai Initiative (CMI) 94–95
Chimerica 16, 24n21
China-ASEAN Free Trade Area 85
China COSCO Shipping Corporation 8, 23n1
China's ability in institutional innovation 8
China's rise 2–6, 8, 12, 15–16, 19, 41, 47–48, 53–55, 68, 80, 126, 139, 153
Chinamerica 16
Chinese reorientation 9
Chinese Version of the Marshall Plan 83–84
clash of civilisations 148
climate change 12, 59, 100, 131–132, 136
cloud computing 108–109, 111, 113–115, 117, 142, 149
cloud network 110
coastal economic open zone 120
coercive power 20
Cold War 1, 4, 11, 16, 30–33, 39–40, 44n22, 45n38, 49, 84, 87
commodity flow 108
Communist Manifesto 27–28
community network of shared destiny 54
community of shared future for humankind 11, 50, 56–57, 59, 62n31, 68, 145, 148
comparative advantage 2, 64, 67–69, 73, 122, 128, 140, 144, 155
Comprehensive and Progressive Agreement for Trans-Pacific Partnership (CPTPP) 154

158 *Index*

Conference on Interaction and Confidence Building Measures in Asia 2, 145
consumerist ideology 29
consumer-to-business 111
Contingent Reserve Arrangement (CRA) 95
COVID–19 134–135, 138n30
cross-border consumption 112–113
cross-border e-businesses 109, 113
cross-border electronic trade 111
Cross-Sea Bridge Project 141
cultural globalization 27, 141
cyber security 12

data technology (DT) 114, 117, 118n7, 142
deglobalisation 12, 14, 26, 29, 31–33, 43n4, 44n20–23, 154, 156n1
democratization 43, 50
demographic dividend 37, 107
developing country 111, 117, 131, 141
development marshes 77
development zones 121–123, 127
digital divide 109
digital economy 109, 114–115, 119n20, 142
Digital Economy 2.0 6, 106–107, 109–111, 113–115, 117, 119
Digital Free Trade Area (eHub) 109
digital infrastructure 114–115
disembedded globalization 6, 41
domino effect 83
Donald Trump/Trump 2, 27–28, 31, 34–35, 43n2, 136n14, 154

e-businesses 106, 109, 111, 113
e-commerce 110, 111–113, 117, 118nn5, 12–13, 119nn15, 17, 129, 152n27–28
E-Commerce Connectivity Index (ECI) 110
economic and technological development zones 121, 123
economic corridor 58, 64, 69–70, 72, 75–80, 88n4, 89n21, 90n29, n33–35, 143
efficiency-driven countries 73, 75
electronic globalization 107
Electronic World Trade Platform (eWTP) 109, 111, 118n7
embedded style of national rise 15
embeddedness 15–16, 18, 24nn20, 23, 25n33, 33, 39
emerging economy 12, 15, 29, 87
epidemic 133–135, 146
European Bank for Reconstruction and Development (EBRD) 94, 97, 101, 103
excessive institutions 83

factor-driven countries 73
The Five Principles of Peaceful Coexistence 49
Forbidden Triad hypothesis 71
foreign aid 20, 71, 84, 131, 136n7, 137n27
four new inventions 114, 119n19
free trade zone 91n52, 123, 125–126, 135n2, 141, 144–145, 150n13, 155, 156n4
free-rider 38, 139

GDP 32, 53, 58, 63, 65–68, 73, 106, 114, 118n3, 130–132, 139–140
General Agreement on Trade and Tariffs (GATT) 15, 40, 58
global climate governance 40, 131–132
global cyberspace 144
global emerging middle class 30
global financial crisis 1–2, 10, 12, 26, 28, 30–35, 39, 41–42, 47, 83, 94, 101, 154
global governance 2–3, 9, 18, 21, 29–30, 36–38, 40–41, 43, 60n18, 63, 65, 67–69, 71, 73, 75, 77, 79, 81–85, 87, 89, 91–92, 101, 105, 130–131, 136n11, 139, 142, 144, 146–147, 150nn11–13, 151n18
global health 131–135, 137nn22, 24, 28–29
global health governance 132–135, 137n24
global inequality 30, 44n11
global order 1–5, 44n17, 120, 139, 155
global power 5, 41, 82, 91n48, 140
global power index 140
global public goods 3, 38, 82–83, 92, 94, 102, 104n3, 105n25, 130–131, 139, 142, 144–146, 150n1
globalisation 1–4, 6–19, 21, 23–49, 57–59, 63, 65, 68, 70–71, 75, 77, 79, 82, 84, 87, 88n1, 90n28, 91n27, 94–95, 104n15, 105n26, 106–109, 111, 113, 115, 117–121, 126, 134, 139, 153–155, 156n1
glocalisation 29
going out diplomacy 96
great national rejuvenation/great rejuvenation 56, 147–148, 151n19, 156n2
great power 3, 5–6, 11, 18, 32, 53, 82, 90n28, 91n47, 92–93, 150n5
the Group of Seven (G7) 101
the Group of 20 (G20) 14, 17, 33, 44n17, 78, 94, 101, 109, 118n9, 127, 132, 134, 137n16, 146
Group of Zero (G-Zero) 32, 44n17
Gwadar Port 79

Index

hegemony 11, 29–30, 38, 41, 53, 57, 60n14, 83–84
high-speed railway 68, 89n16, 140, 144, 146, 150n9, 151nn23, 25
high-tech development zones 121
high-tech industrial development zone 121, 123
hybrid rice technology 141
hydropower 68, 89n14, 140, 150n7

inclusive globalization 6, 41
incremental way 18
industrial park 86, 121, 127–129, 143, 155
industrialisation 58, 76, 78, 103, 111, 131, 141–142
information flow 108, 110
information security 114
Information Technology (IT) 114–115, 142
infrastructure construction 69, 140
innovation-driven countries 73
interconnectivity 19, 69
International Bank for Reconstruction and Development (IBRD) 94, 99
international constitutional order 20
internationalization 9, 14, 26–27, 83
international law 10
International Monetary Fund (IMF) 14, 17, 39, 67, 94, 99–101
international polarization 30
international public goods 38, 64, 83, 93, 136n7, 151n16
internet finance 108
Internet of Things (IoT) 115–116, 146, 149
Internet+ 108, 115, 119n21
internet trade 106
involuted globalization 6, 40
Iranian nuclear issue 146
island chain 72
isolationism 29, 33, 36, 42

joint contributions 57, 59, 65, 84, 92, 154

keeping a low profile and biding time (*taoguang yanghui*) 41, 54, 57, 92

late-starter advantage 139
leapfrog development 102, 155
legitimacy 16–18, 20, 32, 153–154
liberal order 20, 47–48, 153–154

made in China 110, 116
mechanism of reversal pressure 120–123, 125, 127, 129, 131–133, 135, 137
middle-class 12–13, 36, 45
middle-income trap 97, 139

mobile internet 108, 113, 115
mobile payment 106–108, 111, 117, 118n6
modernization 10, 110, 130–131, 142

national interest 10, 19, 91n48, 97
nationalism 10
neoliberal 10, 42, 48
network 2, 19–22, 24–25, 27–28, 37, 42–43, 48, 50, 52–55, 60–61, 63, 65, 68–71, 76–77, 85–86, 89, 94–95, 102, 106–107, 109–110, 114–115, 118, 128, 140–148, 150–151, 156
new Asian security concept 2, 50, 145
new Cold War 33
New Development Bank 2, 14, 93–95, 104nn9, 17
new energy 78, 132
new infrastructure 110–111, 114
new national-level zones 121
new normal 56, 97, 119n18
non-alignment in partnership 54–55
North Korea nuclear issue 146

Occupy Wall Street protests 31, 44n14
online retail 104, 107, 111, 117
online shopping 110–111, 114, 117
open its eyes and take a look 9
Oriental wisdom 50, 148
originated in China 115
outer space 148

Paris Climate Conference 132
Partnership for Quality Infrastructure 83–84, 91n54
Pilot Free Trade Zone 123, 125–126, 135n2, 155
pilot mode 154–155
pivot to Asia 41, 83, 91n49
point to axis to network 76
poverty alleviation 89n19, 131, 142
poverty relief 141
power politics 3, 10, 32, 141
President Xi/Xi Jinping 12, 20, 23nn7, 16, 25n34, 38, 45nn34–36, 47, 53–54, 56, 61n27, 63, 65, 77, 79, 84, 90n38, 91n55, 92–93, 101, 103n2, 105n22, 127, 132, 134, 136n14, 138n30, 139, 151n15, 152n32
principled realism 31
protectionism 12, 29, 35, 37, 68, 154
public-private investment partnerships (PPP) 102

quantum satellites 141

160   *Index*

Rebalancing to the Asia-Pacific 41
reconfiguration 10, 26
reform and opening up 6, 8, 10–11, 43, 120–121, 123–126, 141, 153–155
refugee 12, 79
Regional Comprehensive Economic Partnership (RCEP) 14, 83, 154
regional governance 144
re-globalisation/reglobalisation 2–4, 6–7, 9, 12, 19, 24n24, 26, 33–35, 38–39, 42–43, 47–48, 50, 54, 59, 63, 65, 68–72, 74–76, 82, 87–88, 92–95, 101, 103, 106–108, 110, 113–117, 121, 123, 126, 139, 141, 143–145, 147, 149, 151, 153–155
relationality 20, 51, 153
relational power 20
relational security 52, 60nn6, 16
renewable energy 68, 71, 132, 137n16, 140
responsibility to protect(R2P) 49
revisionist state 15
rural household responsibility contract system 141, 155
Russia-led Eurasian Economic Union 83

scissors gap 33
Shanghai Cooperation Organisation Bank 93, 101
Shanghai Cooperation Organization (SCO) 17, 69, 80, 145
Shanghai Pilot Free Trade Area 8
Shanghai Shipping Freight Exchange Company (SSFEC) 8, 155
Shanghai standard 8
shared benefits 57, 59, 64–65, 84, 92, 154
shared bicycle 115–116
sharing economy 110, 115–117
Shenzhen Special Economic Zone 123, 141, 155
Silk Road Fund 58, 93–96, 101–102, 127
Singles' Day 107, 109–110, 113–114, 117, 119nn16, 18, 147
social capital 19, 21–22, 25nn38, 41, 42
soft power 14, 20, 25n32, 82, 86, 134
South-North Water Transfer Project 141
South-South cooperation 127, 131, 134, 146, 155
Sovereignty 10, 49, 51, 82, 99, 136n9
special economic zones (SEZs) 120–123, 141–142, 155, 156n5
spillover effect 83
status quo power 15
strategic reassurance 41, 46n3

striving for achievement/ striving to accomplish something (*fenfa youwei*) 2, 6, 41, 54, 92
Sustainable Development Agenda 84, 127, 135n4, 146, 151n5
Syria issue 146

Tencent 106–108, 116–117, 119n21, 142
Terrorism 12, 30, 59, 142, 146
Three Gorges Dam Project 141
tit-for-tat strategy 52
trade protectionism 12, 29, 35, 37
trade war 12, 28
traditional Chinese medicine (TCM) 133
Trans-Asian Railway (TAR) 147
Trans-Pacific Partnership (TPP) 31, 154
tripartite pattern 34
Two Hundred-Year plan (*liangge bainian*) 130, 132, 135n5, 144–145

undeveloped growth 40
UNESCO 17, 146
United Nations (UN) 54, 59, 64, 67, 102, 127, 130, 133, 135n4, 136n11, 143–144, 146, 150
United Nations Development Program (UNDP) 64, 136n6
United Nations Sustainable Development Goals (SDGs) 129–131, 142
unmanned vehicle 149
urbanisation 58, 103, 142

virtual network 148

Washington Consensus 11, 30
WeChat Pay 107
Western-centric 1, 5, 153
wide consultation 57, 59, 64–65, 84, 92, 154
winner-takes-all 154
World Bank 17, 30, 40, 67, 70, 73, 89n18, 94–95, 97, 99–101, 103, 105n21, 143, 155
world factory 73, 94
World Health Organization (WHO) 65, 101, 133–135, 137nn23–24
WTO 8, 13, 15, 17, 67, 111, 117, 121

Xiangshan Forum 2, 145

zero-sum game 4, 18, 49, 52, 65, 68, 79, 84, 153–154
zero-sum thinking 79, 84

Printed in the United States
By Bookmasters